Published by
Rajneesh Foundation International
Rajneeshpuram, Oregon 97741 U.S.A.

The Long and the Short and the All

Excerpts from early discourses and letters of

Bhagwan Shree Rajneesh

Editor: Swami Krishna Prem, M.M., D.Phil.M. (RIMU), Acharya
Design: Ma Deva Padma
Direction: Ma Yoga Pratima, M.M., D.Phil.M. (RIMU), Arihanta

Published by:
Ma Anand Sheela, M.M., D.Phil.M., D.Litt.M. (RIMU) Acharya
Rajneesh Foundation International, President
P.O. Box 9, Rajneeshpuram,
Oregon 97741, U.S.A.

First Edition: Delhi, India 1979

First U.S. Printing: July 1984 — 10,000 copies

Printed in U.S.A.

ISBN 0-88050-708-X

Library of Congress Catalog Number 84-42806

INTRODUCTION

Some things in life are as ageless as the stars, as enduring as a smile. Some things in life soar above impermanence and change and carry you to everlastingness. Truth is like this. And the words of Bhagwan Shree Rajneesh are like this.

This volume is a mosaic, a mixed bag of tricks. There are one-liners to shock you, anecdotes to shake you and questions to stir your heart. There are tales to provoke you, talks to inspire you and treatises that will turn you into the very thirst for your own transformation.

This book has everything. It's a tranquil lake; it's a roaring waterfall. It's the nightingale's song; it's the hornet's sting. It's a garden in the sunshine; it's the jungle on the darkest night.

It's the long and the short and the all.

Swami Krishna Prem, M.M.,D.Phil.M.(RIMU), Acharya

1
KNOWLEDGE AND UNDERSTANDING

You ask what my message is? It is a brief one indeed: those who are awake are alive; those who are asleep miss everything.

No man is given manhood ready-made. He has to build it by himself. This is both a blessing and a bane. It is a blessing because he is free to create himself; it is a bane because there is always the possibility he will die without ever having become a man.

Man does not become God by developing himself. If he were able to open himself fully, he would know he is already God himself, here and now. As I see it, the complete revelation of the self is the only development there is.

It is no exaggeration to say that we have forgotten ourselves. Have we not forgotten our own births? Then what else can one say about a life that rests on a foundation of self-forgetfulness? Isn't such a life really just a dream?

What, if any, is the difference between dreaming and

being awake? In a dream the dreamer is completely forgotten. The dream overwhelms him, it happens right in front of him, but he is not present in the dream. In fact, his absence itself is his sleep because the moment he is present he is neither asleep nor dreaming.

Then what shall we call this so-called life of ours? It is certainly not wakefulness because we cannot remember our selves. So is it a dream too? Yes, my friend, this too is a dream. As long as there is insensibility towards the self, life is but an empty dream.

Gurdjieff has said that man is a machine. In all his activities man is nothing but a passive participant. His actions are unconscious, unaware. They are really reactions. A man may love, hate and feel anger, but these are simply expressions of unconscious and mechanical forces at work within him. He is really only an agent through which nature works. He has no conscious vitality of his own. What we can call real life only begins when a man rises above this mechanical state of existence.

A young man came to see me yesterday. He asked, "How shall I conduct my life so I will never have cause to repent anything in the future?"

I replied, "There is only one answer to your question—discover real life. What you know as life is not life at all."

For one who has not yet attained to life the question of using it correctly has no meaning whatsoever. Not attaining real life is to misuse life; attaining it is to use it correctly. The absence of real life causes the need for repentence; living an authentic life results in bliss. What can a man accomplish when his real life is still dormant within him?

A man who is asleep is not one, but many. He is a crowd. Mahavira has said that man has many minds. It is true. Not one, but many individuals exist inside us. And a crowd cannot decide anything. A crowd cannot make a judgment;

a crowd cannot determine anything. To accomplish anything at all it is imperative the soul in each one of us becomes activated, becomes awakened. We must become one, instead of the disorderly crowd we are at present. We must become conscious of our own individuality. Only then will reactions be replaced by actions. Jung has termed this the individual's attainment of his center.

When a man is asleep, unawakened, all of his efforts are futile. There is no sense of direction in such a man. What one part of him creates, another destroys. It is like yoking bullocks to the four sides of a cart, putting the reins into the hands of a sleeping driver and still hoping to get somewhere. The life of the ordinary man is just like this. He thinks he is getting somewhere but he is not really moving at all. Such a man achieves nothing; he simply exhausts his energies.

Mankind must realize that what it has mistaken for life is nothing but a slow form of suicide. Death begins with birth. Death is part of the process of birth; it is not something that happens accidentally. Birth and death are the two poles of life. But there is a greater life, beyond birth, and we must either attain to it or perish.

It must be remembered that whatever occurs at the end of some event was also present in the beginning. The end is simply the beginning in its manifest form. And if life has two poles, then it follows it also has two directions—the possibility of life and the possibility of death. Stagnancy is death; consciousness is life. And man is a combination of these two things. He may be a machine, but there is an element in him that is able to comprehend this fact about himself. If he pursues this understanding he attains to life.

The existence of my consciousness gives me the knowledge that I am. And it is this realization itself that lights the path of existence, that illumines the path to life. The ray of light may be dim, it may be obscure, but still it is visible. And its existence is tremendously significant. That faint ray of light in the darkness is a sign, an indication that there is a possibility of reaching light. That ray of light gives me hope that the sun exists. Cannot the sun be known by a sunbeam? That ray of awareness in man points the way to his enlightenment. This slight indication of consciousness is man's greatest possibility, his greatest asset. Nothing more valuable than that exists in him. If he follows it, he can reach the self, his soul; if he pursues it, he can reach existence. This is the way to life, to the greater life, to God.

Man only has two options; there is no third direction open to him. From this initial spark of consciousness he can move forward to enlightenment or he can regress into a coma. The mechanical and repetitive circle of ordinary life does not automatically proceed towards the peak, towards enlightenment. It is an eternal law that without effort one falls back. Death comes without being invited, but life waits for an invitation.

This ray of knowledge exists in everyone, and one can only move ahead by its light. As a man begins to move inward the dimensions of knowledge begin to unfold before him and he begins to rise above his stagnant, dormant state. And as he becomes more and more familiar with his newfound, growing consciousness, something solid and deep within him begins to take shape, begins to crystallize. It is this process that leads to the individuality worthy of the name man.

It is true that man is not an animal, but is it correct to say that man has become man? His being an animal may be a past event, but his becoming a man is still a future possibility. We seem to be somewhere in the middle. This is our only affliction, our only tension, our only distress.

Only those who are dissatisfied with their miserable existences and make an effort to do something about them can become men. Manhood is not acquired automatically, you have to give birth to it within yourself. But to become a man you have to realize that simply not being an animal doesn't necessarily make you a man. You cannot be satisfied with what you are. Only a deep and fervent dissatisfaction with yourself will become your evolution.

Religious leaders make much of the teaching "Know thyself". But where does this "self" exist? Isn't one's self just the shadow of the universal self? So why should I say to you "Know thyself"? I simply repeat over and over—know, know, know! Know what is!

It makes no difference if no one recognizes me in the darkness that envelops the path of life, but just think of the terrible consequence if I fail to know myself. Many people are not as keen to know themselves as they are to be known by others. That is why life is becoming shrouded deeper and deeper in darkness. How can you shed light around you if you don't know yourself at all?

The prayer of a man of knowledge is, "I will accept death readily—unknown to the world, unrecognized by my fellow men and uncrowned with success—but at least let me know myself."

That single ray of light is enough to lead a man to God. The light of a single man who has the knowledge of the self is more valuable than the light of a million suns.

You want to know how to realize the self? First of all, come to know the non-self. Know what is not the self and understand it completely. Finally, nothing will remain; eventually, everything that is not the self will disappear. That is the self. That emptiness is the self. Only emptiness is really full.

What is this thing called consciousness? The mind is

not consciousness. When the movement of the mind has totally ceased there is another stirring—and this I call consciousness. Only when the mind becomes empty does consciousness manifest itself. The mind is the instrument, the medium. When it becomes involved with the activities of the ego it ceases to be a medium of consciousness because it is otherwise engaged. To become acquainted with consciousness is to bid farewell to the machinations of the mind.

The mind is like a servant who has usurped his master's place in the master's absence. Will such a servant ever desire the master's return? He will never be able to welcome the returning master with sincerity. He will put up every possible obstacle he can to delay the master's return. And the most basic obstruction will be his contention that he himself is the master and no one else. He will simply deny that any other master exists.

Generally the mind does exactly the same thing. This is how it becomes a barrier; this is how it hinders the advent of consciousness.

If you wish to move towards consciousness learn to let your mind relax. Allow it to remain free of activity; allow it to be empty; allow it to disengage itself from its involvements.

The cessation of the activity of the mind marks the first stirring of consciousness. And the death of the mind heralds the birth of consciousness.

It is certainly very difficult to conquer one's self, but it is impossible to conquer anything but the self. And remember, the man who conquers the self can easily achieve victory over everything else in life as well. In life there is only one conquest and only one defeat. The defeat is of the self, by the self; the conquest too is of the self, by the self.

The greatest freedom is the freedom of one's self from

oneself. We usually remain unaware of the fact that we are our own tightest chains and the heaviest burdens on our own shoulders.

Knowledge says "I am emptiness" and in that emptiness it becomes God himself. Ignorance says "I am everything; I am God" and in this fantasy of being God it remains empty. What knowledge realizes, ignorance deludes itself into thinking it has realized. What knowledge knows, ignorance can only admit to, can only accept. What ignorance proclaims, it never becomes.

To know existence, you have to transform the self into a mirror. The shadows of your thoughts distort your mind. But as thoughts subside and the mind becomes empty the mirror that is capable of reflecting the truth is suddenly there.

Nothing is simpler than greatness. Simplicity itself is greatness.

To realize existence one has to come face-to-face with non-existence first. Only when a man is encompassed by non-existence does he realize that existence can be known, can be recognized, can be lived. Only when a man is surrounded by the vast ocean of non-existence can he have the intense experience of existence itself. For the very same reason, those who thirst for the fullness of truth must first move into the realm of the void, into inner emptiness.

I am reminded of something that happened one evening. I was in a remote village and as evening approached a clay lamp was lit in the hut where I was staying. Since darkness had not yet settled in, at first it appeared as if the flame of the lamp were hardly flickering at all. Had the lamp had any consciousness it would have seen at once that it really had no light of its own at all. And had the mid-day sun been blazing down the lamp would not even have known it was burning. But as darkness approached the lamp gradually began to spread its brilliance about the room, and as the darkness thickened the light grew brighter and brighter. As the moon came up, I continued to observe the growing life, the burgeoning vitality in the flame of the lamp. If the lamp knew itself now it would have believed it was no less than the sun.

This little incident sparked a thought in me. The flame and the lamp hadn't changed at all; the change had been in the darkness. As the background of darkness grew in intensity, the brilliance of the lamp manifested itself more and more clearly. The darkness was a friend to the lamp; the darkness had helped it assert itself completely.

This is also true of the self.

When the self is enveloped by existence it is not apparent at all, but when the mind becomes completely empty the full glory of the self shines forth. It is only through the door of non-existence, through the gateway of emptiness, that one can gain access to existence, to life itself.

A set of ethics cannot be religion, but religion is certainly ethical. A moral code is nothing more than an outline, a set of rules to be imitated, to be practiced. It is a disciplinary measure imposed from outside. This is why a moralist is never free, why he becomes more and more mechanical, more and more dependent on his code. His consciousness does not awaken but falls into deeper and deeper sleep. And eventually he becomes nothing more than a sluggish lump.

Like the moralist, the immoral man is also just a slave to his habits. The immoral man follows the dictates of his own nature and the moral man follows those of society. They both live by external guidelines; they are both dependent.

The only activity that is truly independent is the search for the self. And only the man who realizes that self attains real freedom. Freedom is only possible when there has been the experience of the self. How can any kind of real freedom be possible unless the existence of the self is known, unless a man knows who he really is?

From this experience of the self a new kind of discipline arises in a man. It is not imposed externally; it is natural, self-inspired. It comes from within. And the kind of morality that springs forth then is a different thing altogether. It is not the labored imitation of any prescribed set of rules but the spontaneous manifestation of one's inner being. The morality that exists after this is not geared to acquiring anything, it exists for the distribution, for the sharing of what has been acquired.

Remember one truth all your life—to deceive another is eventually to deceive yourself. Whatever you do to someone else always comes back to you.

What is good conduct? Conduct behind which evil intentions, preconceived opinions or selfish motives lurk is certainly not good conduct. Such conduct is both impure and incomplete. It is impure because other things are mixed up in it; it is incomplete because something outside must be added to it to complete it.

Good conduct is complete in itself. It needs no future event to complete it. Good conduct is blissful on its own; its very birth is its bliss. Bliss is inherent in the very existence of good conduct—not in any future fruition, not in any outward achievement.

Once in a lonely forest I came across a man playing the flute. There was no one there to hear him. I had lost my way in the woods and the music of his flute had guided me to the spot where he sat. "Why are you playing your flute in this solitary spot?" I asked him.

"Just to play my flute," he replied. "That is what makes me happy."

Good conduct is an action that is self-inspired; it is not

a reaction to something external. A reaction is something that is done in return, and we make the mistake of looking on reactions as our own actions. Between action and reaction there is a gulf as wide as that between heaven and earth.

Our misunderstanding lies in the fact that activity is involved in both, in reaction as well as in action. But not only are they different, they are diametrically opposed to each other. An action that occurs within an individual as the result of a stimulus from his outer environment is a reaction; that which is inspired by his inner self is the real action.

Reactions imprison us because they are externally inspired; actions free us because they are manifestations of our selves. Reaction is dependence; action is independent. Reactions carry a kind of framework with them and there is always an aspect of helplessness involved, but actions are spontaneous expressions of the soul. Reactions are always redundant, always unnecessary; actions are always fresh, new and full of life.

Being firmly established in action, in pure and complete activity, is good conduct. Reacting is a sort of falling from grace because it is mechanical. In action, on the other hand, there is growth and upward development because it comes from feeling, because it is conscious.

There is no greater affliction than trying to become what you are not. Although this desire has no end to it and offers no fulfillment whatsoever, the majority of people do succeed in their attempts to appear different from what they are.

Recognize your own nature, realize who you really are. Living according to your own nature is heavenly bliss.

A very small lamp can dispel the darkness in a house that has been shut up for years. And in the same way the tiniest ray of self-understanding can erase the ignorance that has been accumulating for hundreds of births.

In the search for life nothing is more fatal than self-satisfaction. Those who are satisfied with themselves are not alive at all. The only man who keeps moving ahead in the direction of truth is the man who is dissatisfied with himself. Remember, real virtue is constant rebellion against self-satisfaction.

On a gravestone it read, "Here lies a man who did nothing in between the great deeds he dreamed of undertaking and the small tasks he hated to perform."

Of course, this is only written on one tombstone, but ought it not to be engraved on many others as well? Isn't this the sum-total of the lives of many men? And I wish to ask you a pointed and personal question, "Isn't this the epitaph you would like to see on your gravestone as well?"

Is there anyone who can deceive us as much as we deceive ourselves? We are our own worst enemies. If you see the truth in this then you should realize that, if you wish, you can also become your own best friend. Religion begins in you when you make friends with yourself.

Do we not use different yardsticks to measure ourselves and to measure others?

A Christian of my acquaintance told his son the good news that a group of Hindus has embraced Christianity. "It is a sign of God's great mercy," he said, "that so many Hindus have shown such good sense."

"But father," his son reminded him, "you did not mention good sense at all when that Christian friend of yours became a Hindu!"

The man was furious. "Don't even mention that rebel's name to me!" he shouted in anger.

The man who leaves one's fold is considered an out and out turncoat, but those who join one's fold are thought to be men of good sense!

Because of this double standard of measurement we see the tiny speck in our neighbor's eye while the mountain in our own escapes our notice altogether. It this proper? Is this a healthy attitude? It is not up to me to ask you, but it is for you to put the question to yourself.

On the path of religion the man with two yardsticks will never be transformed. Because of his double standards he cannot even see the truth of his own life. And this unfamiliarity with himself stands in the way of any transformation. Using two yardsticks is a characteristic of an unrighteous, irreligious mind. When you measure yourself you have to use the same standards you apply in measuring others. The man who does not possess even this much impartiality will never pass through the revolution of the soul.

I do not ask you to believe in others. That is only the result of a lack of belief in yourself.

Man has to struggle against the ego; he has to fight with the "I". He has to start a revolution against the ego. To remain surrounded by the ego is to be trapped in the world; to move out of the ego is to live in God. In fact, man is God himself.

Do not try to run away from your ego, from your "I". It is impossible to run away from it because wherever you go it will be there with you. Rather than trying to run away from it, dive into it with all your energy. The deeper a man goes into his egoism the more and more he realizes that it has no real existence at all.

You want your life to be hell? Then I will tell you about a very easy and totally infallible way to achieve it. It is a method that had been tried and tested by thousands of people for thousands and thousands of years. There is no possibility of error; it is guaranteed to work. It has always proven to be one hundred percent effective. And what is this technique? It is to build your life about "I".

Egoism is the simplest and most direct path to misery. And those who stray from this path will not be able to attain sorrow no matter how hard they try. Without this method no one will ever arrive at misery, because this is misery itself. Without knowing this secret no one will ever reach hell. This is hell itself.

There is no hell except egoism. Egoism kindles the fires of hell. Get rid of your ego and there is no hell.

Pride never allows the flower of knowledge to bloom and a knowledge that is not humble is nothing but delusion. A pompous display of knowledge loudly proclaims that it has all been borrowed.

I knew a man who had never committed an error in his life and I once asked him his secret. He said, "I was afraid to make a mistake, so I never did anything. That is how I avoided making any mistakes in my life."

When I heard this I began to laugh. Somewhat affronted, he asked, "Why are you laughing?"

I answered, "What greater mistake can there be than not doing anything because you might make a mistake?"

To fear mistakes is to fear life. You have to be ready to make mistakes. The only thing is not to make the same mistake again. Only the man who avoids old mistakes but is not afraid to make new ones, lives and learns. And he is also the only one who ever wins too.

What exists can fade into nothingness and what is done

can be undone. If a man can become entangled in worldly activity, he can become liberated from it as well. His dependence can become his freedom.

It is foolishness to expect peace from something you have been longing to possess, from something you have been hankering to own. Even if you obtain your heart's delight it cannot help but be transitory. When the mind that yearns is itself a transient thing then how can any object it cherishes be everlasting?

The gates of bliss are close at hand. But if you set out with violence and hatred in your heart you will find yourself standing at the door of hell, even though you were searching for heaven. The path you take is the important thing. On its own, ambition leads nowhere at all.

There is an invisible inner fire that burns unceasingly, that constantly scorches a man. It is the fire of greed. Greed burns like a torch held aloft in a gust of wind. The man lets himself be scorched by the flame and then puts the blame on the wind.

Where is ignorance to be found? In the ego. That is where lust has taken root.

Lust is endlessly painful because it is insatiable.

Pursuing your lecherous fantasies is a wild-goose chase. It is diving into a wasteland of dreams; it is living a frigid life that only ends in a frozen death. The man who is ruled by sexual fantasies dies a thousand and one deaths in his lifetime, but the man who is ready to court death in a fight against these daydreams will find himself sitting at the deathbed of death itself.

The pleasure of the senses are like delicate flowers—

they fade if you handle them roughly. In your quest for the imperishable pleasures you have to rise far above the body and the senses.

What is sin? Sin is denying your own divinity. There is no virtue greater than constant awareness of your own godliness.

So now you have forsaken evil? That's fine. Now renounce good as well. Your vanity will remain with you as long as you have a hold on either.

What a wonderful creature man is! Side by side within him exist a mound of filth and rubbish and a precious storehouse of gold. What he chooses to dig into rests entirely in his own hands.

Don't be afraid. You will never be free of the person you fear. He will always pursue you. Your defeat is always in proportion to your fear.

To be victorious you have to wage war. But most people plan their victories even before they go into battle. As I see it, these are the people who are always defeated in the end.

Living in the world but not belonging to the world is renunciation. But renunciation has often been compared to the three monkeys—one shades his eyes to escape the evil sights of the world, one caps his ears to shut out evil sounds and the third covers his mouth to avoid evil speech. For monkeys this kind of thing may be forgivable, but as far as man is concerned it is ridiculous.

Running away from the world in fear is not freedom from the world, it is a subtle but very deep bondage. Don't run from the world; just be aware of yourself. If you try to run away even greater fear will grip you; if you stay aware you will find safety. Only fearlessness that has been acquired through knowledge will give you freedom.

Freedom is the form of the soul. If a man has will his dependence can be wiped out in a moment. A man's freedom is in proportion to his will.

Are you aware that no man has ever been deceived by others as much as he has been deceived by himself?

The time and effort spent in seeking the truth, in seeking the self, is never spent in vain. It eventually turns out to be the only time and effort you have never wasted.

The only unbridgeable gulf that can exist between one's self and truth is cowardice.

Get to know the "I" totally, in its fullness, because you have to get rid of it. Egoism is the source of darkness, yet it disappears the second a ray of light creeps in.

If there is darkness inside no outer light will do any good whatsoever.

Not long ago I had a dream in which someone slipped and fell into a ravine in the mountains. A crowd gathered around him. They teased him and laughed in derision at his weakness in falling. A priest told him he must forsake the weakness that caused his fall, and a social reformer told him he should be punished, saying that people who fall must be made an example for others.

I observe all of this in my dream and it bothers me that no one is trying to help him up. Somehow I squeeze through the crowd and reach him. When I try to lift him I see that he is already dead. Then the crowd disperses. Perhaps they have gone off in search of someone else who has fallen. The priest leaves too. Perhaps some other fallen man may be awaiting his advice on some other path. The social reformer moves away as well. Someone else may have fallen somewhere and he does not want to deny himself the chance to punish someone and to see him reform. Finally, I am the only person left near the dead man. His arms and legs look so frail and weak I find it difficult to believe he has ever been able to walk anywhere. It is not his fall but the fact that he has journeyed into the mountains at all that seems a miracle to me.

In this state of dismay I awakened from my dream. And now I see that it was not just a dream after all. All of humanity is in the same condition.

Why is life so purposeless, so meaningless, so mechanical, so sluggish? Why is it so insipid, so boring? It is because we have lost a great power, the sense of wonder. Wonder has vanished. Man has murdered wonder; his so-called knowledge has sounded the death knell on wonder.

We are under the illusion we know everything. We think we know the reason behind every secret, behind every miracle. And naturally, the man who has an explanation for each and every phenomenon under the sun will not consider anything a miracle. To a mind that is filled with so-called knowledge nothing remains unknown. And where nothing is unknown there is no wonder. There are no miracles where there is no sense of wonder. There is no charm; there is no joy. But this is the bliss of life; this is the very point of life.

I urge you to discard this so-called knowledge. It is dead. It is a thing of the past, an obstacle that stands between you and the miraculous unknown. Let it go and allow the unknown in. Awareness of the unknown is wonder. It is also the doorway to God, to the greatest unknown.

What is known is the world; what is unknown is God.

That which always exists in the present is truth. And that which is closest to you is ultimate truth. Seek to understand that which is closest, not that which is afar. How can a man who is ignorant of what is near know what is far away from him? For him who understands what is close at hand nothing remains distant at all.

One moonlit night I stood alone on the bank of a river silently gazing at the sky. Suddenly I heard a sound, and turning, I saw a young monk standing beside me. He was weeping. I asked him to sit with me and for some time we sat quietly together, my hand resting on his shoulder. There was nothing I could say to him yet my silence seemed to bring him consolation. I have no idea how long we sat there like that but at last he spoke. "I want to see God," he said. "Tell me, does he exist or not? Am I just chasing a dream?"

What could I say? I drew him closer to me. "I know no other God than love," ran through my mind. "Anyone who ignores love in his search for God will surely miss. Anyone who seeks any other temple than the temple of love is simply moving further and further away from God." These were my thoughts. But still I said nothing.

"Please say something to me," he implored. "I have sought you out with great expectation. Can you show me God?"

What was there I could say to him? I kissed his tear-filled eyes, drenched in hope, overflowing with the fervor of his desire to see God. But is God something external, something one can see?

Finally I spoke, "That very question you have put to me was also asked of Shree Ramana," I told him. "He replied that God could not be seen, but that if a man wanted to, he could become God. I say the same thing.

"It is meaningless to say you want to find God. How can you find something you have never lost? How can you find that which you yourself are? The one thing you cannot see is your self. And the idea of visualizing God as an external being simply separates him from the self. God is your self; he is your soul—and so you will never be able to see him. And my friend, if you do see God then know well, he is just a figment of your imagination. The human mind is capable of giving form to all its fantasies, but when you lose yourself in these creations of your mind you move further and further away from God, away from truth itself."

I am reminded of this incident because you also want to see God. You have come to hear me for that reason and so I must say something about it to you as well.

In the past I myself sought God in the same way, but I have since come to realize the futility of this kind of search. I realized that it was because of my ignorance of my self that I was unable to know truth, unable to know God. You have to know your self before you can know truth. And once the self is known you realize there is nothing more to be known. The door to truth is unlocked by the key of self-realization. Truth pervades existence, and the self is the door.

The man who is unable to discover his self, who cannot find something so close at hand, won't be able to find anything off in the distance either. Seeking some remote goal is an attempt to avoid that which is near. And this pursuit of worldly things begins as an effort to escape oneself, which is the same thing as trying to escape from God. All quests, except the investigation of one's own inner being, are attempts to escape from one's self.

What exists inside us? Inside there is darkness, loneliness, emptiness. And aren't you just running in circles, looking for shelter from this darkness, from this loneliness, from this emptiness? But escapism only results in suffering, nothing more. Any man who tries to avoid his self will find nothing anywhere else. All pursuits, except this inquiry into the self, lead nowhere.

There are only two alternatives—escape from the self or awakening to the self. To escape, one needs an outer goal; to awaken, one must be totally disillusioned with everything on the outside.

As long as your God remains external he is your illusion, your hallucination. Man has invented this God to escape from the self. So the first thing I wish to say to you is that there is no need to search for God, for truth, for liberation, for emancipation. You must investigate the investigator himself. That investigation alone will ultimately lead to God, to truth, to liberation. No search, other than the search for the self, can be termed religious.

The terms "self" and "self-realization" are very misleading. How can one know one's self? To know something, duality is required. So how can one know something if there are not two separate things involved? How is visualization possible; how is realization possible? Both knowledge and perception belong to the world of duality, and where there is oneness they lose their meanings, their credibility.

As an act, "self-realization" is an impossibility; the term is self-contradictory. And yet I also say to know the self. Socrates said the same thing, and so did Buddha, so did Mahavira, so did Christ, so did Krishna. Even so, you must realize that what it is that can be known is not the self, but the non-self. That can be known. The self is the perceiver, the one who realizes; it can never be the object perceived.

So, you ask, how can the self be known? Since only the object can be known, how can the knower be known? Where there is knowledge there is both subject and object, there is both the knower and the object that is known. And isn't trying to know the knower like trying to see your eye with your eye? Have you ever noticed a dog trying unsuccessfully to catch its own tail? The tail moves away from him as quickly as he tries to grab it. He can never catch it; it is impossible. In the same way, you cannot make the self the object of knowledge. I cannot know myself in the way I can know everything else.

Self-knowledge is so simple, and yet it is so complicated, so difficult. Self-knowledge is not the same kind of knowledge with which we are familiar. Not at all. It is not a relationship between the knower and an object. It is supreme knowledge, because after it there remains nothing else to be known. We can also call it supreme ignorance, because there is really nothing to be known. Objective knowledge is the relation between the subject and the object; self-knowledge is the absence of both subject and object. When this happens, only pure knowledge remains, unqualified.

It is through knowledge that all worldly objects are known. Through knowledge the object is known, but the one who knows is separate from the object. And our understanding of material things is this very relationship between subject and object.

Where there is neither subject nor object—without an object the subject no longer exists—there is knowledge of the self. Self-knowledge is the purest state of knowledge there is. We call this state self-knowledge because, as Buddha explained it, neither self nor non-self exists in this state.

To most people the word "self" suggests ego. But this is not the case. As long as the ego exists, there can be no self-knowledge.

But how can one attain to this knowledge? Where is the path to be found?

I was once a guest in a house that had so many things in it there was hardly any room to move about. The house was large, but because it was so overcrowded it seemed quite small. In fact, the house was really invisible. A house is the empty space enclosed by the walls, not the walls themselves. The space is the house; it is that space in which we live.

During the evening the host complained that there was no room in his house. He asked how he could make more space. I laughed and told him there was all kinds of room in his house. It was there; he had just filled it with things. If he got rid of some things, I told him, he would see how much space he really had.

The process of self-knowledge is not unlike this.

"I" is always there. Whether awake or asleep, whether sitting or walking, whether in pleasure or in pain, "I" is there. Whether one is knowledgeable or ignorant, "I" is present. No one doubts the fact that he exists, that he is. A man can doubt everything else in the world but he cannot doubt his own existence. Descartes has said, "Even if I doubt, I am there. Who else is there to doubt besides me?"

But who am I? What is this "I"? How can I know it? I can accept that I exist, but what is this "I"? Who am I? I do not doubt my existence; I do not doubt that I am able to know, that I possess consciousness, perception. There is a possibility that what I know may be false, may be fantasy, but my capacity to know is real.

Let us consider these two facts. First there is the fact of your existence, and secondly, there is the fact that the ability to know exists within you. You can set out on your search on the basis of these two facts alone.

You know that you are, but you do not know who you are. So what is to be done? You must first investigate your capacity to know. You have no other alternative. Knowledge is a tremendously powerful force, but it is hidden by objects, by the things you know through it. Over and over again, in the same way one thought gives way to another, one object is replaced by another. No sooner has your knowledge been freed from one object than it is trapped by another.

But if this knowledge were freed from objects, if it simply existed without anything outer on which to focus, then what would happen? In such a void, where there was nothing to comprehend, wouldn't knowledge then turn towards itself, wouldn't knowledge then know itself? When knowledge is freed from any object it settles on itself. When it is not tied to any object it is pure. That purity, that emptiness itself is what self-knowledge is. When one's consciousness is without object, without thought, without focus, this experience is what we call self-realization.

In this realization neither ego nor object exists. Nor is there any word for this experience. Lao Tzu has said, "Whatsoever you may say about truth, it becomes a lie as soon as you have uttered it." Yet, is there anything man has said more about than truth? When we say it is indescribable we are also describing it. Knowledge is beyond words, but as with love there is an urge to talk about its bliss, its light, its freedom. However incomplete the comparisons may be, however unsatisfying the answers to your questions may be, every man who knows wants to say something, even if it is only to explain to you that he wishes to say something but cannot. The problem is that these statements, these suggestions about truth can create great misunderstandings.

The man who searches for the self as one searches for an ordinary object is on the wrong path. The self cannot be the object of knowledge. The self is not an object at all. It cannot be aimed at, like some target, for it is the intrinsic nature of the seeker himself. The investigation and the investigator are one and the same. Only those who do not search for anything else can search for the self. Only those who empty themselves of all knowledge can come to know the self. And when all searching has finally been abandoned, one's consciousness reaches its natural state, the state in which it has always been.

Once someone asked Buddha what he gained by meditation. Buddha replied, "Nothing. I have lost much, but I have gained nothing. I have lost my passion, my thoughts, my struggles and my desires, and I have only gained what I have always been since time immemorial."

You cannot lose your innate nature. You cannot lose God.

And what about truth? Truth is without beginning, without end. To find your intrinsic nature you have to erase all that is untrue from your consciousness. You only know what is true when you have lost everything that can be lost. The truth is attained when you have lost your dreams.

Let me say it again—the truth is attained when you have lost your dreams. When all your dreams have gone, what remains is your self. That alone is truth. That alone is freedom.

You cannot become a rose. But that is no reason for you to become a thorn. You cannot become a twinkling star in the sky, but do you have to become the dark cloud that covers its light? Let me tell you a little secret—the man who does not become a thorn becomes a flower, and the man who does not become a dark cloud becomes the shining star itself.

"Who am I?" you ask. Rather, ask yourself "Where am I?" Search for "I". Look for it in yourself. When you are unable to find this "I" anywhere you will realize who you are. The secret of who you are lies in the annihilation of "I".

A man's life is really counted by his actions, not by his years. Thoughts give birth to actions. And actions are deeper than breath. The breath just drags the years along in its wake. Feeling and emotions are even deeper than thoughts, but there is an unfathomable depth that is even more profound than any of these things. And that is a man's soul. The man who goes deeper and deeper into himself rises higher and higher in life. The proportion is the same. A tree that aspires to touch the sky must first fix its roots very deep in the earth.

I cannot walk the path to truth for you. Nor can anyone else. You have to undertake that journey for yourself. Know this and know it well, otherwise you will spend your precious life in vain. The path of life is shrouded in darkness and no other light but the light of self-understanding can illumine your way. You are your own darkness and you can also be your own light. No one else but you can envelop you in darkness, so how can you expect anyone else to be a light for you?

What shall I say about *dharma*, about religion? Whatever I say will not be religion. That which is beyond words cannot be expressed through speech.

Don't mistake the scriptures for religion; they contain only words. Words divide. Words have divided humanity. The walls that exist between men are not of stone, they are built of words. And the same wall of words stands between man and truth. Anything that has separated man from truth has separated him from everything. Words are mantras that have hypnotized us into straying from our authentic natures, from our real selves.

The man who is unfamiliar with himself is far from the truth. This is because the understanding of one's self is the nearest thing there is to truth. Everything else is distant, far removed. Words hide the self as the waves camouflage the ocean; the turmoil of words shrouds the inner music as smoke smothers a fire.

We spend our lives caught up in exploration of the outer shell, ignoring the man within. I look inside myself. I see words—thoughts, memories, images, dreams—words. The real me is buried beneath this layer of words. Is this it? Is this all? Or is there something else within me, beyond this cloud-cover of words? Everything depends on your answer to this question. If the answer comes from words, from thoughts, then you will never know *dharma*, you will never know what religion is. Thought cannot know that which is beyond thought. Thought is its own limitation.

Generally, in the search for the self, this is where people turn back. They run up against this invisible wall and retrace their steps. It is very frustrating. It is like digging a well and only finding more rocks, more and more stones. But to be confronted by this layer of stones, of words, is quite natural. This is only an outer layer, only a veil.

To find the self you have to pierce this veil. You must move on until you arrive face to face with the naked truth. You must keep on digging through the layers of words until you hit the well of wordlessness. You must brush away the dust of thoughts until the mirror of the self is reflected. This is not easy. You not only have to remove your clothes, you also have to strip away your skin. This is penance, this is real atonement.

Have you ever peeled an onion? You have to peel yourself like that. After the layers and layers of peel have been removed the essence remains. That is your authentic being. That is you.

You have to drive all thoughts away; you have to know, to recognize, to understand everything that is not you. You have to dive deep.

And there is to be no choosing between good and bad. These are intellectual evaluations and do not lead beyond thought. This is the difference between morality and religion. Morality is the selection of what is good, as opposed to what is bad. In religion, there is no selection; religion is beyond all choice.

When there is nothing left to choose, all that remains is one's self. When a man becomes free of choice, thought evaporates. And only awareness remains. There is no object any more, there is only consciousness. At this point the wisdom that has always been latent in you manifests itself, and the gates of religion are thrown open to you.

I invite you to meet your self. What the scriptures cannot give you is already within you. What no one else can give you, you can attain yourself. The truth is realized as soon as you go beyond words.

Man is a journey, a journey to the infinite. Nietzsche has said, "Man's greatness is this: he is the bridge, not the destination." I say the same thing.

When I look into myself do you know what I realize? I realize that salvation is nearer to me than the ground under my feet.

The physical body is a sacred temple. Instead of fighting with it, go inside; the path to God lies through it. The body is a place of holy pilgrimage; God has chosen it as his abode. The true seeker after spiritual perfection acknowledges his body, cooperates with it in gratitude and directs all its energies towards the ultimate merger with the universal soul.

2
TRUTH AND SCIENCE

The experience of truth is neither a thought nor a feeling. It is a vibrating and a throbbing of all the vital components of your entire being. It is not in you: you are in it. It is your whole being, not just an experience that is happening to you. It is in you yourself, but it is larger than you because the whole of existence is included in it as well.

You ask me for a definition of truth? There is no definition of truth. How can one's self define one's self? Pilate asked Christ, "What is truth?" and Christ simply looked at him and remained silent. Truth has no words, no sounds. Truth is an experience of the extreme depths of the self. It is total identification with what is.

Truth is not the opposite of untruth. The opposite of untruth is still untruth. All extremes are untruths. Truth is the mean between extremes. In other words, truth transcends all extremes.

As I see it, mankind has lost all sense of direction. And this has happened because man has chosen investigation of the physical world over exploration of his own inner being. Nothing should be more important to a man than himself. His first and fundamental inquiry should be into himself.

Unless a man knows himself all his knowledge lacks authenticity. In the hands of an ignorant man nothing can be creative, but even ignorance can become a creative tool in the hands of a knowledgeable one. If a man can understand himself, can master himself, only then will his other achievements have real merit. Unless this happens he is simply digging his own grave.

That's what we are doing. We are digging our own graves. Previous civilizations were destroyed by external attack; ours is threatened by a great internal danger. If the civilization of the twentieth century is annihilated, it will be by suicide. This is what we will have to call it, if there is anyone left to call it anything. It is possible this final war may never be written into human history. It will take place outside history's ken, because it will destroy all of humanity. Those who came before us made history; we are preparing to unmake it.

We are in control of infinite material power, but we know nothing of the depths of the human heart, we know nothing of the poison and the nectar that lies hidden there, side by side. We know the atomic structure of matter but nothing of the atomic structure of the soul. And this is our great misfortune. We have achieved power, but no peace, no enlightenment.

There is great power in the hands of the unenlightened, of the unawakened. But these are the people who should not be allowed to possess power; if it is misused, power can wreak great evil. Our whole search has been for power. And this is man's mistake. He is in danger from his own achievements, from his own successes. The world's great thinkers and scientists should be made aware of the pitfalls of this preoccupation with the question of power. It is just this sort of blind, thoughtless investigation that has brought us to the brink of the present crisis. The aim should be peace, not power. And if the aim becomes peace, then the focus will be on the mystery of man himself, not into the secrets of nature. There has been much research and exploration into unconscious matter, but the time has come when we must concentrate on man himself, on his mind.

The science of the future will be the science of man, not the science of matter. This change must occur before it is too late. Those scientists who are committed to the investigation of the inanimate are orthodox men, with minds bound by tradition and convention. Men of awareness must come forth to alter the direction of scientific research. Science must strive for knowledge of man himself.

In their efforts to master the material world modern scientists have attained results unprecedented in human history; there is no reason they cannot be equally successful in achieving the same insight into man. Man can be known. He can be mastered; he can be transformed. I see no reason to be discouraged. We can come to know ourselves, and on this knowledge we can build a totally new consciousness.

A new man can be born; a new life can begin. This has been attempted by various religions in the past, but to see it through, to perfect it, a scientific approach is needed. What religion has begun, science can complete.

In relation to the world of matter, the attitudes of conventional science and orthodox religion have always been dissimilar. In fact, religion has not been concerned with matter at all. In this area, science reigns supreme. But this does not mean religion has nothing of value to contribute. Traditional science must be abandoned and science and religion must join forces. Only this kind of marriage can save mankind. What we have acquired through our knowledge of matter is nothing compared to what we will gain by knowledge of the self. In the past, religion has only made it possible for this knowledge to be possessed by a very select few; with a scientific approach, this knowledge can be available to all.

In the human mind there are latent powers and infinite possibilities as yet undeveloped. And the reason mankind is so miserable is because of the confused state of these untapped energies. When the mind of a man is in chaos, his individual confusion automatically multiplies by the time it merges with the collective consciousness, by the time it mixes with the universal mind. Society is much more than the sum-total of its individuals—it is its individuals, multiplied; it is the expanded effect of our personal interrelations. You must remember that whatever happens in each individual will be reflected in society in a greatly magnified form. The cause of all war, the roots of all social degeneration are within the individual human mind. If we are to change society we have to change the men who exist within it; if there is to be a new base for society we have to offer a new kind of life to the individual.

I said earlier that both poison and nectar exist within the hearts of men. The confusion of energy is the poison; the control of energy is the nectar. And the way in which a man's life can be transformed into harmony and bliss is through yoga.

The ideas and actions that go against this inner harmony are sins; those that help create it, that help nourish it, are virtues. When a man is out of tune with life he lives in a state of anarchy, and a mind that knows no harmony is in hell. When this harmony is sublime a man is in heaven. And when an individual becomes one with the harmony within him, his outer actions reflect his accord with the universe. Whatever is within us is what flows from us; it is what we give out. It is also what we receive.

We must create a science that can fill the inner world of man with glowing health and celestial music—not for any future kingdom of heaven, but for this world, for life on this planet. If this life is bountiful, why worry about any other! One's imagination is only fired by visions of another world as an escape from this one. Authentic religion has nothing to do with other worlds, with other lives. But that is what has happened to this world. Religion's concern for the other world has been detrimental to mankind because it has taken his attention away from this one.

Religion, philosophy and the scriptures have not been concerned with the physical world at all, not as science has been. Matter has been conquered, but the man for whom this has been done has been completely ignored. Man must come first. Man must become the center of both science and religion.

Science must disengage itself from matter; religion, from the other world. This rejection of their individual attachments will be their point of meeting. This will give birth to the greatest event in human history; this will give birth to a great creative energy. This union alone will save mankind. There is no other way.

From this joining, from this coupling, the science of man will come into being for the very first time. The life, the future of mankind depends on this. On this alone.

Truth liberates. But the truth that liberates is manifested in the very breath of one's being. The strongest chains of all are borrowed truths. Nothing in the world is more untrue than these.

I see a lie as a pile of straw. It has no might whatsoever. The tiniest spark of truth can reduce it to ashes.

Belief and non-belief are closely related. There is really no difference between them at all. Their bodies may be different, but their souls are the same. And the man who seeks truth must beware of both of them. One is a well and the other is a ditch. Both are fine if you wish to fall, but if you want to move on towards truth you have to take the in-between path. The mind becomes liberated only after it frees itself from the two, from belief as well as from non-belief. Only the man who is neither a theist nor an atheist, neither a believer nor a non-believer, can undertake the journey to truth.

In a small village one moonless night everyone was fast asleep when the sound of weeping and crying suddenly broke the stillness. It awakened everyone, and the villagers, confused and shaken, ran towards the small hut from which the shouting came. From within they heard, "Fire! I am on fire! My house has caught fire!"

Some of the villagers immediately ran to fetch buckets of water, but on closer examination and to their great amazement they could find no sign of fire anywhere in the vicinity of the hut. There did not even seem to be a lamp burning inside. Someone brought a lantern and they pushed open the door and crowded into the hut. They found the old woman there, still yelling, "Fire! I am on fire! My house has caught fire!"

"Have you gone mad?" they shouted back at her. "Where is the fire? Show us where it is and we'll put it out."

The old woman's shouting stopped and she began to laugh instead. "I am not mad," she said, "But you are. You have all gathered here to put out a fire that has broken out in your own houses. Go back to your own homes and look for the fire there. The fire I am shouting about has broken out within me and you will not be able to extinguish it. Only knowing myself can put out this fire. If the fire had been outside you could have doused it, but what I am shouting about is the inner fire."

And once again she began weeping and wailing that her house had caught on fire and that she was burning up inside.

I was in that village on that particular night—and all of you were there too. You may have forgotten the incident but I have not. I saw you all returning to your houses, upset by the old woman's behavior, annoyed that she had disturbed your sleep. When you arose next morning you had forgotten all about it. Actually one could say the whole world has forgotten that incident, since that village is also the dwelling place of the entire human race.

You all went back to sleep but I could not. That old woman shook me out of my sleep once and for all, because when I looked inside to find that invisible fire I found nothing at all. I did see, though, that my sleep had been only a dream, only an illusion, and that the illusion itself was the fire of which she spoke.

Most people's lives are simply consumed in flames because of this illusion, because of this ignorance of the reality of life. But that ignorance itself is only an illusion, and it is this illusion that causes you pain, that makes you miserable. But you cannot see the fire, and so you go back to sleep, back to you dreams. Dreams are good companions of sleep, but they make it difficult for you to awaken. Dreams are, in fact, fuel for this fire of illusion.

Painful dreams may make you uncomfortable, but then you simply turn over. You tolerate bad dreams in expectation of nice ones. But the absence of painful dreams does not guarantee pleasant ones. It just makes you hope for better dreams to come. But pleasure and pain are yoked together; they are like a pair of bullocks pulling the cart of dreams. And so a man wastes his life in sleep, in dreams. And one who is asleep cannot be called alive.

This is the very old and very painful story of humanity. It is as old as creation. But whenever a man says that he is on fire people say he is mad. They ask where the fire is and then rush to him with buckets of water to put it out. But the fire is not on the outside, and so those whose eyes are only accustomed to looking outwardly cannot find it. And how can outer water extinguish inner fire anyway?

Whether the fire is visible or not, every individual feels at some point that his life is consuming him. And where there is fire, there is flame—whether we can see it or not. Its existence does not depend on our sight.

The truth is that the fire only exists because we cannot see it. It's very existence is due to our unawareness. It lives only in our ignorance. But when a man feels the heat of the flame he thinks he is burning up and instead of looking for the cause of the fire he rushes madly about in search of water. This quest for water is also an illusion. Everyone is running here and there in search of water—be it in the form of wealth, fame or salvation.

Water is outer, and to find it requires an outward approach. But this outer race only adds fuel to the flames; it only stimulates the fire. Any outer search only fans the flames and as one is running about looking for water on the outside the flames get higher and higher, the inner fire grows hotter and hotter. It is just a vicious circle. But even this vicious circle is also an illusion. And you can never find the water you are looking for. All the wells are illusory too. How can any outer effort extinguish this inner fire?

The man who thinks he has found water and the man who cannot find any at all really share the same defeat. Illusion and real success can never exist together. One's lack of success is really fuel for the fire of illusion.

When Alexander the Great died, millions of people came to pay homage. And they found, much against tradition, that his hands were visible. In almost every country it is customary to place the hands inside the coffin. When people asked about it they were told Alexander has expressly wished his hands be visible so that people could see that he too had left the world empty-handed. A great conqueror like Alexander also leaves the world with nothing in his hands! How nice it would be if every corpse's empty hands were exposed so mankind could witness again and again the truth that worldly possessions have nothing to do with life at all.

Nothing outward can ever extinguish the inner fire. No outer happiness can ever cure inner pain. No amount of outer light can ever dispel the inner darkness. But up to now all attempts to remove this inner darkness have been made by outward approaches. And it is this very effort that has given birth to science.

I am not against science. On the contrary, I am a great friend of science. But I wish to assert that science can never bring peace, joy or anything of real value to mankind on its own. Alone, it can never truly serve mankind. It can provide comforts, however, but all these comforts do is help us forget our misery for a while. Within a very short time we get used to them. We soon take them for granted and then we are miserable once again. All they do is suppress mankind's misery, not cure it. And then we seek new answers in even greater comforts. It is an endless merry-go-round. It causes neuroses, agony, misery, and ultimately culminates in madness.

Science is relative only insofar as life on the physical level is concerned. And really, scientific knowledge is quite essential, because it can help to improve things on the physical plane. Pain is felt on the outside, for example, and an outer remedy may appear to work, but in actual fact pain is not the source of human agony at all. Pain is simply the outer boundary of an inner agony, and the center of that agony is one's own inner conflict. Outward remedies may help us to escape from pain but they can never cure it. And because of the numbing effect of these outer remedies, the inner conflict goes on increasing.

The higher the outward trappings of happiness, the deeper is one's inner poverty. It is not at all suprising that Buddha and Mahavira, in the midst of their worldly riches, felt their inner poverty so keenly.

SCIENCE

Because of the great riches science has brought mankind, people are gradually waking up to the fact that outer wealth does not guarantee inner peace and freedom. The advances of science have slowly shattered this age-old conviction. The progress of science has not only shown man the benefits of science, it has also bared its faults. Science is not as useless as the orthodox religious leaders used to believe, nor is it as infallible as its blind supporters once thought it was. Whenever this kind of blind faith exists, things are never perceived as they really are.

Faith has always been a great blindfold. Blind faith smothers facts with ready-made formulas, clouds the truth with cut and dried theories. Shrouding a fact in theories is running away from the fact itself. Looking squarely at facts as they are is to widen one's vision, and what one learns then does not constrict life but liberates it from all narrow-mindedness. By viewing life through this haze of preconceptions, humanity has reduced itself to a crippled and stagnant state. Man cannot view life as a whole. He has never looked at life except through the veil of his own subjective selection; he has never seen life as it is, in its perfection, in its unity.

Religion has denied the outer in many ways, and in reaction others have denied the existence of an inner being. Science has done this. And so religion and science have long been each other's rivals. But this competition has not really been between religion and science, it has been a war of one mental state with another, of one human tendency with another.

The human mind is motivated by its predispositions; it swings from one state to another like the pendulum of a clock. One mental state simply gives birth to another, but the truth is not to be found in any of these conditions. No condition can be perfect; it is not in its nature to be perfect. Reality only exists in between these mental states, in between these conditions. Reality is only present when all conditions have dissolved, when all is still.

Reality is only to be found in the absence of conditions.

Life is neither inner nor outer. Life is both. If a man concentrates on the inner, then he sees only the center and loses sight of the periphery. But how can there be a center without a circumference? The center only exists because the circumference exists. And if a man only concentrates on the circumference then the center is lost to him. And how can there be a circumference without a center? Life is both. Life is never just inner or outer, never one particular state on its own.

Science is research on the circumference, into man's environment, religion is an inner inquiry, focused on the self. Science is concerned with the material world; religion is concerned with God. And though exploration of the outer and the quest for the inner may at first appear to contradict each other, they are really just two faces in the search for one total truth. The controversy only exists in man's imagination. Life is whole, total. Only the perversity of human nature has created this division.

Life is the totality of inner and outer. The breath one inhales is the breath one exhales. The in-breath and the out-breath are just the two sides of the same coin. And what is air? Is air outer or inner? It is neither and it is both. From a subjective point of view we can call it inner; from an objective standpoint we can call it outer. But as far as breathing is concerned it is both. It is all relative. And life is the same. If you look at life from one angle it is an inner phenomenon; if you look at it from another, it is outer. Science is the objective angle; religion, the subjective.

The reality of life can only be perceived by one who can view life from both perspectives, by one who is outwardly and inwardly calm, tranquil and still. Only the man who is free of opinions and preconceived ideas can see the unity and integrity of life. No one can ever experience the totality of life as long as he is bound by concepts and fixed ideas, because this fragmenting of life creates space for the ego.

Where there are no points of view, no concepts, no ideas, there is no ego, no "I". Then what is, simply is. That is truth. Truth is not a viewpoint; truth manifests itself when all viewpoints have dissolved. And where no changing circumstances exist, reality exists. And that is truth. The realization of truth is the only water that can extinguish the flames of life's frustrations.

When a man identifies himself with objects, with possessions, he divides his heart. He is in inner conflict and he is in outer conflict. But people always find themselves caught up in this duality. This duality, this split, is caused by identification of the self with something outer, and it is because of this identification that the duality exists. It is another vicious circle. But we all live with and suffer this dichotomy. And the man who is able to look at his life objectively will find that the tension arising from this feeling of duality just keeps on increasing, because the wheel of identification keeps revolving by its own momentum.

Science has a beginning—it begins with the circumference of life—but it has no end. And so it keeps moving further and further away from the center. Science is a single-pointed quest. It is simply a means; it is not an end in itself. It sets out in search but can never attain a final goal.

Religion is an inner state. But it is not really a state. Religion is inner peace and emptiness, but the roots of all states, of all human conditions are only found on the periphery.

Religion is an inner search. But the word "search" is not really accurate, because this search is effortless.

Religion is inner watchfulness. But the observer, the act of observing and the observed only exist as long as there is duality, as long as man is centered on the circumference. The heart makes no such distinctions.

Science is technology. So can religion also be called technology? No, religion is not technology at all. What exists on the outside can be explained by technological terms, but what exists at the inner core is beyond all explanation. In fact science starts where explanation begins—on the outside.

Science is words; religion is silence. Because the circumference consists totally of expression, of manifestations, science exists in words; because the inner is unknown, invisible, silent, religion needs no words at all. Science is like a tree; religion is the seed.

Science can be known; religion cannot be known. But although religion cannot be known, a man can be religious and can live in religion. Science is knowledge, but a religion has to be lived. And so science can be taught, but religion can never be a subject for any kind of instruction.

Science is the search for the known; religion is the discovery of the unknown. Science aims to widen the scope of human happiness within the world, while the aim of religion is for one's individual identity to dissolve into the unknown. That is the reason there are so many different sciences, but only one religion. Science is progressive; religion is unchanging and eternal.

To seek security by looking for happiness on the circumference is to move even further away from the reality of one's being. Yet the great mystery of life is that when a man moves closer to his center, closer to reality, he becomes happy on the circumference. But the process is such that when he reaches his center the circumference disappears, happiness and all. This happens because his center, his self, dissolves as well. When worldly happiness exists, the self exists, when the self dissolves, worldly happiness ceases to exist as well. The center only exists because the outer exists. Their existences are relative.

As it approaches the center the circumference grows smaller and smaller until it is finally reduced to the point where it coincides with the center completely. And then the identity of both is lost. This point of meeting is the door to truth. It is neither the center nor the circumference, but a state wherein the seer and the seen, the observer and the observed, become one.

This is why I say that science can be at odds with religion, but that religion can never instigate any kind of argument with science. The outer can be at odds with the inner, but this is not possible for the inner. The inner knows no outside at all. The son may be at odds with the mother, but for the mother her son's existence is her own.

Religion cannot be in opposition to science; if it is, then it is not real religion. Nor can religion stand against the world. The world may oppose religion but the opposite can simply never happen. Religion is absolutely non-controversial.

Religion is a song of a freedom; where there is, controversy or antagonism there is bondage. And where there is controversy there is no peace. There is only fire.

So that old woman was quite justified in shouting, "My house is burning. I am on fire." This is why she laughed when people came running with pails of water—just like scientists who go on searching for outer remedies. She must be still laughing because the world is still in the same dilemma today. At this very moment the world's quandary is the same. This is the same moonless night.

Right now the villagers are being awakened from their slumber but not out of their lifelong hypnotic sleep. Right now they are rushing about with buckets of water. Right now they are asking, "Where is the fire? We cannot see it. Show it to us and we will put it out. We have buckets of water to throw it."

Every night the same thing happens over and over again. But the fire is inner and the water is outer. So how can that fire be extinguished? The fire blazes higher and higher every day and humanity continues to be consumed in its flames.

There is a possibility that the fire may one day reach a crescendo and that humanity may finally surrender itself to it. Another possibility is that as the fire reaches its climax, mankind may finally see the truth, may finally be transformed, may finally achieve wisdom. But remember, science can never extinguish that inner fire. So far, with all its inventions and innovations, science has only succeeded in fanning the flames.

And what has science really done for humanity? Great effort and much research have brought science to its present state, but the inner fire continues. All the miraculous discoveries of science have simply given man great power, reinforced the circumference, added more fuel to the already-blazing fire.

Would you find it strange if the tremendous strength science has placed in the hands of the ignorant finally proves to be man's downfall? As I see it, the last two world wars have just been rehearsals for the eventual and total destruction of humanity. Approximately one hundred million people lost their lives in these two wars. And yet preparations for warfare still continue. The Third World War will be the final one. I do not mean that mankind will wage war no more, I simply mean there will be no one left to attack, no one left to defend.

This desire for self-destruction that mankind continues to display is not without cause. Man's outward quest has not brought him anything satisfying or substantial, and perhaps this may be the underlying reason behind his desire for the total destruction of the world.

Despite everything he has at his disposal man is exactly where he has always been. His life is empty, aimless. It was only at the hour of his death that Alexander the Great realized his hands were empty, and by having them visible in his coffin he wanted to help his people understand the mystery of death. Could it be that because man has had a glimpse of death he wants to destroy himself? Could it be he wants to save God the trouble? When one's hands are empty and one's soul is shallow what is the meaning of life, what is the aim of life, what is the purpose of life?

A man's life is pointless because he does not know life at all. And there is no question that what he knows as life is pointless. It is not worth living at all. If a man lives his life without paying any attention to the inner, by looking for solutions to his misery outside, his life is bound to become purposeless. This is because the only things that are left for him are material things, objects. If a man seeks security in material things at the expense of the inner he causes his own sickness, misery, poverty and frustration—and ultimately invites his own death.

And the man who simply denies the outer world and looks for security in the inner is equally helpless. He creates mental conflict for himself at a sub-conscious level and is also deprived of inner peace and freedom. Only a man who lives in love and beauty can really reach his inner core. Denying the outer only brings sorrow and frustration and the resulting conflict carries inertia and stagnation along with it. This kind of subjective conflict only strengthens the ego. And when this happens it is impossible to attain to one's innermost being.

Life is a unity, a merger of both subject and object. Life is the rhythm of subject and object. Where suppression, domination or tension exist, there is no life. Life only exists in peace, serenity and simplicity. And these only grow out of awareness—awareness towards life, awareness of what really is. Awareness is the lack of ignorance; awareness is consciousness. In a state of total awareness there is a constant flow from the object on the circumference to the subject in the center. And then there is the kind of quest that is neither subjective nor objective. This is an authentic quest.

That is why I say over and over again that ignorance, unconsciousness and unawareness are a fire in which life is being consumed, and that understanding, consciousness and awareness bring about a totality in which one's life is transformed into bliss. The very energy that consumes a life of ignorance is transformed into bliss through awareness. There is nothing worse than ignorance and unawareness, but if a man lives in awareness every power he has becomes blissful. Energy is neutral, impartial. How energy is used depends totally on the individual.

To a really religious mind, the inability of science to achieve fulfillment on its own is not a source of frustration. It can be turned into a medium for inner contentment. It can help make the world a paradise. The union of science and religion can give birth to an entirely new vista, to a totally new dimension for mankind.

A king once said to an ascetic, "I have heard that sleeping too much can be harmful, but still I sleep a great deal. What is your opinion?"

The ascetic replied, "It is bad for good people to sleep too much, but it is good for bad people to sleep a great deal. The more active bad people are the more they work to bring frustration to the world."

Where there is inner peace activity is always constructive, but where there is inner conflict, dullness and lethargy are good things.

In the hands of the righteous, science can be a means to achieve great good, but how can one justify the existence of science when it is in the hands of monsters? When power is coupled with understanding the result is bliss—but the combination of power and ignorance is certain to end in disaster. And humanity is caught up in just such a sorry state of affairs. Science has given man power, but where is the right understanding to enable mankind to use this power properly? There will be disaster if peace is not achieved. It is only in peace that man moves on energetic, creative and constructive paths. But now all we have is outer creativity and inner frustration. The mathematics is simple; the combination is very dangerous indeed.

A mind that is frustrated and disturbed only derives pleasure from torturing others. An unhappy and discontented mind values nothing more than this kind of perverted pleasure. We can only give that which we possess. An unhappy man feels even more unhappy when he sees others who are content. His only desire is to see that others are as discontent as he. This is what has been happening; this is what is happening.

Science has put great power into the hands of ignorant and frustrated men, and this power itself will most likely be responsible for the total destruction of life on this planet. Such men have been and are in positions where they control the possibility of global destruction. If mankind becomes engaged in this kind of holocaust can it be said to be accidental? Aren't we all involved? Aren't we all heading in the same direction? Where are all man's efforts invested? What are we living and dying for? Is it only to invite death, to invite mass suicide?

In the past, so-called religious people used to meditate to escape life. Now science has provided new avenues for people of all walks of life to escape life collectively and instantaneously! Who would want to miss such a golden opportunity?

We are all co-conspirators, fellow-comrades in this march towards planetary suicide. And even those who talk of peace are ready to destroy each other. They are even prepared to forfeit their own lives for peace. And they talk of the great sacrifices they are willing to make to protect the world! They are also enemies of peace, they are also partners in this inevitable annihilation of the human race.

Do I mean by this that all of humanity has gone mad? Perhaps. But this statement is not quite accurate because it may create the impression that man, at one time, was in his right senses! If the truth be known, man is now as he was before, as he has always been. The only difference is in the power he possesses today. In the past that power was not his. And it is this newfound power that has brought all his hidden frustrations to the surface. Power and prestige do not necessarily result in madness, but under the aegis of power a man's hidden madness finds the opportunity to show its true colors. And all man's frustrations are surfacing.

We should be grateful to science for such a tremendous breakthrough. All man's facades have been stripped away and now he stands there, naked and insecure. He is in a dilemma. But at such a crucial point he can either perish or awaken into a new way of life.

To come face to face with reality and to remain oblivious to it is to bring any further evolution of life to a standstill. Mankind previously labored under some very false and dangerous notions, but it is better to face the facts now than to indulge in more intellectual escapism. False notions are not only harmful to others but to one's self as well. And it is because of this self-deception that man has been unable, in the past, to break through the barriers that hemmed him in. The time has now come when man can see his frustrations clearly. The time has now come when, whatever the disease, a way can be found to overcome it.

In a short period in human history, in three thousand years, there have been approximately fifteen thousand wars. Five wars every year! Is this not perverse? And these wars were all supposedly fought for peace! If this is not the summum of perversity then what is? Since mankind has come into existence this planet has only been through two particular phases—war and preparation for war. There has never been a period of peace. The span between wars cannot be called peace; it has only been a breather to allow for the preparation of the next war! If this is not pathological, then what is? Does mankind live just for war?

Because of science this disease has reached its climax. There is no doubt about it. But the disease must go. If mankind wants to survive it must rid itself of this affliction no matter how close it may be to its heart. The older an infirmity is and the more used to it one becomes, the more pleasant it seems. This particular disease is hereditary; it has become habitual. The older something is, the more solid its claim, the more one will defend it—and the sickness of war is as old as man himself. It is deeply and firmly rooted in the culture of mankind.

I would like to tell you a little story. It is absolutely untrue, but what it has to say is very true.

After the Second World War was over, God was quite perturbed about what he had seen—man's treatment of man in particular. But his concern reached a peak one day when a messenger arrived to inform him that mankind was preparing for a third global war. The perversity of human nature brought tears to his eyes. And so he invited the representatives of three major powers—Great Britain, the United States and the Soviet Union—to call on him. When they arrived God said to them, "Have I heard correctly? Are you preparing for a Third World War? Did you learn nothing from the second?"

Had I been there I would have pointed out to God that mankind is always learning its lesson. For the Second World War, man learned his lesson. For the Second World War, man learned his lesson from the first! And for the third, they have already acquired all the knowledge they need from the second! But I was not there. However I am here, and I am telling you exactly what I would have said to God.

But, being God, he said with divine benevolence, "I will give each of you anything your heart desires on the condition that you avoid this suicidal war. The Second World War was quite sufficient. I have already repented enough about creating mankind, and I would be grateful if you would harass me no further in my old age. Haven't you noticed that after I created mankind I didn't create anything else?"

Had I been there I would have said, "You are quite right, God. As they say on earth: once bitten, twice shy." But I was not there.

The American representative said, "Almighty Father, we

have no great desire at all. We have but one trivial wish. If that is fulfilled there will be no need for another war as far as we are concerned."

God seemed quite pleased at this. But when the American ambassador added, "Our only wish, trivial as it is, is that there should be no trace left of Russia on the face of the earth," God was unhappier than he had ever been since creating man.

Mankind seems to want complete revenge on his creator!

Then God turned to the Russian. "Comrade," the Russian spokesman said, "first of all I would like to point out that we don't believe in you at all. Our great nation forgot about you years ago. We have annihilated every trace of you from our world. But we are prepared to revive worship in you; we are prepared to allow you once again into the devasted and dilapidated churches, synogogues, and mosques, but you will have to do something for us in exchange. We would like to have America wiped off the face of the world map. If you feel you are not in a position to do this, don't worry. It may take us a bit of time, but even without your help we are quite prepared to do it on our own. We may survive or we may not survive. That is unimportant. We will do it anyway. We will do it for the common welfare of all men. The future of humanity lies in the destruction of America."

And then God raised his tear-filled eyes to the British ambassador. Can you possibly imagine what the Englishman said? No, probably not. He said, "Oh Lord, we have no desire of our own at all. All our wishes would automatically be fulfilled if the desires of both our friends were satisfied at one and the same time."

Such is the state of affairs!

Is this really such an untrue story? Can any story be more factual than this?

This incident is not only about these three countries. All nations have the same notions. Where nationality exists, war exists. The very concept of nationality ultimately results in war. And this is not only true of nations. The situation between individuals is the same. If this kind of perversity is not already present between men, then how can it possibly exist between countries? The individual is a part of everything that happens to the whole human race. Whether a collective action is one of love or one of hatred, the source is always individual.

If the entire world were blanketed with clouds of hatred one would only have to look into the heart of each individual to find the source of the personal anger, ambition, pain, misery and hate that have combined to form those clouds. When one man stands against another in hatred or in violence the effect multiplies. It spreads all over. It becomes like a shadow of death, encompassing the earth. And the totality of this hatred and violence is far greater than the sum-total of individual hatreds, of individual acts of aggression.

But what has happened with hate can also happen with love. There is the possibility of a love that can be many times greater than the total contributed by each individual. That love is God. But what we have now is a monster, hatred itself. You can call that Satan. But remember neither God nor Satan is separate from the totality, from the whole. They are nothing but human creations. What is good in man is God. What is beautiful in him is paradise; what is evil in him is hell.

A man constructs his own world. What I am is my contribution to the world. And by that very offering I become a participant in the creation of the world, in the creation of my environment. In that respect every man is a creator. It is essential to understand that each individual is a contributor to the ugliness of the world, that each individual is equally responsible for whatever happens in the world, be it violence, anger, hatred or total annihilation by war. The responsibility for this condition rests on each and every pair of shoulders. Everyone is responsible. No matter how unimportant he may be, every man is responsible for every war, even the most major catastrophe. The collection of individuals is what constitutes a society. What else is society? The individual himself is society.

Man is drunk with ambition. Everyone would like to be something other than he is. But in this race to become something he forgets what he really is. To be something more than one is, is impossible. What is not in the seed cannot be in the tree, yet every individual is in search of what he is not. And this is the very cause of the illness of society. It is this desire that results in violence and anarchy.

For his natural evolution man requires nothing from outside. No searching, no tampering, no outer interference whatsoever is necessary. Man is gifted with a silent, mysterious and natural evolution. But this evolution is so natural that even the results of this growth are not visible on the outside.

In the process of trying to become what he is not, a man expends great effort—but in the end he accomplishes nothing at all. Tension, struggle and unhappiness are the results of this attempt to be what one is not.

When a man remains simply as he is there is no struggle, no conflict. Such a man is simply what he is. He is not in any kind of competition with anyone. There is no trace of any other personality in him; nothing has been imposed on him from outside. His heart is free of tension, free of competitiveness—and he evolves naturally. In this way, he stops expending his energies in pointless struggle and competition and becomes a great, natural reservoir of energy. It is this very stockpile of energy that directs his innate evolution. And then there is no tension in him whatsoever.

An individual who spends his life comparing himself to others does not live his life at all. Life is an inner phenomenon. It is not to be discovered by forgetting about oneself. When a man compares himself with others he feels envy, anger and aggression. That is not life; it is a living death. And it is unavoidable that a world populated by walking corpses has become as ugly as this one is now.

When a man tries to live with all this ambition and competitiveness he is unable to find any inner peace, and in the deeper levels of his subconscious mind the conflicts and frustrations continue to multiply. And eventually, out of his despair, he begins to take revenge. He becomes destructive. The reaction of one who is unable to understand himself is destruction. The lack of self-understanding manifests itself as destruction, violence.

This is why I say that a world based on ambition can never be non-violent, whether a man's ambition is for this world or for the other world. Wherever there is ambition there is aggression. Ambition itself is violence. And science has placed immense power in the hands of ambitious people. Destruction is inevitable unless religion can erase ambition from the hearts and minds of men.

Why is there all this ambition? Where does it come from?

Ambition is the result of an inferiority complex. Inside himself every individual feels weak, ineffectual. Inside he feels shallow and empty, as if he is nothing. He feels a kind of non-existence, an emptiness. And it is this emptiness he is trying to escape.

In reality he is not running towards something, he is trying to escape from something. But it is impossible to escape from one place without fixing one's sights on another—and that is why he focuses on material objects. The root cause of man's escapism is his inner emptiness, but outwardly it takes the form of trying to attain something, of trying to reach somewhere else. In fact he is running to escape from his self.

But to accept this as a fact is to expose our own escapism and so we indulge ourselves in theories about freedom from the wheel of birth and death. This self-deception is very deep-rooted and unless one breaks this chain of deceit he will never free himself from ambition.

If a man fails at one ambition he simply selects another.

If he fails in the world he will create an ambition for God. A businessman who cannot free himself of wordly ambitions becomes a sannyasin—but it is the same ambition in a new garb. And is not ambition itself also an illusion?

The birth of religion in a man's life only takes place at the moment he begins to look at and understand the reasons he is trying to escape. Realizing that the root of ambition lies in trying to escape one's inner emptiness opens a new vista in a man's life. Thinking one can flee from one's inner emptiness is just another illusion, but being aware of one's inner emptiness is religion. Escapism is illusion; awareness is religion.

The man who tries to escape finds the inner emptiness quite shallow, but the man who lives in awareness finds no shallowness there at all. What appears as shallow in one's ignorance becomes deep, whole and profound in awareness. Trying to escape means increasing this feeling of shallowness because you move further away from your self. And the further you go the more shallow you will feel. The degree of this feeling is your distance from your self. Remember, a man is as ineffectual as his ego is strong.

A man's sense of emptiness increases as he tries to escape from his self—and the basic cause of this attempt to escape is fear. To escape is to accept your fear; to escape makes your fear secure. And whatever you accept, whatever brings you a sense of security ends up dominating you. As you try to escape, your fear does not decrease; on the contrary, it increases. Your fear grows to the same extent you lack understanding of your self. You feel more and more shallow, and this ultimately becomes very painful.

The man who does not try to escape from the self and who becomes aware of the self finds he has entered a whole new world. He does not feel shallow at all. He does not find his life empty. His whole life is one of unfathomable love and joy.

The man who is aware of the self finds no shallowness within himself whatsoever. He finds God there. There is no shallowness in the self. Shallowness is only to be found in one's ignorance of the self. If you are unaware, that unawareness itself is your feeling of shallowness; if you are aware, there is no shallowness—just like there is no darkness in the presence of the sun.

The moment you become aware nothing like shallowness exists. The moment you become the sun there is nothing like darkness to be found anywhere. I say this after having become awareness; I say this after having become the sun; I say this after having been filled with the totality. Come, look at my hands. Are they not full? You too are the sun. Your hands are also full.

But you are asleep. Your eyes are closed. Because of your slumber you do not see that your hands are already full, and so to try to fill them you spend your life in dreams. But I ask you, how can you fill hands that are not empty? How can you fill an inner emptiness that is already full? This is why all your efforts are futile. And this futility, this failure, is the cause of all human agony.

A man who is in mental anguish wants to torture others. One who suffers wants to share his suffering with others. A man can only share what he possesses. It is impossible to live without sharing what you have. Flowers share their fragrance because fragrance is what they are; stars share their light because they are light themselves. A man shares his suffering if suffering is what he is.

But man can also share joy, because man can also become joy. And religion is the road to unimaginable joy. Religion is awareness of the self, and one who is aware of his self finds there is no shallowness in him at all. He is filled with unfathomable joy, because now nothing remains to be achieved. In the self, one finds that whatever is worth achieving is already there.

The self is not shallow. The self is the fullness of joy. To be aware of the self is to be joyous; to be aware of the self is to share one's joy with others. The heart that scatters the fragrance of joy is a religious heart.

In the hands and hearts of truly religious people, science and its power could be a truly glorious thing. Such a collaboration, such a merger of science and religion has long been awaited. Are you prepared to support that union? Each man must be a vehicle. Each individual must become an instrument. Such a partnership can bring a period of great glory to the earth. It is not an era that has been and gone, it is an era that is yet to come.

There is a world of difference between the experience of truth and an interpretation of truth. When you try to interpret truth you stand outside; when you experience truth you are completely inside it, in total communion with it. This is why it is impossible for those who have had the experience of truth to define it. If a man can give you some explanation of truth it is a sign he has never experienced it. People ask me what truth is. But what can I say? I have to remain silent.

What is truth? Is it a creed, a cult, an organization, a scripture, a word?

No.

A creed is dead and truth is life itself.

Truth is not a cult. There is no path leading to truth. How can a path that is known lead to the unknown?

Truth is not an organized religion either. Truth is an experience that transcends time. It is extremely individualistic, totally personal. How can it be confined in the limited circle of time?

Truth is not a scripture. All scriptures are man-made. Truth is unformulated, uncreated, beginningless and endless.

Truth is not a word, not a sound. Sounds are born and die out, but truth exists forever.

Then what is it?

You will never find truth in the language of who, what, where, when or why. Truth simply exists, and what is just is. Truth cannot be thought about or pondered over but it can be lived. All thought and deliberation are obstacles to being in truth.

In the cadence of music, in the fullness of love, in the beauty of nature the individual virtually disappears—and what exists then is truth.

The individual himself is untruth; the non-individual is truth. The "I" is untruth; God is truth.

What so-called spiritual men call renunciation is ignorance to me. How can there be any renunciation where there is no knowledge? There can only be detachment where there is still hidden attachment; there can only be virtue where there is still sin. And these only exist in ignorance.

The man of knowledge is free from the entanglements of attachment and detachment both. In that state of realization there is no conflict between attachment and detachment whatsoever. This is the state of oneness, of non-duality, of the realization of truth—and there are no worldly pleasures, there is no renunciation. This is the state of absolute truth, of pure existence.

Ignorance lives and breathes in duality. And in this state the mind wanders from one extreme to the other. If a man drops enjoyment then renunciation steps in. But what is this renunciation? Isn't it just the opposite of attachment? And what is detachment? Isn't it simply the other side of attachment, just escaping from the world in the opposite direction? But don't forget, this kind of man becomes just as entangled by whatever it is he is trying to escape from. Detachment is just another kind of slavery. But it is not independence, not by any stretch of the imagination.

Independence is not attained by opposing untruth or by running away from falseness in life. Independence lies in the knowledge of truth. And it is truth and truth alone that makes us free.

If you do not consider the truth worthy enough to be lived then it is improper of you to consider it worthy of being honored.

For the acquisition of perfect knowledge nothing is more essential than a mind that is humble and free. But as a rule the mind is neither humble nor free. It is usually afflicted with egoistic pride and tightly hemmed in by obsessions and feelings of prejudice. Egoism constricts it from within and obsessions and prejudices restrict it from without. And imprisoned thusly, the human intellect gradually loses its capacity to rip open the seal that covers truth.

Someone once asked Albert Einstein, "What is the most important principle in scientific investigation?" Do you know what Einstein replied? Even in his wildest dreams the questioner could never have imagined the reply he was given. Einstein said, "The absence of egoism."

Without a doubt, the key to perfect knowledge is the absence of egoism. Egoism is ignorance. The mind that is filled with the notion of "I" has almost no room left to welcome truth as its guest. If it were free from this I-ness there would be lots of room for truth. The house of the heart is too small for two to obtain adequate accommodation. Kabir was not at all wrong when he said the path to God was narrow.

The ego is an avid collector of obsessions and prejudices. Can you think of an easier way to appear wise in one's ignorance? The ego gathers bits and pieces of knowledge for its own growth, for its own further development. It steadfastly holds on to its own notions and pet ideas as a way to protect itself.

You will notice that any intellectual discussion very quickly evolves into a battle of egos. It doesn't take very long before it's *my* truth, *my* religion, *my* scriptures, *my*

God, and not just truth, religion, scriptures, God. The ego thrives on this kind of thing; its whole existence is centered in these kinds of notions. How can truth be present when "I" asserts itself? How can there be any religion there? How can perfect knowledge find any room? To the extent "I" is present, truth is absent. In this sort of situation the ego simply accepts the precepts and words of the scriptures as truth and remains quite content with itself.

But there is always an element of fear in this contentment. There is always the possibility, always the suspicion that what has simply been accepted as true may turn out to be untrue. And this is why the ego proclaims a belief it has accepted as its own; it is done in order to solidify its own belief. It is even prepared to die for its sake. It is even afraid to listen to anything contradictory, because at any time some fact may come to light that could prove the truth it has accepted is really false. Under these conditions the egoist neither wants to listen nor to think. He wants to retain his complacency; he wants to continue in the blind belief he has already accepted.

For a man who wants to search for truth this attitude is fatal. No one has ever found truth at the price of cheap contentment. To reach truth complacency has to go. One's aim should be truth, not this pseudo satisfaction. When truth is attained real satisfaction follows in its wake like a shadow.

The man who girds his loins and sets out to find truth at any cost also attains satisfaction, but the man who wants satisfaction first is denied access to truth. And eventually he also loses the satisfaction he thought he had found.

Someone once asked a venerable sage, "Is there any advice no one has ever given? Is there any teaching no one has ever taught?"

The old man replied, "There certainly is. There is one teaching that has never been taught and one bit of advice that has never been given."

The man began to ask, "Can you tell me what it is?" when the sage laughed and added, "But it is not an object you can see, or a thought you can put into words."

Truth cannot be taught through any word. Understand well that any truth that can be taught through words is not truth at all. Truth can be known but it cannot be uttered. To know truth you have to become wordless, silent, empty. How can something that is known in emptiness be put into words?

I have heard that when Adam and Eve were expelled from the Garden of Eden, the first words Adam uttered were, "Eve, we are going through a period of great revolution!" Even if those were not his exact words, the idea certainly crossed his mind. He was about to enter a world that was totally alien; he was being forced to leave the known for the unknown. And it was only natural he should feel like that. This idea has been expressed by men of every age, because the procession of life is always from the known to the unknown.

One must leave the known to discover the unknown. Lacking the courage to leave the known behind is stopping at the door of the unknown itself. Staying with the known indicates the absence of knowledge, because until a man has perfected himself he will always have to bid farewell to what he has known, to the familiar. It is a passing through darkness. But it is necessary. The sun must set to allow a new sun to rise. The process is difficult—but there is no birth without pain.

At this point in time we are going through an unpredented revolution in human consciousness, an upheaval heaval unlike any that has ever taken place before. There has always been change, sometimes to a great degree, sometimes to a lesser degree, because unless there is change there is no life. But every once in a while this eternal process of change reaches a zenith—and then there is a real revolution.

The twentieth century has brought mankind to such a peak, and his consciousness is now ready to evolve, to turn in a totally new direction. It is probable we will have to travel along entirely new paths and that what we know, what we are acquainted with, will disappear. The principles and values by which we have lived are no longer applicable; the grip of tradition is weakening. This is in preparation for a great change. We are being uprooted from the past; we are awaiting transplanting into the future.

Through all of this I see man knocking at unfamiliar doors, trying to fathom the mysteries of his existence. The well-trodden paths that led in repetitive circles have been abandoned and people are trying to light the darkness of the future. These are all very good signs and they fill me with hope. These efforts herald the good news that the consciousness of mankind wants to scale new heights, wants to set a course in a new, uphill direction.

We are close to some new stage in man's evolution. Man will be different from what he has been before. Those who have eyes to see, can see what is coming; those who have ears to hear, can hear what is coming. When seeds break apart and the tiny sprouts poke through the ground in search of the sun there is a feeling of agitation, a kind of anxiousness. And there is a similar sense of expectancy within us, a restlessness. It is nothing to worry about. This state of confusion is part of the period of transition. To turn back in fear now is suicide. Life only moves forward; it is not possible to go back. As darkness is deepest before dawn, the pain and confusion are worse, at their most intense, just before birth.

The reason behind this restlessness, behind this revolution of consciousness, behind this possibility of a new age, is science. Science has opened our eyes; it has shaken us out of our slumber. It has shattered many of our most cherished dreams; it has shown us our own nakedness; it has awakened us from the darkest night. Science has given man maturity and has taken away his childhood.

Its inventions and the conclusions it has drawn from its experiments have freed us from traditional concepts, have liberated us from conventional patterns of thinking. We were living in falseness, because thinking that is not free is not real thinking at all. We were enmeshed in the blind faith of centuries past as if caught in the web of a spider. Science has broken these bonds and now it is possible for mankind to proceed towards understanding, discrimination and awareness.

Science has also freed man from the slavery of faith. The era that has just ended can be called the age of faith; the coming period will be the age of awareness. This progression from blind faith to discrimination is science's greatest gift to mankind. It is not a change in faith that we have been given, but freedom from faith itself. In the past, beliefs changed—new faiths simply replaced the old—but through science, something is happening today that is completely new, that has never happened before; the old beliefs have been shattered, and they have yet to be replaced. This emptiness, this vacuum, is unprecedented in human history. It is not that faith has changed focus, but that it is disappearing altogether. A consciousness that has nothing at all to do with faith or with belief is coming into being.

In changing one's faith, nothing basically different happens. One belief is simply replaced by another just as a man shifts the weight of a coffin from one shoulder to the other. The tendency to believe is important, it is this propensity of his for belief that is the real factor. Science has not given man a new faith, it has broken this habit completely.

This tendency to believe leads men to follow blindly; it makes a man stick to his prejudices. A mind that is stuck in prejudice cannot know the truth. To acquire knowledge, a man must be totally free from bias. One who simply believes in something possesses no knowledge, and his very belief itself is a kind of slavery. For a man to realize the truth his consciousness must be free. It is discrimination, and not belief, that leads a man to truth.

For the awakening of discrimination in a man, there is no greater obstacle than belief. Remember, a man who believes never investigates. Doubt, not faith, leads to investigation. All knowledge is born out of doubt. And do not think that doubt is only lack of belief. Lack of belief is nothing more than the negative aspect of belief itself.

To embark on a real search for truth a man needs a mind that is not only free but one that is also full of doubt. The scientist questions accepted knowledge, and it is his doubt that paves the way for further investigation. As science discards prevailing beliefs it proceeds towards the truth. Science has no use for belief or for disbelief; science is free from such prejudices. It accepts nothing but that knowledge which has been acquired through experiment. It is neither theistic nor atheistic; it has no preconceived ideas. It has no belief of its own to prove. Science is non-sectarian; its findings are universal.

When a man sets out with preconceived notions, no matter what he is investigating, the result is always sectarianism, never truth. The only thing that is universal is truth itself. This is the reason there are so many religions, each opposed to the other, but only one science. When religion is based on pure discrimination and not on beliefs, it will be one as well. Beliefs can be many; real discrimination is one. Lies can be many; truth is one.

The essence of religion in the past was faith. And faith entails the acceptance of precepts without any kind of verification at all. If a man had no faith he was considered irreligious, because faith was looked upon as the shadow of religion. The essence of atheism, the opposite of religion, was lack of belief. This is only the other side of faith; as opposed to acceptance it involves rejection, but without any verification either. Without faith, neither atheism nor theism could have existed. Mankind has always swung between these two extremes, between these two polarities.

But now, science has given us a third option. It is now possible to be neither atheistic nor theistic, now possible to be absolutely free of belief. Now, mankind can free itself from those so-called principles that have been hammered into its unconscious through generations of tradition, through centuries of teaching.

The various societies and the different schools of thought always imprint their ideas on young minds in the most formative years. Whether parents are Hindu, Jain, Buddhist, Christian or Mohammedan, all implant their views in the minds of their children. And by constant repetition these ideas become firmly ingrained in the unconscious minds of these youngsters. This negates any opportunity for free thinking. The same approach is used to promote atheism, to spread communism.

This indoctrination of innocent children is one of the greatest crimes against the human race. The young mind is stuffed with ideas, imprisoned by them. When he grows up a man is like a train on a track; he only appears to be functioning of his own accord. He is only under the illusion that his ideas are his own.

This kind of ideological indoctrination simply allows people to relate to each other within the framework of their own beliefs. This is tremendously detrimental; this stands in the way of the development of a man's free and uninhibited consciousness. It results in a kind of mental slavery. Like a bullock turning a waterwheel, a man moves within the boundaries of his own beliefs and is unable to think for himself.

One's latent power of thought only develops when one's mind is totally free. And this alone can lead to truth.

Science has been of great benefit to mankind by its attack on the static belief-mentality. It has laid the foundation for mental freedom. And this will give rise to a new religion, to one based on discrimination and not on belief, to one whose essence will be knowledge and not faith. Religion will become the science of consciousness.

Authentic religion has always been scientific. The experiences of Mahavira, of Buddha, of Christ, of Patanjali, of Lao Tzu were all based on experimentation, on investigations conducted with discrimination, with awareness. Belief followed, but there was no belief in their beginnings. Their experiments were based on knowledge; faith ensued. The truth they propounded was their experience itself, the essential and unique experience. Their words may have differed, but the essence of their truth is the same. Truth cannot differ from person to person.

This science of religion has always remained in the hands of a few enlightened beings; it has never spread to the masses. The religion of the people has always been fettered by blind belief. But now, the advances of science are finally eradicating this blindness, and this is to the great good fortune of true religion. The fire of science will purify religion, and religion in turn will enlighten human consciousness. A religion based on wisdom and discrimination can lead mankind to superhuman consciousness. The consciousness of man can only rise above itself in this way. And when a man rises above himself he becomes one with God.

Truth can only be realized. It cannot be explained or understood.

3
RELIGION AND EDUCATION

What is the aim of religion? It is to awaken the slumbering superman in the ordinary man. This and this alone is religion's goal.

You ask for proof of the existence of God? Isn't the existence of consciousness sufficient proof? Doesn't a drop of water prove there is an ocean?

At dawn I watched the sparkling drops of dew gently and lovingly settling on the petals of the flowers. They made not a sound. When one's heart is ready God also descends like the tiny drops of dew. You have no inkling of his coming until he manifests himself before you.

If you wish to know God the path is silence. Whatsoever is said about God becomes untrue because it has been said in the first place.

To which religion do I belong? To none. Only in the sense of virtue, piety, justice, fairness, simplicity and like qualities has religion any real existence, but in so-called religious cults and sects it does not exist at all. And it is the very existence of these cults and sects that have obstructed the manifestation of real religion in the world. To give birth to a true religious spirit all cults must disappear. That is why I do not belong to any particular religion, to any sect or cult.

The man who aspires to real virtue need not belong to any religion. The organized religions really only exist to encourage the evil that lives and flourishes in the name of religion. Evil may have some cause for anxiety when it encounters virtue, but the existence of today's religions must make it positively jubilant. I do not belong to any religion because I have no wish to join Satan's party.

I have heard that Satan and his disciples had for some time been keeping their eyes on a man who was engaged in the quest for truth. They were understandably anxious and had been watching him closely. One morning, however, the disciples rushed to Satan to inform him that the man had attained truth. They were quite upset.

Satan consoled them, saying, "Don't worry. Just wait until this news spreads from city to city. People will flock to this man; they will take the truth he has attained and frame it in codes and creeds, and then they will organize themselves into a sect. You have nothing to worry about at all."

Religion is a path. No path can be traveled just by knowing about it. You can only travel a path by walking it.

The greatest respect a man can show religion is to live it, to use it. The man who only talks about it but does not live it betrays his non-belief in his own words and thoughts.

A religious life is not an impractical one. Nor is a virtuous life.

The truth of religion can only be known to the degree

it is lived. Unless it is lived it cannot be known. Living it is knowing it. To those who imagine they can know religion without living it, a religious life may appear impractical, but unless they live it they will never be able to understand it.

When a man is walking in the darkness the lamp he carries only lights a few feet in front of him. Only as he walks along is the path ahead of him illumined. The path of religion is the same. But if the man with the lamp stops and says to himself, "This is such a tiny lamp. Its light is so weak, the way is so long and the night is so dark," is it any wonder it seems impractical to him to continue on his way by the light of his lamp?

It is very easy to die for religion but very difficult to live for it. Actually, it is always easy to die for some cause. All that is needed is a kind of madness. Dying happens in a moment, so even a single moment of insanity is quite enough. But to live, awareness and wakefulness are essential.

Only those who live for religion know religion. Those who martyr themselves for religion do not know it at all.

Whatever drive there is in a man's life, whatever evolution there is, whatever touch of glory there is only comes as a result of daredevil courage. What I mean by daredevil courage is accepting life's invitation to insecurity, possessing a love for the new and the unknown, finding joy in risking one's all. The man who is not prepared to take risks may exist but he is not alive.

And what is the greatest way to apply one's daredevil courage? It is to seek God, to seek the universal soul. Nothing is more insecure than the path to God. There is nothing stranger, nothing more unfamiliar, nothing more unknowable. What bigger stake, what riskier gamble, what more perilous adventure can there be than seeking the universal soul? I say unequivocably that daredevil courage is the greatest of qualities, the greatest of virtues. The man who lacks it is not meant for religion and religion is not meant for him.

You have to forsake both good and bad to realize God. Only then will your consciousness rise above differences and establish itself in oneness.

Religion means death, the death of ego. But, you ask, how can a man whose ego is dead attain God? I say, just forget about the ego and start to let self-worship go. Forsaking self-worship is worshipping God.

There is one man I have known for many years. He used to chase money; now he pursues religion. But the race is the same. The only difference is that before he was a businessman and now he is an ascetic who has renounced everything. Whenever I hear of things like this I am surprised. In the depths, is not his desire to reach God the same as his former desire to amass riches? The ways of greed are very subtle, and is not the desire to realize God the ultimate development of greed? Man's greed is boundless; he is even greedy for salvation. But the fact remains that a man can never become liberated as long as his mind desires to acquire anything at all. The desire to acquire is the fundamental obstacle that stands in the way of liberation. And how can someone who is not free know God? What a man knows when he is liberated is God!

What connection do "I" and "mine" have with truth? Or with religion? How can truth be *my* truth? How can religion be *my* religion? Truth cannot be *my* truth; *my* truth cannot be truth.

Are you so poor that you have no religion? Wordly poverty is not such a big thing, but having no religion is real poverty. In spite of his gold and riches a man can be poor, but if he has the treasure of religion he can never be a pauper. The greatest thing that can happen to a man is not his worldly success, not his building of empires—it is nothing of this sort—it is his setting out in search of the wealth that lies hidden within him. That riches is religion. Outer wealth is nothing but soiled banknotes; inner wealth is the only real virtue. Those who seek worldly wealth are really seeking poverty but those who are seeking virtue are searching for real riches.

What is the meaning of religion? Religion is moving from the mud to the lotus. Wherever there is mud, the lotus is there as well. But what a difference there is between them!

Religion is not a formless concept. Religion is a concrete activity. It is not a thought, it is an experience. Living your life so that whatever causes you misery should not befall others is religion.

I dreamed the Day of Judgment had come. Everyone rose from his grave to be questioned. The inquiry was conducted by God himself. Standing next to me was a pundit, a scholar I knew quite well. He had a very carefree attitude. He knew the Gita, the Vedas, the Upanishads, the whole lot. He felt he could pass any examination in religion. But as God moved down the line he became less and less sure of himself and more and more anxious. He turned to me and cried, "This is too unjust! Nothing whatsoever is being asked about the scriptures! God is only asking about life! But I know what I'll do. You know what I'll say? I shall say I know nothing but the scriptures, that I have spent my whole life trying to know them."

Scriptures and dogmas are like dry leaves. There is no sap in them. Nor can there ever be. Only the tree of the self produces green leaves and blossoms that are full of life.

On my search I found no greater scripture than silence. When I had dug through all the scriptures I realized how futile they all were and that silence was the only thing that had any point to it whatsoever.

If the truth is not known to you the knowledge of the scriptures is useless. If the truth is known to you the knowledge of the scriptures is also useless.

It is completely ridiculous to delve into the scriptures in the hope of realizing truth. The scriptures may well have grown out of truth, but they have never been known to generate the experience of truth in anyone. People are so silly—they shelter the blackest ignorance in a living heart and dig among dead words trying to unearth the truth!

Words, scriptures, creeds and cults conspire to keep the soul tied to the shore of slavery. And the man who is moored by the rope of slavery is denied the freedom of the limitless ocean. To sail the open sea you have to untie yourself from the shore. To attain freedom you have to break your chains. To catch a fish, anglers put a lump of dough on a hook and the fish is tempted by the dough and caught. The hook of mental slavery is baited with the dough of promised security.

It is always on the hook of security that people lose their freedom. This is one of the oldest conspiracies. And people who are not vigilant, who are not alert to this web of intrigue will never attain to that life and that bliss that go hand in hand with freedom of consciousness. Life and bliss are both hidden in that freedom.

Nothing is of greater value than freedom. No other experience or acquisition can compare. This is because it is only through freedom that truth can be realized. Whoever is opposed to the freedom of man's soul is an enemy of mankind.

The temptation of security is freedom's principal foe. An excessive desire for security becomes a prison for one's soul. This mad craving for security feeds the blindly-accepted superstitions and traditions that can so easily fetter the mind. And even when a man is able to drop these things a vague kind of fear seizes him. The familiar ground shifts and quakes under him and he has no choice but to walk on strange paths.

This is why all vampires, be they political leaders or the priests of the religions, never want to see a man's heart free of fear. Fear and fear alone is the mainstay of their extortion activities. It is out of fear that people cling to what is well known, to the most popular beliefs, even if they are untrue. A man with an eye on his own safety does not dare stray a single inch from the accepted traditions and recognized values of the masses, even though these things may be founded on ignorance and blind belief. This fear ultimately dulls and deadens his capacity to think. It is safer; thinking will lead him to rebellion.

As long as this web of extortion envelops man and this well planned and carefully executed conspiracy to destroy his individuality goes on, the only important thought a man can have must be how to achieve his freedom. Political and economic slavery is nothing in comparison to the slavery that chains an individual's consciousness to words and scriptures in the name of truth. This slavery is subtle; it cannot be seen or felt. It goes so deep that the individual accepts it in his very marrow.

I oppose this slavery. Because of it, millions and millions of souls have been deprived of the dazzling brilliance of truth. Their hearts have not known freedom. And without that freedom a man is deprived of the bliss and harmony that is his own birthright. A subservient mind can never encounter God. God is brilliance itself; the servile mind is the blackest night.

If you wish to hear the sweet voice of God then turn a deaf ear to the verbiage of the world. Those who are deaf to the external world hear him clearly, those who are blind to mundane things see him distinctly and those who are lame and crippled in the earthly sense keep pace with him easily.

Do not keep religion in your mouth. Let it go to your belly; let it be absorbed into your blood. You will never fill your belly if you keep a piece of bread in your mouth.

People worship words and think they are truth. They mistake a milestone for their destination and settle down beside it. Isn't man's great lethargy at the root of this self-deception? Only a lazy and insensitive man could accept empty words as truth and think of a stone idol as God.

I watch you repeating mantras and incantations, muttering words you have memorized from the scriptures, and my heart is filled with sympathy for you. What are you doing? Do you take this drugging, this self-forgetfulness, this soul-destroying slumber for some kind of religious practice?

This chanting of mantras and the repetition of words will drown the mind in a pleasant kind of sleepiness but please do not confuse this drowsiness with meditation. There is a very wide gulf between sleep and meditation. In this sleep of self-forgetfulness you may have some sort of experiences, but these experiences are nothing but dreams. Your mind is a master at creating dreams. They may be highly pleasing to you, very satisfying to you, but they are not real just because they make you feel good.

But most people are not looking for truth at all, they are only seeking satisfaction. And so it is very easy to get caught up in any kind of illusion. The mind that is seeking satisfaction is likely to be satisfied with any sort of intoxication, with any kind of self-forgetfulness. This self-forgetfulness can easily be attained through so-called mantras, through recitation of the scriptures, through concentration. Repeating anything over and over again can subdue your consciousness.

Religion is not concerned with self-forgetfulness or with stupefaction. Not at all. Religion is the state of total sensitivity, of remembering the soul completely, of absolute wakefulness.

Salvation is neither achieved by prayer nor by worship. It is not even achieved by faith in religious teachings. Salvation is attained by leading a peaceful life. To remain peaceful in thought and deed is prayer and worship. It is also the only spiritual discipline that is necessary.

If I step into a river to bathe I leave my clothes on the bank. And the man who wants to wash himself clean in God must leave all of his clothes on the bank as well—all of the apparel that masks his individuality, all of the garments that hide his personality. Only those who are stark naked have access to that great ocean—only those who have nothing left at all. But blessed are they who can leave everything behind them. By doing so they receive much more than the sum-total of all.

How can you desire *nirvana* or *moksha*? Nothing is more impossible than the desire for *nirvana*, than the desire for emancipation, because nirvana is the state where there is no desire at all. And if desire is the absence of liberation, if it is your unliberated state itself, then how can you desire *moksha*? But there are people who desire *moksha*. So it is only natural that their so-called spiritual renunciation becomes a form of bondage and chains them even more securely to the world.

Moksha is attained naturally, without asking, without desiring, when the futility of desire is known, when desire is recognized as misery, when the bondage of desire is understood in the subtlest of its subtle forms. When the pointlessness of the race is understood, the race finishes.

An understanding of what the pursuit of desire is all about is enough to be liberated from it. And then what remains is *moksha*.

Aren't we all just like floundering, flailing fish that have been caught in a fisherman's net? It seems to me. And yet this is no reason to feel desperate, because I also see something else—not only are we the fish, we are the net and the fisherman as well. And there is the door to freedom. We ourselves are the creators of all our bondages, of all our miseries. They are the creations of our own minds. And now, from this truth, don't you see the possibilities of salvation?

What is religion? If you wish to know religion you will have to forget about religions. Unless you can ignore religions you will never know religion.

Am I to proclaim God to you? Is he not proclaimed all around you? Isn't nature itself God's clearest and loudest proclamation?

Look at the Ganges. It rushes to the ocean from the mountain peaks. It is the symbol of a righteous life because it has only one aim throughout its whole journey, and that is to unite with the ocean. It wants to lose itself, to lose its individuality in the universal sea. Its bliss lies in its merger with the ocean. And there, there is no difference, no loneliness; there, there are no petty boundaries. There it is complete. There it has attained its fullness. As long as it still exists as the Ganges it is incomplete.

Become like the Ganges. Seek an ocean. Let there be a single aim in life: the vast ocean; let there be one passion, one zeal: the limitless ocean; let there be a single song in your heart: the boundless ocean. And then just keep flowing.

If the currents of your being are impatient for the ocean

your feet will find the path. The river's search for the ocean is its search to lose itself, because this is the only way it will truly find itself. In this single precept all spirituality, all religion and all yoga are united. This is the only bliss, the only truth that man can attain.

I am the poorest of the poor. There is nothing I can call mine. Even I myself am not mine. Whatever there is belongs to God. God himself is all. But the moment I realized my utter poverty it vanished completely. I am now God too, for "I" am no longer there. God alone exists.

What is this search for God? It is the search for one's lost home. In this world man is but a homeless wanderer, a stranger in a foreign land.

When I look into your eyes my heart weeps at the agony and disillusionment I see in them. What have you done to yourselves? Man is born with such possibilities, and see how he dies! He perishes with nothing! His consciousness has the potential of scaling the peaks of divinity and he simply wanders about aimlessly in the valley of the animals. You never experience that perfect happiness that is your birthright; your lives are heavy with the weight of darkness.

Man is in agony because he has not developed his potential, because he has not achieved that which is in his nature to achieve. Education can be the means, the medium for allowing that which is contained in the soul of man to manifest itself.

Socrates once said, "I am like a midwife. I will bring out what is hidden in you." This is a tremendously apt definition of education. Fortune and misfortune are both hidden in man; nectar and poison exist in him; God and the animal both dwell in him. And this gives man the glorious freedom to choose whatever it is he wishes to become.

The right kind of education will be the one that shows him the path to godliness.

But it must be remembered that when a man does not strive towards the achievement of a better life he automatically sinks to a level even lower than that of the animal. The fact that a man has been born is enough to achieve this kind of fall. It is always easy to slide down; it requires work and constant application of oneself to rise. It takes effort, courage, determination. Rising upwards is an art, the greatest art in life.

The aim of an authentic education must be to teach this art, to teach the art of becoming one with God. The goal of education must be life itself, not merely providing instruction in how to earn a livelihood. In itself this means nothing. It is often mistaken as the aim of education, but this is tantamount to saying that man does not eat to live but lives to eat. Yet, considering the status of modern education this kind of conclusion is unavoidable.

Is this the only failing of the present form of education? If I were to say so, it would be the same as saying that everything is just fine in the body of a dead man except that life is absent. Today's system of education is just such a body. It is totally without life. The means of a man's livelihood is only the existence of his body, and education will only be alive when it teaches life itself.

To teach life is to teach knowledge of the self. A man may know everything else, but if he is unaware of the existence of his self then all of his knowledge is negated. Of what use is knowledge that does not have the self as its center? The illumination of the whole world is useless if the self is in darkness.

To begin this ascent to consciousness, the first step must be in the direction of self-knowledge because that is the ultimate aim of all knowledge. The extent to which a man begins to know himself is the extent to which his animality declines. The perfection of self-knowledge establishes a man in God. Only in that attainment is there fulfillment.

Each man carries the seed of that supreme development, of that ultimate perfection within him. And unless those seeds are fertilized he will remain barren. His situation is not unlike that of seeds sown in the earth. Only when they are watered and cultivated do they sprout; only then do they poke through the soil and reach the light of the sun. And the sense of anxiousness, the feeling of restlessness that exists between the sowing and the harvest is an excellent sign, because only after restlessness can there be peace. And education can intensify, can sharpen this wonderful time of restlessness in young people.

When education moves towards real knowledge and real peace, a new man and a new humanity will be born. Our future depends on this. The fate of mankind is in the hands of education. If man is to be saved from himself it is essential he be reshaped, re-created. If this does not happen the animal in man will destroy him. The only escape from this nightmare is for mankind to establish itself in God.

I am against that kind of education that tries to shape an individual in a predetermined mold. That kind of education does not sharpen one's individuality, it blunts it. I do not favor an education that is based on temptations or on the fear of punishment either. What is more poisonous than fear! I also condemn outer disciplines. What are they, except preparations for slavery?

Do not tie yourself to disciplines. Real discipline happens when discrimination awakens in you. Then you are liberated. It can never happen if you tie yourself to anything.

How can I find the words to tell you how much our present so-called educational system distresses me! Knowledge that is taught destroys one's ability to think. The power to think is crushed under the burden of acquired thoughts.

The memory may be trained but the springs of real knowledge are never set free. And then the trained memory gives the illusion of knowledge.

The individual who has been educated under this so-called system must learn to think from a whole new standpoint. He has to unlearn everything he has learned thus far. I had to do this. But it was a tiresome job. It was not as easy as taking off my clothes, but more like stripping off my skin. But it had to be done. It was the only way I could look at life through my own eyes.

I had to forget everything I had learned, everything I had been taught. To attain my own vision, I had to get rid of all those second-hand points of view. To think my own thoughts I had to free myself from all the borrowed ideas that had been pumped into me.

If you want to learn to walk you have to stop leaning on someone else's shoulder. And only when you stop looking through someone else's eyes will your own eyes open. Remember, the man who sees life through the eyes of another is even more blind than the man who is born without sight at all.

The aim of education is to bring out what lies hidden in the individual. Education is not some external ideal, not some outer imposition, it is a revelation of one's inner being.

I would like to tell you about something that happened to a *fakir* I know. He was a very lonely man. One night he met God in a dream. Much to his surprise he saw that God's loneliness was even greater than his. He said to God, "Are you alone too? But so many people believe in you! Where are they all?"

God replied with serenity, "I am always alone. This is why only a man who is also alone can see me. And as far as those who believe in me are concerned, as far as those so-called religious people are concerned, when have they ever been with me? A few are with Ram; a few are with Krishna. Some are with Mohammed; some are with Mahavira. But none of them is with me. I am always alone. And only a man who is not with anyone else, who is with himself, is with me."

The *fakir* awoke in great bewilderment and rushed to see me. He woke me up, told me of his dream, and asked, "What does it mean?"

I said, "If it had only been a dream I would interpret it for you, but it is a fact. Since when does a fact require interpretation? Be aware; just look at it. Those who are attached to any ism, be they Hindu, Mohammedan, Christian or Buddhist, are not religious. Religion is one; only where there is oneness there is religion. To a real religious mind, all these human divisions are false. In the state where one experiences God there are no cults.

"What are the scriptures? What are all the religious organizations? How can you put such boundaries on the boundless? Where are ideologies to be found in that state of inner silence? In that void, where are the temples? Where are the mosques in that emptiness? Rid yourself of all of these things—and what remains is God."

Before I say anything on the topic of "religion and education" I wish to clarify one point. When I use the word "religion" I do not mean the organized religions. To be religious is different from being Hindu or Mohammedan. Being traditional is being non-religious. It is, in fact, a great barrier to being religious. As long as a man is Hindu or Moslem it is impossible for him to be religious. Those who talk about religion and education and wish to unite them are speaking of Hindu, Mohammedan or Christian when they use the word "religion". This kind of religious education will never result in authentic religion. It will simply make man more irreligious. Mankind has been given this kind of education for the last four or five thousand years but it has neither improved mankind nor brought about any radical change in our society.

More violence, injustice and bloodshed have been perpetuated in the names of Hindu, Mohammedan and Christian than in any other. You may find it hard to understand that the heretics, the non-believers in these religions, are not responsible for very great sins at all. It is the theists, those who follow these religions who have committed the truly great sins. Heretics never burn temples or murder for religion, but those who belong to these religions are responsible for incredible massacres. It is those who claim to be religious who have divided humanity.

Words, ideologies, creeds and codes of conduct have set man against man. Isms and organizations have brought chaos and misery to the world. Humanity has been divided, and man's mind has become exceedingly narrow. Continuing to impart such an education in the name of religion is a very dangerous practice and will be even more so in the future. Such an education is not religious at all. Nor can it ever be. Those who have been educated in this manner prove my point. This ideological instruction has given birth to violence, anger and hatred. It has stunted the hearts and minds of men.

So in the first place, I wish to say that by "religious education" I do not mean instruction by any religious organization—not in its likes and dislikes, not in its dogmas, not in its so-called spiritual know-how. If we want to marry religion and education we have to divorce ourselves from the concepts of Hindu, Mohammedan, Christian. Only then can religion and education become a unit, a single entity. Organizations should have no relation with education whatsoever especially those who do so under the guise of religion.

In this context it is preferable to remain non-religious. For the non-religious man there is at least a chance of his becoming religious, but the heart and mind of the so-called religious man are always closed. A man whose mind is closed can never be religious. To discover truth you need a mind that is always kept open, a mind that is completely free.

If you want to find a civilization in the true sense of that word, that civilization can neither be Hindu nor Mohammedan, neither eastern nor western. Such a civilization will have to be total. It will have to be of every individual, of the whole of humanity. Such a civilization cannot be aligned to any particular sect, because so long as there is any division in humanity, any categorization at all, mankind will never be free of frustration or war.

It is very difficult to create such a civilization as long as there is a wall between me and you. As long as there are walls between individuals how can we create a society that can live in love and joy?

The society we have created thus far can certainly not be called a society of love. Fifteen thousand wars have been waged on the earth in three thousand years. In three thousand years, fifteen thousand wars! How hard this is even to imagine! And fifteen thousand wars cannot have been fought in three thousand years without some cause.

What is the meaning of this ratio, five wars a year? It means that in the last three thousand years there has only been a small span of three hundred years in which there have been no wars. But that period of three hundred years was not continuous. Between wars we have only had short lapses—one day here, two days there, a week, ten days. And these brief intervals add up to three hundred years. Three thousand years of war and three hundred years of peace! And it isn't even correct to call those three hundred years peace. At the most they have been a truce. And whatever peace we have today is as unreal. What we call peace is nothing more than the preparation for the next war.

I divide the history of man's evolution into two stages—war, and the preparation for war. We have never had peace. And it is this kind of human behavior that is responsible for the disintegration of mankind.

Who has divided mankind? Who, I ask? Have not the religions done it? Haven't ideologies, codes of conduct and organizations split man asunder? Hasn't the whole petty concept of nations and nationalities separated man from man? But religion is the worst culprit.

All controversy has some identifications with a particular sect inherent in it. And these sects may be religious or political. No matter which, their existence causes controversy and controversy ultimately results in war. Today, Russian communism and American democracy are the new religions.

But I ask if it is not possible to stop this discrimination, to end this division in humanity? Can it not all be traced to our personal ideologies and to our private dreams? Do you think it is right that there should be "my ideas" and "your ideas" when all they do is corrupt the hearts and minds of us both? Up to now this is what has happened.

No organization based on religious and national preferences can ever be an organization of brotherly love. They are, in fact, organizations of brotherly hate. You must be aware that anyone can be made to join an organization if the poison of hatred sufficiently pollutes the general atmosphere. Adolf Hitler said somewhere that to unite a community it was necessary to create hatred for another community. Not only did he say this, he put it into action and found the formula to be very effective indeed. And any revolutionary who has ever wanted to create chaos on earth has found it as true and as applicable as Hitler did.

You can unite Mohammedans by shouting "Islam is in danger" and Hindus will rally if they hear the same cry about Hinduism. Danger produces fear, and whatever makes a man afraid becomes the object of his hatred. It is his way of reacting to the fear. All organizations and alliances are based on some aspect of his fear and hatred.

All religions say they want to foster love in the world, but since they want individual organizational unity they must ultimately take shelter in hatred. And so they only pay lip service to love. Their hatred of each other is the backbone of each and every one of them.

The religion I am talking about is not an organization at all. It is meditation. It is a *sadhana*; it is the journey to self-realization itself. It is an experience, an individual experience. It has nothing whatsoever to do with amassing large groups of followers. The experience of religion is a totally individual one.

All these organizations we call religions are based on hatred. But what possible relation can there ever be between hatred and religion? Whatever makes me hate you cannot be called religion. Only something that allows love to flow between you and me can be called religion. How can anything that divides man from man ever unite man with God? But what we call religion does just this—it separates us from each other.

Although the religions all talk about love and say they stand for unity and brotherhood, it is all just hot air. No matter what they have said to date, it has simply resulted in hatred and hostility. Christianity preaches the gospel of love, but no other cult can possibly compete with Christianity in numbers of lives destroyed. Islam is supposed to be a religion of peace and tranquility, but do you know of any other sect that has created more unrest in the world? Perhaps they believe fine sentiments are a good way to cancel out evil deeds!

If a man would like to kill people, then it becomes quite easy to do so in the name of love. And if one wants to indulge in violence it is a simple matter to strike out in defense of nonviolence. If I wished to take your life I could easily convince myself that it would be for your own good because you are going to die anyway. You are going to die one day so why should I feel like a criminal? You would never complain about it to anyone. Man is a very logical animal and can always find a rational excuse for anything he does or wants to do.

Perhaps Satan has led man to believe, from the beginning, that if there is any bad work to be done all he need do is find a good banner under which to do it. The worse the deed, the better the slogan he requires.

Those organizations that exist under the banner of religion have no relation whatsoever with God, with love, with prayer or, indeed, with religion. Mutual hatred and envy hold them together. Otherwise how could there possibly be so much desecration of mosques, burning of temples, smashing of idols and killing of people? How can all this happen? But it has happened, it is happening and it will continue to happen. If this is religion, then it is beyond me to imagine what irreligion is!

A traditional attitude is not religious. If the truth be known, it is the shadow of irreligiousness. That is why the first requirement for a religious education must be total freedom from all organized religions.

So-called religious people say they want their children to learn to live together in harmony, but they insist this be learned under the mantle of their own particular religion. Why is this so? Is it because they are so very interested in religion? No, they are definitely not interested in religion at all. Their concern is only for their own religion. And this kind of self-interest is completely irreligious, because anything that has to be identified as "mine" or "yours" is not religion. Religion is only present when there is no "mine" or "yours". And that is the beginning of the wisdom that leads to God.

Whenever religion is taught by so-called religious people there is always a selfish motive underneath. This selfishness has very deep and ancient roots. And these very roots themselves are responsible for many different kinds of exploitation.

The younger generation, however, is capable of effecting a radical change in society if it is able to free itself from the vicious circle of its conditioning. This revolution must be one of total deconditioning. Such a revolution will have far-reaching and adverse effects on those who thrive on the promotion of conflict between men. And those whose livelihood depends on perpetuating this vicious circle of the organized religions will find themselves unemployed. Then the selfishness and exploitation that are based on the differences between men and carried on under the fatherly eye of religion will be greatly undermined.

Under the pretext of religious education the older generation endeavors to pass along all its blind faiths and its ignorance, all its illnesses and its enmity to young people. And that very transmission itself brings great satisfaction to the ego. It is this very ego that does not allow a man to break through the barriers of his conditioning. In the process of human evolution there is no greater obstacle than the ego.

There is only evolution where there is revolution. But the older generation cannot accept the fact that evolution comes through revolution. It prefers the status quo; it wants to keep its old faiths, its old disciplines, its comfortable submissiveness. It wants to hold the younger generation down so that all of its creative energy is destroyed, so that the energy that is capable of discarding the old and creating the new has no chance to grow. This is cold-blooded murder. But it is done invisibly, in secret. Perhaps they are not even aware of what they are doing; perhaps their actions are completely unconscious. Their fathers and their fathers' fathers have done the same thing; they have behaved as unconsciously towards their children. This vicious circle is a very ancient one indeed. But it must be brought to a halt! This is the very thing that prevents the union of truth and religion.

What is the basis of this vicious circle? Parents plant the seeds of their own beliefs in their children before the young people have a chance to mature. And for a preconditioned mind to think for itself, to think new thoughts, is an almost impossible task. Faith and creativity exist in opposite dimensions. Faith is blindness; creativity is self-understanding. And children are deprived of any possibility of understanding themselves by this parental imposition of ready-made answers. And it is in support of something this sinister that so-called religious people are anxious to impart "religious education" to their children. This is a great misfortune. There is no greater sin than the destruction of creativity. But parents are always committing this crime and it is one of the basic reasons why real religion does not exist in the world today.

Children have to be taught how to think, not how to believe; they need to be helped to understand themselves, not to have blind faith in someone else's ideas. And only when religion is based on self-knowledge and not on blind faith can it be united with education. And the result will be sheer bliss! When tested with right-thinking and self-understanding, and not simply accepted blindly, even scientific facts can also bring a man bliss!

Did you know that a man who just believes what he is told eventually becomes incapable of any kind of creativity whatsoever, and that all he sees around him then, wherever he looks, is frustration? And these are the people who want to educate their children with ready-made formulas so they do not appear stupid! It is so easy for these people to believe they are right. And if someone awakens and realizes the significance and magnitude of this vast network of deception, then what do they do to him? They do the same thing to him they did to Socrates and to Christ.

When you consider the question of religious education, it is essential you ask yourselves whether you are not, in fact, bringing darkness to these young minds under the illusion you are bringing them light. Cut and dried concepts have corrupted the vision of many in the name of sight. Any kind of belief is ignorance; any kind of belief is darkness.

Children must be saved from these blind beliefs, but they can only be saved if they are given clarity of mind. They must be helped to think clearly; they must be helped to think creatively. Do not give them thoughts, give them the ability to think. Giving them thoughts means you are giving them your thoughts, but giving them a chance to be creative is giving them something that is their own. That energy is what must be generated. That energy, that energy of creativity, is enough to bring your children lives that are new, fresh and real.

Thinking is the way. Beliefs bring nothing but frustration. That is why I say that a man who is conditioned by beliefs cannot think freely. One who is a Hindu cannot be really creative; one who is a Jain cannot be creative; one who is a communist cannot be creative. His belief itself is his conditioning.

Because thinking can destroy his beliefs, a believer chooses not to think. And this becomes his security. But all this security is, is a denial of himself. Do you not see that belief is an obstacle to creative thinking?

This murder of young minds is being carried out both consciously and unconsciously. A Hindu father wants his son to be a Hindu and a Mohammedan father wants his son to be a Mohammedan, yet this is all decided when the child is an infant and incapable of thinking for himself. But this kind of corruption is only possible during that period; to accomplish this in later years is very difficult indeed. When the ability to think exists, deception is impossible.

A man's capacity for rational understanding becomes his self-awareness. It is no wonder the so-called religious people are opposed to such reasoning, to such understanding. If the truth be known, they are not even in favor of intelligence. Wherever there is intelligence, creativity and reason, there is revolution. And revolution means the quest for a new way of life. Revolution means leaving the known in search of the unknown. Revolution means breaking through the barriers that separate every older generation from every younger one.

As I see it, revolution is the nucleus of a religious mind. There is no greater revolution than religion. Religion is a life-transforming process. It is the most radical transformation there is. So, religious education cannot be an education in dullness, in ignorance—it must be an education in profound and creative thinking. A religious education must spark deep reasoning abilities; it must foster creative intelligence.

An innocent child should not be burdened with pat answers or conditioned in ways that go against his basic intelligence, he should be encouraged along paths that will allow his intrinsic intelligence to function freely, actively and with constant awareness. He should be helped to reach a point where it is impossible for him to be conditioned by anything or anyone at all. Only such a mind can be capable of joy, of love. This is what truth is.

Freedom is the path to truth. So allow children to be free. Awaken a sense of freedom in them. Help them to be alert to all possible enslavement of their hearts and minds. This and this alone is what real religious education is.

The various religions, however, do not impart this type of education. What they do is exactly the opposite. They provide an education in slavery. This is not an education in creativity, it is an attempt to promote the worship of belief. It is not an education in intelligence, it is an education in ignorance. It is founded on blindness and not on self-understanding.

Why are all the religions so afraid of creativity? Their fear is definitely not without foundation. There are many fundamental reasons, but the most important one is that if there is too much creative thought many religious organizations will not be able to survive for very long. Religion will endure of course, but religious organizations would be in certain danger.

Any move towards effortless creative thinking is a move

in the direction of truth. Just as the rivers flow naturally towards the sea, creativity moves towards the totality. And there in the totality, only truth remains unidentified with anything and unattached to anything.

There cannot be many paths to truth—the truth is one. There is no separate truth for Hindus and Christians, but when their so-called truths are based on blind faith there is no possibility of their having any common denominator whatsoever. Beliefs are obstructions to creativity. Beliefs are imprisoned within their own narrow limitations and because they are static and do not move towards the totality they can never attain oneness. It is because they are confined within such rigid and private structures that there are so many different beliefs in the world.

Thinking is creativity; belief is conditioning. Thinking is self-revolution; belief is self-programming. A thought may start out from any point but it ultimately leads to deeper realms, towards the center, towards the truth; a belief simply blocks the way to God.

I have heard that there is even a Jain geography! And this type of foolishness exists in other religions as well. Can there even be a separate geography? If it is based on a belief, yes—then it is possible. Where there is no creative thinking there is fantasy, blind faith and gullibility—and these things all differ from individual to individual.

The truth is one, but each man's imagination is different. No two person's desires are the same; no two people dream the same dream. The truth that exists within the self is universal. It is not someone's dream, not someone's projection, not someone's interpretation.

To perceive truth one needs enormous capacity; one needs a wide-open mind that is constantly alert. The creative totality can only be perceived by a man with great clarity of mind. That is why I say over and over again that if you want your children to know the truth you must give them the chance to think creatively. Stop conditioning them with beliefs; allow them to understand things for themselves. Creativity will become their capacity for life; creativity will become their wisdom. That capacity and that wisdom will lead them to the uncharted sea of truth.

Did you know that Aristotle, that a man of his stature has written that women have less teeth than men! How could he write such a thing? Was there no woman around so he could count her teeth? Although there was no scarcity of women, he simply accepted the traditional belief and saw no reason to check things out for himself. And he even had two wives of his own! All he had to do was ask either the first Mrs. Aristotle or the second Mrs. Aristotle to open her mouth so he could count her teeth! But he never bothered. He never doubted tradition. He simply accepted the belief that women have less teeth than men. If the truth be known, the male ego is not prepared to accept that women can be equal to men in any respect, not even in the number of their teeth! And when a man like Aristotle did not doubt a popular belief then who else would?

Doubt is the beginning of discovery. Real doubt is the first step on the path to the discovery of truth. And that is the beginning of an authentic religious education. Doubt, not faith, is the real foundation of religion. Doubt is the beginning; faith is the end. Doubt is the search; faith is the fulfillment.

The man who sets out in doubt ultimately reaches God, but the man who starts out in faith reaches nowhere at all. He has put the cart before the horse. You can only begin at the beginning. How can you begin at the end? Where there is no doubt there is no thinking, where there is no thinking there is no understanding, and where there is no understanding there is no truth.

Religious organizations teach belief, not doubt. They teach how to follow not how to explore. But an authentic religion will teach how to doubt, how to think, how to discover.

Real perception only comes through self-discovery, and

that very discovery itself brings about that radical transformation we know as truth. Truth is discovery, constant discovery. It is a continuing revolution in creative inventiveness. Truth cannot be passed from one hand to another; it can only come from one's own direct experience. Truth cannot be borrowed; it is the result of one's own effort.

Any activity directed towards the discovery of truth is part of a religious education. But as long as religion is hung up on belief, there is virtually no hope for religious education at all. You can call it religious education if you wish, but all it will really be will be Hindu education, Christian education, Mohammedan education. This kind of education is not a religious education at all. This is an education in narrow-mindedness; it is definitely not the way to become broad-minded.

Anyone who has been given this kind of education cannot help but be prejudiced. His intelligence has not been freed; it has become stale, stagnant. He has grown old in heart and mind. To make any kind of discovery a mind that is young and fresh is needed. And a man who is free of prejudices is always young. A man who is free from ideologies and preconceived ideas is forever fresh. A biased mind ages quickly, and a man is conditioned to the same extent he is prejudiced. This kind of mind is not religious, but the man who is free from all these ready-made theories and structures lives in religion, in a flow of natural creativity, in self-understanding.

A man's ideologies grow out of his identification with his environment, but these are simply outward expressions. Like dust covers a mirror, ideologies veil one's consciousness. The mirror of consciousness must not be coated with the dust of stock answers, blind beliefs and preconceived ideas, it must be clear.

An authentic education in religion and in meditation gives birth to an aspiration for freedom. Religion is the way to free the intelligence from all of its complexes. But the religion that is offered in the marketplace is not real religion at all, and before religion can enter the domain of education it must free itself from virtually all other involvements. Only then it can bring a new creativity and intelligence to the younger generation.

Young people have to learn to live in religion. It has to become part of their daily lives, and until this comes to pass their lives will remain crippled, twisted and out of harmony.

If we think only in terms of our outer environment, our inner being will remain unknown, undiscovered. As long as our attention is towards material things alone we are deprived of God. This a costly affair, this forsaking of diamonds for pebbles. Of what value are outer comforts when you compare them with the inner experience? Can you compare worldly pleasures with the unfathomable joy of God, with the bliss of the unknown? You have to come to know the heart, the core of your being. The heart and soul of all your activities must become the discovery of your inner being. As long as this urge towards inner discovery is missing in you, your life will never be total.

I do not want to see religion and education joined together in name only; I want to see the core of life become the focal point of education as well. And the unknown is the foundation. Unless a man is in communion with the unknown, with God, there is neither meaning nor significance to his life. And how can there be any joy in a life that is empty of all meaning? There is joy in life only when there is meaning to life.

Science is the discovery of things useful to life; religion is the discovery of the significance of life itself. Science is incomplete on its own, and religion is as incomplete. There can only be perfection and joy in the union, in the combined virtues of the two. The same is true of religion and education.

One universe exists outside man. But that is not all. A universe exists within him too. One is the goal of objective research; the other, of inward discovery. But subjective discovery must not be ignored at the expense of objective research. If this happens we will have power but we will have no peace, we will have outer comforts but no inner serenity. And what is the point of possessing worldly riches at the cost of inner peace? This kind of success is tantamount to defeat and failure.

There was once a holy woman named Rabiya. One morning someone called to her from outside her hut, "Rabiya, come out! The sunrise is so beautiful. The morning is exquisite. Come out!"

Rabiya replied, "My friend, I invite you to come in. In here I am looking at the creator of that very sun, of that very morning you are admiring outside. Shouldn't you be inside too? I have seen the outer beauty. Have you never seen the beauty that is inside?"

One world is the objective one. It is very beautiful indeed, and anyone who wants to pit mankind against the outer world has no intelligence whatsoever. This outer world is tremendously beautiful, and those who reject its splendors without understanding are against the welfare of humanity. The beauty of the outer world is beyond question, but there is a world inside that is infused with a beauty that has no limit. The man who stops at the outer world has stopped halfway.

Such a man has been in a hurry to settle down; he has confused the means with the end. He has mistaken the door for the palace and is standing on the staircase. He must be shaken up; he must be awakened. He has to be directed towards the goal so he can continue on his way.

Children must be given a sense of the same goal so they won't stop somewhere en route. It must be the aim of a religious education to help children understand the goal so their lives don't grind to a halt at the half-way mark.

It is absolutely essential to understand that learning is only concerned with the exploration and discovery of the outer world. On its own, objective research is incomplete. The concentration of education must be on subjectivity, on inner discovery. But the search of religion as we know it is not subjective at all. The religions may talk a lot about the inner, but their talk is empty, useless. Their temples are outside, their mosques are outside, their idols are outside, their scriptures are outside, their ideologies are outside, and every day we see them fighting over external things. Their whole insistence is on the outer. These so-called religions do not lead mankind towards any sort of subjective exploration whatsoever.

One morning a Negro approached a clergyman standing at the door of his church and asked permission to enter. Now how can a man with black skin enter a church that belongs to men with white skin? The very people who talk about subjectivity all the time never fail to notice whether a man's skin is black or white! And those who go on and on about God in this country are also very aware of whether a man is a Brahmin or an untouchable!

The priest said, "My friend, what would you do in church? So long as your mind is impure or restless, what good will it do you to go in?"

Times have changed and along with them, the priest has changed his way of putting things. In the past he simply would have obstructed the man, saying, "Begone. Your sort is not allowed here." But times have changed and he has had to change his tone. But his heart has not changed. He stills manages to keep those he considers undesirable out. He did not say "You are untouchable and unchaste, so go away" but he did say, "My friend, what good will it do you? So long as your mind is impure and not at rest, how will you understand God? Go and purify your mind first." This is what he said to the Negro. But if a man with white skin had come to the church he would have said nothing at all. As if having white skin guaranteed peace of mind!

That innocent black man withdrew. The clergyman must have rejoiced. He must have thought the man would never attain peace of mind in a million years, and so would never come back again. The Negro never did come again in fact—but he did attain tranquility.

A year rolled by and one day the priest saw the Negro walking down the street in front of the church. He looked totally different. He radiated a divine glory and was surrounded by a celestial glow. The priest thought he was going to try to come into the church again, and the idea upset him greatly. But his fears were groundless. The Negro continued down the street without so much as a glance in the direction of the church. The priest could not contain himself. He ran after him and asked, "Where have you been? I have not seen you around here in quite some time."

The Negro laughed and said, "My friend, thank you. I followed your advice. For the past year I have been trying to attain peace of mind so that I might come to church. But last night God himself appeared to me in a dream and said, "Why do you want to go to church? To see me? Let me tell you, I have been trying to get in myself for the past ten years. If the priest won't let me in, he'll never allow you to enter!""

I would like to say that not only has God been unable to get into that particular church. He has never been allowed into any! Any church or temple built by man cannot be greater than man. And those man-made churches and temples are so small and insignificant there isn't enough room for God! A temple built by someone whose mind is not a temple itself is of no use whatsoever.

One who has never experienced God within will never find him somewhere outside. God makes his first appearance to a man within the man himself. And that first appearance is total. There is no outer way to reach the totality; the inner is the only route.

One's self is the closest thing to God; instead of searching for him far and wide one has to discover him within. If a man cannot find something so close, how can he expect to find anything that is far away? God is not experienced in the temples; God is experienced within. Because of this, the religions of the temples and mosques can never be united with education. Nor should they. Their influence is just more insistence on the outer, and any insistence on the objective world is an obstacle blocking the way to inner discovery.

I feel like laughing when I hear them talking in the universities about the education imparted by religious organizations in the temples. Doesn't man learn anything at all from history? Haven't we already seen what the religions of the temples and mosques can accomplish and cannot accomplish?

There is no need for any kind of outward religious formalities or rites whatsoever. If they were only useless there would be no problem, but they are really very harmful. Religion is not to be found in any kind of externalization, and so any type of outward ritual is a non-religious act. This should be as easy to understand as two plus two equals four.

There is also a real temple of God, but it cannot be built from bricks and mortar. A temple built of stone can be Hindu, Christian, Jain or Buddhist, but it cannot belong to God. Something that is the private property of some organization cannot belong to God as well. There cannot be any limitations to God's temple because he is limitless. There cannot be any structure to God's temple because he is whole, total. God's temple can only be the temple of consciousness. That temple is not in the sky or on the earth, it is in the soul itself. And it does not have to be built. God's temple is already there. It need only be unveiled.

So for an education to be integrated with religion, it cannot have anything to do with the religions of the temples and mosques. It must only be associated with that religion that can unveil the temple hidden within the self.

What exists within is what has to be understood, because

to understand that can bring about a revolution in one's life. To understand truth means to effect a radical transformation in one's life. An education which does not uncover the inner truth, which does not discover God, is not only incomplete but also very dangerous. And it is this incompleteness itself that is the root cause of the failure of today's educational system.

The education of the young man who has just completed his university training these days is thoroughly incomplete. He is absolutely unaware of what throbs at the core of his being, at the heart of life itself. He has no understanding of truth or of beauty; he is totally unacquainted with love. He enters the world with certain trivial facts he has learned and these are all he has to live with, all he has to live by. This kind of a life never brings him peace, and his consciousness gradually becomes suffocated by a sense of purposelessness, of superficiality, of futility. The living creativity that is life is lost in a desert of pointlessness—and his reaction to this is anger and frustration towards the world in general. This is what happens to a non-religious mind.

A religious mind, on the other hand, is filled with bliss and with a sense of benediction. A religious mind is grateful to all. But this only happens when a man is total, when his whole being pulsates with joy. This joy and this feeling of totality are only available to the man who has understood his self, who has come to know his inner being. Until it merges with religion there can never be such a thing as real education, because the consciousness of one's inner being is the foundation of life itself. To understand this, to be open to this is indispensable if a man is to live his life to the full. Religion is the education of the inner man.

So what should we teach? Should we teach what is contained in the scriptures? Should we teach codes of moral conduct? Should we tell our children our ideas about God, about the soul, about heaven, about hell, about salvation? No, absolutely not. Such an education will not be a religious education at all. Such an education can never lead a man inside. Such an education is first passing along one's own prejudices; such an education is simply memorizing words and trite phrases. All this does is give birth to misconceptions which in themselves are even more dangerous than ignorance.

Wisdom only comes from self-understanding. Knowledge that is acquired from others is not wisdom. Knowledge acquired from others is simply the illusion of wisdom. This illusion only acts as a veil over one's own ignorance and shuts the door on creative discovery forever. To understand one's ignorance is a truly beautiful thing, because it leads a man to the discovery of his own creativity. But to accept acquired knowledge as gospel is very dangerous indeed. The contentment that borrowed knowledge brings is a barrier that can stop a man from making any further attempts at discovery.

I once visited an orphanage where some hundred children lived. The administrator informed me they also gave the children a religious education, and so to show me he began putting questions to the youngsters.

"Is there a God?" he asked.

The children answered, "Yes, there is a God."

"And where is he?" the administrator inquired.

The children pointed their fingers towards the sky.

"And where is the soul?"

The children said, "Here" and put their hands on their chests.

I watched the whole thing. The administrator and the teachers were very pleased with themselves. They said to me, "You may also ask something."

I asked one small child, "Where is your heart?"

He looked around, a bit confused, and then said, "They haven't taught us that yet."

Can you call this religious education? Is the repetition of memorized answers what education is? Wouldn't the world have become religious long ago if it were that easy? I informed the administrator and the teachers that the education they were giving those children was not a religious education at all, that all they were doing was training the children to become parrots. If an individual learns to memorize certain things and to repeat them mechanically his intelligence suffers greatly. And then when life faces him with a challenge, the type of challenge that could be a doorway to the discovery of truth, he will repeat what he has memorized and be quite satisfied with it.

"Your teaching techniques are murdering their sense of inquiry," I said. "They know neither the soul nor God and this putting their hands on their chests and pointing to the sky to show where they are, is a complete sham. And you say you are giving them a religious education!

"But isn't your own understanding the same as that of a child's?" I asked. "Aren't you just repeating what someone has told you?"

And they began looking around in confusion, just like that child.

From generation to generation we continue to pass the same empty words along—and we call them knowledge. Can truth be taught? Can truth be memorized? Is truth something to be repeated by rote?

In the material world, these techniques can be of some use, just as symbols are effective in indicating knowledge man has acquired about the objective world. But as far as God is concerned, symbols are meaningless, valueless. God's dimension is not one of symbols; it is the realm of understanding alone. It is the dimension of direct perception. One can be there, can live there—but this cannot be taught. When one is there, both teaching and learning become play, just like being on a stage.

Can anyone learn love? If a man thinks he has learned love somewhere then it is not love at all, it is just an act. This is the reason that all acquired knowledge about God and dogmas is so phony; this is the reason worship and prayer have become so false. If love cannot be learned, how can one learn how to pray? Prayer is a deeper aspect of love. And if a man cannot learn about love, then how is there the remotest possibility he can be taught to understand God? The fulfillment of love itself is God.

The truth is unknown, and with what is known—with rules, codes of conduct, words—one cannot reach the truth. To enter into the unknown a man must leave all he knows behind him. Freeing oneself from the known is the beginning of facing the unknown. Unlearning all one knows is better than receiving a so-called religious education. In this case, forgetting is better than remembering. Nothing more should be imprinted on one's consciousness; what has to happen is that everything already written there must be erased.

When the consciousness is freed of words it becomes the mirror of truth. One's consciousness must not be allowed to become a storehouse of ideologies, it must be made the very mirror of truth itself. Only then will religious education become less education, in the ordinary sense of the word, and more an active *sadhana*, more a direct journey to truth itself. Preparing a man for this *sadhana* is what a religious education is.

An education in religion is not like an academic education, and so no examination is possible. The test of religious education is life itself; life is its examination.

After completing their university educations three young men were preparing to return to their homes. They were examined in all their subjects, but not in religion. They had been surprised at not being examined in religion; they had simply been given passing grades.

When they left the school, night was beginning to fall. As they walked along they came across a thorny branch that had fallen onto the road from a nearby tree. The first youth jumped over the branch, the second skirted it, but the third picked it up and placed it safely out of the way.

The others asked, "What are you bothering with that for? It's getting dark and we should hurry if we want to be out of the forest before it's pitch black."

"That is exactly why I'm removing the branch," he said. "If anyone else comes along in the darkness he won't be able to see it and might step on the thorns."

At this point their teacher stepped out from behind the tree. To the third youth he said, "My son, you may go. You have passed your religious examination." He led the other two back to school to complete their educations.

Can there be any other examination for life except life itself? Religion is life itself. Those who think they are educated, simply because they have passed some exam are living in illusion. Where examinations end one's real education begins, because the end of schooling is the beginning of life.

Then what is to be done about religious education? The seed of religion exists in everyone. Truth exists in each of us; life exists in each of us. An environment that allows the evolution of that seed must be created and barriers that stand in the way of its development must be removed. If this can be accomplished, then with its own spontaneous and inherent capacity for life the seed will find its true course. For its natural evolution no effort is required at all. And that instinctive activity itself is what life is all about. When a man evolves naturally his life will be full of joy, full of beauty, full of love.

All we must do is to create the correct environment and let life take its natural course. This will be a real religious education. Educational institutions are quite capable of providing the kind of atmosphere necessary to allow religion to find its own natural and spontaneous route. And as well, circumstances can be created to remove all the barriers that stand in the way of this natural evolution of religion.

To create this opportunity there are three fundamental requirements. The first element is courage. An individual needs tremendous courage. The first requirement on the road to the discovery of truth, in the search for God, is courage. To discover God a man needs more courage than he does to climb the Himalayas or to plumb the depths of the ocean. There is no loftier deed, no effort more profound than the discovery of God.

But so-called religious people are usually not courageous at all. In fact, their religiousness is generally an escape from their cowardice. Both religion and God are masks to hide their fear. A mind that is afraid can never be religious.

To be religious fearlessness is essential. Courage grows out of fearlessness, so the first thing is not to teach fear, not to teach children any kind of fear at all! And the second thing is to instill a sense of fearlessness in them. Fearlessness is such a glorious thing. It is so radiant, so tremendous! Real religion can only be built on a foundation of fearlessness.

The so-called religions exploit men through fear, and it is because of this and this alone that religion is in the state it is in today. It has not been able to transcend the material world at all. Can there ever be any kind of transcendence when fear is so deep? Whenever I go to a temple, to a mosque or to a church, I see people huddled together in fear. Their prayers are nothing more than reactions to their fear, and the God before whom they kneel is nothing more than a personification of that fear. A man runs to God in times of crisis because that is when he is most afraid. And at the end of his life a man rushes headlong to God because death terrifies him even more than anything else.

Go to a temple and look. Visit a church. You will only see people there who are either approaching death or who are already dead. Such fear should not be taught. We should teach fearlessness instead. Only then will religion become the religion of the living.

Why are you so afraid to teach fearlessness? One of your fears is that young people will deny God. But this only frightens you because your God is based in fear.

What is wrong with denying God? I say it is wrong just to accept him. I am so keen on fearlessness that I say it is fine to deny God—if we do not know him ourselves.

Where there is no denial there is no fearlessness. And unless a man denies what is false for him how can he ever discover what is true?

As I see it, an atheism that has arisen out of a man's fearlessness is just the other side of theism; it is a fundamental factor in the growth of theism. How can a man who has not been an atheist ever become a theist? It is much more difficult to be a theist than to be an atheist. But if a man is afraid of atheism then his theism is totally false; then he is a theist simply because he is afraid of being an atheist. And of what value is his theism?

I prefer an atheism based on fearlessness to a theism based on fear because there can never be real religion where fear exists. A religion is only creative when fearlessness exists. Passing through atheism is a joy; it makes one's being more vital, more energetic. If a man becomes a theist without first having gone through a period of atheism his theism is empty. The atheist will always be there, hidden in the deeper regions of his mind. But if one passes through atheism completely he is free of it forever.

Atheism is denial. If a society is against God and against religion, then in that society it will be atheism to believe in God. The denial of what is generally accepted and believed is atheism. This period of denial is very useful, a very valuable stage in the maturing process of an individual. One who has not passed through this period of denial will always remain immature. And maturity only comes through one's own personal experience, through one's own fearlessness, through one's courage to experience life.

What is the greatest courage? The greatest courage is to deny what is false for you. If you are not convinced that God exists then do not accept his existence. Though someone may try his utmost to convince you, may tempt you with heaven or threaten you with hell, do not let yourself be convinced if you are not sure. It is better to lose heaven and prepare for hell than to be afraid. It is ruinous to be afraid. Only a man who possesses great courage is capable of discovering the truth.

What does a man who is afraid do? Such a man is ready to accept anything and everything because of his fear. In a theist society he becomes a theist; in Soviet Russia he becomes an atheist. He is dead, a shadow of the society. He cannot be called alive. Only fearlessness can bring an individual's creativity to the fore.

A few people came to see me yesterday. They said, "We believe in the eternity of the soul," but their faces betrayed their fear of death.

I said, "Don't you just believe this because you are afraid of death? Those who are afraid of death always feel consoled when they are told the soul is eternal."

When they heard this they looked perplexed. One of them said, "Is the soul not eternal then?"

I said, "No."

What I said to them makes no difference whatsoever. And it makes no difference whether the soul is eternal or not. The question is whether one who is afraid of death can ever discover or understand life! Fearlessness is the most essential factor on the path to the discovery of truth.

And I want to say to you as well that those who are the most afraid of death are those who have the greatest faith in the eternity of the soul. Their faith is equal to their fear. Are such people ready to open their eyes and face the facts? The truth can never be experienced unless one is fearless.

Yes, the soul is eternal, but this is not the belief of a frightened mind, it is an experience of consciousness. A frightened mind does not want the truth, it wants to escape into whatever makes it feel secure. A mind full of fear does not really want to know truth, it wants consolation. And such a man will grab onto any belief which gives him the security and consolation he is looking for.

But how can beliefs, persuasions or past experiences give

any security or consolation? There is no security except in truth. Only in truth is there contentment and peace. To discover the truth one needs a mind that is free from this desire for false security and well-being. This is why I say infinite courage is the greatest religious virtue.

A priest was giving a sermon on courage to a group of children and the youngsters asked for an example. He said, "Suppose twelve children are staying in a hill-station. It is a very chilly night. All the children are tired from their journey and ready to go to bed. Eleven of the twelve children jump into bed and snuggle down into the blankets immediately, but despite the cold one child kneels down to say his prayers. To me, this is courage. Don't you find this courageous?"

One child spoke up. "Suppose there were twelve priests in the inn," he said, "and eleven kneeled in prayer. And suppose the twelfth priest covered himself with a blanket and jumped into bed. Wouldn't this be courage too?"

I have no idea how that priest handled that young boy's question, but I do know that just to be oneself takes great courage. To stand on one's own, free of the crowd, is courage. To help a child to be as he is, is to give him courage. Courage is confidence in oneself, in one's self. Courage is self-confidence.

Along with courage, give children understanding, give them self-awareness. This is the second fundamental requirement of education. If there is no understanding, then courage can be dangerous on its own. Then, instead of helping a child to become self-confident, courage can pervert him, make him egoistic. Courage is an energy; understanding is vision. Courage is a force; understanding is sight.

Have you heard the story of the lame man and the blind man? Once the forest they were in caught fire and they were both trapped. Naturally each of them wanted to escape the flames. The blind man could run but he could not see. And since the forest was on fire what chance would he have anyway? The lame man could see but he could not run. So of what use was his sight? There was no way he could run from the fire! But they found the solution and they both escaped death. The answer was very simple, quite straightforward. The blind man carried the lame man on his shoulders.

This is not only a tale of the blind and the halt, it is also a story of courage and understanding. If a man wants to rescue himself from the fire of ignorance, from the burning forest of his environment, he needs courage that is guided by understanding.

Most people live their lives in ignorance. Man is asleep, in a deep hypnotic sleep. He is in the deep sleep of self-forgetfulness. Becoming conscious, becoming aware of one's self, rouses one from this sleep—and self-understanding is born. Children must be educated in awareness. They must become aware of their whole beings. And they must be helped to develop self-understanding.

Generally, all of our conscious activities are outer ones. We are only aware of what goes on outside. But that very energy can be directed inside, towards the self, towards an awareness of one's self. This understanding results in an awareness that awakens a man from the sleep of ignorance to the reality of his own being.

Nothing that is perpetuated in the name of religion, be it hymns or prayers, brings any kind of self-understanding of awareness whatsoever. These things bring nothing but self-forgetfulness. The contentedness a man feels through this kind of religious activity is akin to the enjoyment he gets from a good night's sleep, like the happiness he feels when he's had a few drinks.

Educational institutions are the perfect places to begin instilling awareness in young people. And this awareness must be all-encompassing, on all levels—on the physical level, on the mental level and at the level of the child's inner being, at the level of his soul. If everything is done in awareness, done with understanding, life can be filled with consciousness. Alertness to each and every aspect of a child's mental creativity will bring total awareness and understanding to his life. Constant awareness of one's inner being results in self-awareness and self-knowledge.

The third fundamental requirement in a religious education is stillness, silence, tranquility. Words are the worst offenders. Words disturb the mind; they make it tense. The mind is always thinking. It thinks and thinks and thinks. It is never at peace.

By stillness I mean peace of mind. Being in a state of stillness and watchfulness generates freshness, youthfulness. In a state of stillness, of total silence, the mind becomes crystal clear. It becomes a mirror in which truth is reflected.

Tell me, what can a disturbed mind understand? What can such a mind ever discover? Such a mind becomes so caught up in its own machinations it has no interest in exploring any new avenues whatsoever.

The discovery of truth requires a mind that is totally still, completely calm, empty of thoughts. This mental state is meditation. And children can be easily directed towards this calm and quiet state of mind, towards meditation. The mind has a natural tendency towards tranquility, an intrinsic attraction towards silence.

The mind must be totally calm. It must be as peaceful as a man is when he is simply floating on the waves—not swimming, simply floating on the waves. Just floating. No movement at all. And this action of complete inactivity will lead a man to a silence he has never known before. And in that peace, in that silence, the mystery and the joy of life appear before him. It is then he perceives the truth.

In fact, truth has always been there. Because of his frustrations it was invisible to him. In silence, in total peace, his self is revealed.

Religious education then is an education in courage,

understanding and peace. Religious education is an education in fearlessness, in awareness, in stillness, in thoughtlessness. And without a doubt, such an education can be the foundation of a new generation, the foundation of a new humanity.

I hope you will meditate upon what I have said to you today. I do not want you just to believe what I have said, I would like you to meditate on my words, to experience them for yourselves. You only require an attitude that is free of prejudice; you only need to test what I have said by your own experimentation.

When tested in the fire of self-experience, the truth becomes pure gold.

I have forgotten what I have learned. I have realized the only thing worth learning but it is something that cannot be taught. In order to realize the truth are you ready to forget everything you have ever learned about it? If your answer is "yes" then come, the door of truth is open for you.

4
THOUGHT AND VISION

I know only two types of men— those who have turned their backs on truth and those who have opened their eyes to truth. There are no other types of men.

The power of thought is as great as the power of electricity. We have understood the power of electricity, but most of us know nothing at all about the power of thought. And those who do know it cannot use it, because to use the power of thought you have to transform yourself at your very roots.

Try to think of things about which you are unable to think at all—and you move outside the sphere of thinking. Doing this is entering the circumference of the self.

The door to truth, immortality and eternity is neither a languishing love nor an unquenchable thirst nor an insatiable passion. In fact, neither the mind nor anything of the mind is the pathway that leads to truth. Truth exists where the mind has no access whatsoever.

There is no greater power than the power of thought. Thought is the essence of individuality. The flow of a man's life is centered in thought; all that is manifested within him is expressed through thought. It is thought that separates man from the animal.

It must be remembered, however, that there is a great difference between possessing the power of thought and being overpowered by thought. Not only is there a difference, there are also great contradictions involved. When a man is overpowered by thought he becomes incapable of thinking. Being overpowered by thought can reduce a man's mind to madness, which is nothing more than a disordered state of thinking. It is possible that the roots of all madness lie deep in the evolution of this kind of thinking on a global scale. Under the chaotic burden of thoughts the spontaneous and natural ability to think is stifled, the inspiration to think is killed. And this tumult of thoughts is mistaken for the actual power to think.

The error of confusing one's thoughts with one's capacity to think is the basis of human ignorance. Collecting ideas is no proof of one's ability to think. But what it can do, though, is compensate for one's inability to think. There is no easier way to satisfy one's ego than with false knowledge acquired in ignorance. The greater the lack of thinking-power a man senses in himself, the more he is inclined to hide it with the thoughts of others. It is hard work to acquire the ability to think for oneself, but it is as easy to amass the ideas of others as it is to collect shells on the seashore.

Although the power to think is innate within us most of our thoughts belong to other people. Developing one's power to think involves an inner search; borrowing the thoughts of others necessitates looking outside oneself. This is why I say there are two different approaches, two contradictory journeys.

The man who is preoccupied with the study of knowledge negates his own ability to think. Real knowledge cannot be acquired outside oneself. Only knowledge that grows out of one's own consciousness is genuine.

When a man attempts to hide his ignorance, he does not eradicate it. Nor does he attain knowledge. It would be much better were he to face his ignorance in all its nakedness and try to understand it. Isn't knowledge that is acquired in an attempt to conceal one's ignorance more detrimental than ignorance itself? Surely a foe disguised as a friend is more dangerous than an out and out enemy! Knowledge that is not born out of oneself is the enemy. It is false knowledge.

Why do we want knowledge that is false? Why do we chase dreams? Nothing happens without cause, and in this case the ego is the culprit. To hide our ignorance we want instant knowledge, right away, and so we accumulate the ideas of others. The ego's drive is strong, and this is what pushes people into memorizing scriptures, into blindly accepting all sort of doctrines. False knowledge makes the ego feel stronger. The awareness of one's ignorance breeds humility; the illusion of being knowledgeable enhances the ego.

To acquire real knowledge it is essential to annihilate the ego. The core of the ego is possessiveness; it has no real existence, no real center of its own at all. Being in the state of non-possessiveness means the extermination of the ego. and so it wants to possess as much as it possibly can. As long as the mind has this tendency towards acquisition it cannot know itself. Its frantic race after knowledge does not allow it the time to come to know itself. Whether this race after status, fame, religion, knowledge, renunciation or the nature of the soul is irrelevant, because wherever there is desire of any kind there is ego. And where there is ego there is ignorance.

The quest for knowledge is the same as the search for wealth. Wealth may be a gross possession and thoughts may be subtle, but all outer possessions are simply indications of inner poverty. It is this feeling of inner poverty that drives a man to explore the external. And this is mankind's basic mistake. This outward search negates any possibility for him to draw any real conclusions. Because of his inner poverty a man hankers for outer riches, and this creates a disharmony in him that is tremendously disruptive. It is also completely futile. Outer prosperity can never eradicate inner poverty. There is no relation between the two whatsoever. The poverty is inner, and if we want prosperity we must look within for that as well. Only knowledge that comes from within can dispel ignorance.

Do you want wealth or do you just want to appear wealthy? Do you want knowledge or do you just want to hide your ignorance? All outer wrappings are deceptive, yet you cannot really deceive yourself in this way. As soon as you realize the truth of what you are doing to yourself, a basic and radical change in your outlook takes place. If you see the reality of your ignorance, don't run away from it. What will you achieve by this attempt to escape? What is the point of all this hiding behind doctrines and scriptures? What purpose will you serve by trying to cloud your self in a haze of borrowed ideas? This is no remedy. All it does, under the pretense of treatment, is worsen the disease. A quack doctor can be more dangerous than the illness he diagnoses, and the medicines he prescribes can set off a whole new chain of diseases. Wanting to stuff yourself with a whole lot of ideas just for the sake of knowledge is like falling prey to the promises of some cure-all medicine. And being bound to the scriptures for the sake of freeing yourself from your ignorance will only lead to greater bondage. Truth does not exist in words; truth is inherent in the self.

To attain truth it is necessary to free yourself from all doctrines, from all formal structures. The realization of truth only happens when one is totally free. Attachment is a sign of dependence; it indicates a lack of confidence in oneself. Faith in others and none in oneself is a form of slavery. Only the man who is free from faith in others is really free.

Faith in priests, in sects or in scriptures means you are dependent; faith in words or in creeds is dependence too. I tell you, only real freedom leads to truth. You have to discard all thoughts and all beliefs you have acquired from others, no matter from whom.

It is part of a man's natural growth for him to come to realize his ignorance. And once he realizes it, he must never forget it. This tendency to forget is self-deception: it is an attempt to brighten the dark emptiness of the self. An inferiority complex is the child of this emptiness, and those who suffer from a sense of inferiority hanker after status, strength and power. They are like lame men longing to accomplish great feats of physical prowess.

Hitler was a concrete example of this age-old truth: the greater a man's fear of death, the greater is the violence that develops in him. By killing others, he feels he has risen above death. Exploitation and war only exist because people with disturbed minds are trying to escape from the madness in themselves, and society is stagnating because we are not even able to see the magnitude of our mental unrest.

This race after power and possessions is a fatal disease. The illness is not external, but internal, and so man cannot escape from it. His ignorance of it simply makes him run all the faster. But this cancer is within. And running away from it only intensifies it. This course ultimately leads to madness. Insanity is the natural result of any attempt to accomplish the impossible.

It is impossible to escape from one's self, and to make the tension bearable, a man needs intoxicants—be they wine, women and song, the repetition of mantras, prayer or worship. The desire of wealth, for power and knowledge is the desire to forget the self. And to do this a really strong wine is needed. Some turn to religion, and for them it becomes a powerful opiate. This is the reason, in the so-called affluent societies, for the upsurge of interest in religion. But it is still a race. The basic question is not how to change the direction of the race, but how to finish it completely.

The philosopher escapes through thought, the artist through his creation, the politician through power, the wealthy through riches, the ascetic through renunciation and the devotee through God. But the truth can only be realized by the man who does not try to escape from his self at all. Think about this. Isn't the desire to amass things, to collect things, to own things, just trying to escape from one's self? And learning is the same. Studying others' ideas is simply another attempt to conceal one's own inner ignorance.

I am in favor of the power of thought, but I am not in favor of thoughts at all. No thought touches the core of an individual. Nor does any kind of wealth. All wealth is external. Wealth cannot reach the soul. It can simply create an illusion of riches.

Last night I met a man who said, "I am a beggar." His eyes and his words both betrayed his poverty, but yet I laughed. "Why do you call yourself a beggar?" I asked. "You may have no money, but is that reason enough to call yourself poor? I know people of great wealth, yet they are really poor. If you call yourself poor for lack of money alone, you are mistaken. As far as the deeper poverty is concerned, all men are poor, all men are beggars."

One who does not know the truth of the self is poor. He is a beggar. And one who is unfamiliar with his inner being is ignorant. Remember, fine clothes do not mean prosperity and knowledge is not gained by cloaking oneself with great thoughts. One thing just conceals your poverty and the other simply hides your ignorance. For those with deeper insight, lordly garments are a manifestation of poverty and grandiose thoughts are a sign of ignorance. Consider this for yourself. Are you not depriving yourself of truth? Is anything worth attaining at the cost of your self, at the expense of your soul?

Once I stayed with a *maharajah* and I asked him, "Are

you under the illusion you are a king?" "Illusion!" he said, "I know I am a king!" He said it with deep conviction and I felt great compassion for him. Every day I meet learned men and find they have nothing but the illusion of knowledge. I also meet monks and find them living in the illusion they are ascetics. The illusion of knowledge is created by thoughts. The illusion of kingship is created by a title and the illusion of ascetism is created by renunciation. If one has outer wealth but is inwardly poor, how can one become an ascetic simply by giving up one's riches? There is no truth to be found in possessiveness, nor is there any to be found in the renunciation of possessions either. Truth lies in the awareness of what is hidden beyond both.

Knowledge is not to be found in thought or in the absence of thought. Knowledge is to be found where the seer is, where the one who witnesses both thought and no-thought exists. Thoughts are only memory, and we mistake the training of the memory for knowledge. The memory simply provides answers to external questions and we incorrectly assume this is thinking.

Do you understand the difference between thought and memory? Memory is totally of the past. It is a dead collection of past experiences. Then where are the answers to the questions of life to be found? Life is a riddle, a puzzle, because the old solutions are incapable of solving new problems. There is no relation whatsoever between the old solutions you have accumulated and the fresh problems that arise from day to day. And so the mind loses touch with life, and so a man ages and dies long before his physical body actually perishes. To investigate truth you need a mind that is never too old to face the mysteries of life. When a mind is tied to the past it loses its freshness, its inspiration, its power of thought. It becomes closed to life. The possibility of pure and unbiased thought only exists when one's mind is not bound to the memory, when it is not tied to the so-called knowledge that has taken the form of the memory.

Looking at life through the memory is viewing the present through the veil of the past. Only when the mind is freed from this slavery does it attain the capacity of real perception. And real perception leads to real knowledge. If your vision is pure, the latent power of self-knowledge awakens within you. Your vision is freed from the past as soon as you liberate yourself from the burden of the memory and focus on the present.

Never mistake memory for knowledge. Memory is just a mechanical process, just an aid to thinking. The invention of computers has shown clearly that memory is a mechanical thing. Given the appropriate knowledge, given the correct facts, these machines provide the correct answers. There is no margin of error whatsoever. We feed our minds in the same way—with the Gita, with the Koran, with the Bible, with the words of Mahavira, of Buddha, of Mohammed and even with the daily newspapers—but the memory can only print out what has been put into it. The memory cannot think of its own accord. It is important, but its role should not be misunderstood. It should not be taken for what it is not. Real thought is always original; memory is always mechanical.

Thought born of memory is neither original nor alive. Knowledge, on the other hand, is totally different. Knowledge is not a mechanical process, it comes out of conscious awareness. And because the nature of knowledge is such, it cannot be produced by machines. Wisdom is never mechanical, but learning is. And the most stagnant of minds belongs to the so-called learned man. This type of mind provides the answers to questions even before they arise. This is nothing more than a repetitive process, relying on faith rather than on initiative. Thought that is dependent on memory needs faith to stand on, and faith, in turn, is supported by repetition which depends on memory. It is a vicious circle.

Only this morning I met a so-called learned man who had memorized the entire Gita. He has read it over and over for the last forty years and now he recites it night and day and whether the occasion calls for it or not. People avoid him because of his learning. He is restless and argumentative. He does not see this about himself and yet he is filled with ideas on how to bring peace to the world. He is typical of such a mind—mechanical, rather than creative. Such people become slaves to doctrines and it is in this way that the scriptures become sources of sectarianism and violence. How is it possible for the words of Buddha, Christ, Mahavira and Zoroaster to separate one man from another? How is it possible for their words to become the basis of hostility and violence? It happens when their words are exploited and twisted by uncreative minds.

A learned mind is stale, and although the problems of life change continuously, the solutions these minds have to offer do not. They are totally uncreative. If the world moves on to Marx this kind of mind will remain with Manu, and when the world moves beyond Marx this kind of mind will stay with him. Whether he looks to the Bible or to *Das Kapital*, an unoriginal man needs the reassurance of some kind of scripture. Doctrines and ideologies are more important to him than real life. The mature intellect will approach a problem from a fresh angle, from a new point of view, and not from some preconceived position, but the so-called learned man cannot imagine there could be any mistake in the scriptures. Out of his lack of wisdom this kind of man says the error must be in life. He is like a tailor who blames your body when something he has made for you does not fit.

Because of the great burden of scriptures and traditions that have been passed down from generation to generation for thousands of years, mankind has become incapable of solving anything. Man's mind has become paralyzed. And not only are we unable to find answers to our problems, we are not even able to see where the roots of these problems lie.

Man must rise above his memory; he must awaken his power of thought. To accomplish this you must reduce the profusion of thoughts you have accumulated to the absolute minimum. Your memory must not be allowed to be a dead weight any longer. You must learn not to view your problems through the veil of memory but to look at them directly, as they are, each in its present context. It is fatal to put the scriptures between you and life, between life and yourself. The more direct your contact with the self is, the greater your capacity to understand your problems will be. To solve a problem you must live it. No doctrine will help because the solution is hidden in the problem itself. It can only be uncovered by a totally unprejudiced mind.

The power of thinking will only begin to stir in you when you free yourself from the ideologies of others. You only learn to think by thinking for yourself. Then a new power will awaken in your inner being; then, a new and unfamiliar energy will manifest itself in you. It will be as if a blind man is suddenly able to see, as if a house that has been in darkness is suddenly brilliant with light.

When the power of thought awakens in your inner heart it is filled with light. And with this illumination, comes bliss. When this light exists, within you, no obstacle is hidden from you. In the light of pure thought the misery of your life becomes a symphony.

I urge you to light the lamp of free-thinking in your life. Do not become anyone's slave by accepting his thoughts. Truth belongs to him who is his own master.

Thought cannot travel beyond the known. No matter how high it may soar it is impossible for it to cross the frontiers of the known. Thought is the source of all that is known and the extent of the known is its whole existence. Thought is the essence of one's past experiences and the memory is its abode. But the memory is dead;

it is of the past. And thought is also lifeless. Although the truth is unknown, it is what life really is. And this is why thought can never lead a man to truth.

Thought is forbidden to enter the realm of the living, to enter into the unknown. Fish may be able to survive out of water for a few moments, but it is not possible for thought to take even one single step beyond the circle of dead memories that orbit the known.

In intellectual pursuits the power of thought exists, but not experience. Experience happens in the heart, in the most vital part of a man's being. Thoughts that are not based on experience are dead. But lifeless words and notions are continuously reverberating in our heads and we are staggering under the burden of their weight. They do not free us; they enslave us.

Experience that is of the heart is essential for freedom; it is imperative if we are to shake off this heavy load. This is why I tell you not to look for the meaning of truth, not to look for some interpretation of truth, but to seek the experience of truth itself. Seek life. Dive into the depths of truth, become totally immersed in it and then you will be free from untruth. The intellect only allows you to float on the surface; the heart submerges you completely. The heart, not the intellect, is the way to liberation.

What is it that I speak? Words? No, not at all. Those who only hear the words do not understand what I am saying. Are we pondering great thoughts? No, not at all. We are not pondering any kind of thoughts. In fact, we are not engaged in deliberation of any sort. Not at all. What we are doing is seeking a certain side of life, a particular aspect of existence. We are seeking an entry into pure existence itself.

Besides the idea of comprehension, the word "understanding" also carries with it the concept of entry, of penetration—and life can only be understood if one can penetrate into it. Life can only be understood by going through the doorway of love, not down the empty halls of thought and deliberation. Life has to be lived.

Am I making you understand my words? But if you do not understand them, don't worry. Worry will be a block; it will stand in the way of your comprehension. Just stop for a moment and see what I am saying.

Look at the flowers that blossom on the *Gulmohr* tree outside. Do you ponder over them or do you just see them? Do you hear the cuckoo calling? Do you think about it or do you simply hear it's song? Just listen to me and see what I say.

It is not deliberation, but sharp and penetrating vision that will lead you to an understanding of my words. Deliberation drowns in words; vision pierces through silence. Deliberation ponders in vain; vision unfolds meaning. Vision is a much deeper understanding, because it is free from the binding process of deliberation. Deliberation involves time and action, but in realization, in inner vision, neither time nor activity is present at all.

Inner vision is the crowning of understanding; it is understanding developed to the optimum. Have you not seen this in moments when you have experienced beauty, love, bliss? Isn't it only deep and profound awareness that is present in you at those moments? Aren't those the moments thoughts have bid you farewell? Truth, beauty, happiness—whatever is authentic in life—can only be known in silence, in waveless thoughtlessness, and never in the billows and breakers of thoughts.

Where are you going? What you are seeking is close at hand. If you keep on walking to find what is near you will be going astray. Stop and look. To realize what is so close it is enough just to stop and look.

Doesn't the intellect know anything at all? No, it certainly does not. All the intellect can do is explain; it can only comment. As far as the outer world is concerned, the senses perceive and the intellect clarifies; in relation to the inner world, it is the heart that perceives and the intellect that explains.

The intellectuals who accept the intellect as the knower are mistaken. Through the intellect nothing at all has ever been known. It is not the way to knowledge. But because of the illusion that it is the route it has become an obstacle, a hindrance in finding the true path.

Then what, you ask, is the reality of the intellect? The answer lies in not allowing your intellect to become a hindrance. When your intellect does not stand between you and life, between your self and life, an open and understanding attitude is created in you. And this becomes the eye of truth.

I am opposed to superstition and to blind belief. In fact, all belief is blind. If a man hold beliefs his power of discrimination never sharpens, never becomes a flame.

If a healthy child is made to walk on crutches when he is young his legs will never function properly when he grows older. He will be lame. And the same kind of habitual dependence on belief cripples the intellect. Can there be a greater affliction in a man's life than an infirm intellect? But this is what belief causes.

No society or nation ever really wants its citizens to develop their faculties of thinking. All tyrants and oppressors who hold the reins of administration face great danger if men develop their abilities to think. Then there is the possibility of revolution, there is always the fear that men may begin to search for the truth. Organized societies, the so-called religions and all kingdoms have been built on foundations of untruths.

The moment a baby is born a collective effort is made to chain him to servile dependency on various beliefs. This is all the educational systems have ever done, and yet they say their aim is to liberate man. But what really happens is that a shrewd and subtle mental slavery slowly overtakes the mind of the individual. This system does not teach people how to think, it simply pumps them full of beliefs. It does not encourage doubt, it does not allow rebellion, and the products of such an educational system are usually unable to think for themselves.

An active, vital quest for truth springs out of doubt, not out of belief. In the quest for truth there is no greater support, no stronger impetus than a healthy sense of doubt. Faith is not the beginning of the search of doubt. Faith is not the beginning of the search for truth; faith is the outcome. Doubt chracterizes the beginning. Any well-planned investigation begins with doubt and ends with faith. The badly planned investigation starts on faith and is both conducted and concluded in doubt. This kind of faith cannot be founded in reality.

How can any faith founded on belief be real? Only perfect knowledge gives birth to real faith. Perfect knowledge and real faith go together. Belief is ignorance; true faith is perfect knowledge. Belief is a faith that is borrowed; belief is a faith that has been thrust upon you, thrown over you, superimposed.

A faith you have to work at is just a belief. Only that faith that awakens within you, that faith that comes to you naturally and on its own through the illumination of perfect knowledge can be called true faith. You don't have to go looking for that faith somewhere. You don't have to learn it, it comes of itself. What you do have to learn is doubt, the right kind of doubt. The right kind of doubt is the beginning of the process of attaining true faith.

Doubt is not disbelief. Disbelief is merely the negative aspect of belief. If one's doubt is only disbelief, it is both unhealthy and incomplete. Doubt is neither belief nor disbelief, it is unbounded inquisitiveness. It is the irrepressible desire to know. It is the urge to attain knowledge; it is unceasing investigation. It is the firm resolve not to stop anywhere before reaching the truth, before reaching the truth that comes out of your own experience.

As I see it, both belief and disbelief are impediments on the search for truth. Doubt is the only way to achieve truth. Only doubt can ultimately lead a man to truth.

There was once a man who was in search of the truth. After years of wandering he came to a holy man who lived in a cave crammed with volume upon volume of sacred books. The topics they covered were infinite. Everywhere one looked were scriptures, scriptures and more scriptures. The sage said to him, "All the knowledge of the universe is preserved in these books. These volumes, full of mysteries and secrets, have been collected and are being kept here only for those who come in search of truth. Each seeker can take away with him one book of his choice. Which of the scriptures would you like to have?"

The young man looked over the endless pile of books, thought for a moment and said, "Please give me the volume that supplies everything all the others profess to contain."

When he heard this the old man laughed. He said, "Of course I do have such a text, but it is rare that anyone asks for it." Then he gave him a volume entitled, "Scripture of the Greatest Doubt."

I would also like to give everyone the same book, because this is the only one that can free the seeker from the chaotic muddle of all the other scriptures and lead him to the eternal truth.

I noticed a lute in one house I visited and it struck me how much the lute and the human mind resemble each other. The mind is an instrument too; it can produce either harmonious or discordant notes. But whatever note your mind produces you are responsible for it. So make your mind an instrument of harmony and truth. Keep your mind open and keep it in tune. Keep it free from the ego. Nothing produces a more discordant note than the ego.

Only the man who is filled with the inner music can approach truth. It is not the man who intellectualizes about point and counterpoint but the man who is a full symphony unto himself who will find his way to truth.

I do not speak to you of light, of illumination, because that is not the question. The question is one of vision. With vision, light exists; without it, there is no light at all. You cannot perceive what is beyond your vision, and so the issue is not one of knowing existence but of your capacity for knowledge. Your perception of existence is proportionate to the extent to which your knowledge is awakened.

Someone asked me earlier whether the soul existed or not. I answered, "If you have eyes to see it the soul exists; otherwise, it does not."

Normally, you are only able to perceive the objective reality. Your senses are only attuned to that. Through the medium of the body, it is not possible to know anything apart from the body itself. The soul is beyond the body; its essence is totally different. The soul must be approached another way.

Religion is the way to know the soul, the way to know the self. Religion is the disciplining of one's inner eye, of the inner vision that enables you to see beyond the objective world, that allows you to surpass your physical existence. Religion is not thinking, however; it is an experience that requires practice to attain.

Thought is always related to the senses; all thoughts are grasped through the senses. The inspiration for thoughts comes from without, not from within. Thoughts belong to others, not the self. The culmination of thought is science, and like science, thought is always centered on objective things.

Thought can never lead beyond the objective world. By its own very nature any possibility for thought to perceive the soul is negated, because all thought is born of and experienced through the senses. What exists beyond the senses does not enter into the realm of thought at all. This is why any thought that attempts to describe or depict the soul seems both illogical and incoherent when given utterance.

Religion is beyond logic: it is beyond both thought and the senses. And with religion comes coherence.

Religion is not an experience that comes through thought, it is an awakening into thoughtless consciousness. The terminal point of a thought is an object: the ultimate perception of a consciousness devoid of objects is the soul. All thoughts that pertain to the soul are, therefore, futile. The only path which is meaningful is the path that leads to thoughtlessness.

The state of being awakened, of discrimination and of intelligence, exists beyond thought, but the man who is preoccupied with thought is not aware of this at all. Thoughts smother the underlying reality as smoke envelops a fire, and so the individual remains ignorant of the real nature of existence.

Thought is the domain of the multitude: the real fire of knowledge is uniquely personal. Thought is not knowledge, but if it did not exist we would be blind—and the blind man is neither aware of darkness nor of light.

A monk once explained light at great length to a blind man, but the man would not accept what the monk said at all. He was right to disagree, and as far as thinking goes his arguments were coherent. To him what he could not see did not exist. Most people possess this same kind of logic. The blind man was a thinker and his disagreement was in absolute accord with the rules of thought. The monk finally said to the man's friends, "Why have you brought him to me? He needs medical treatment more than he needs explanations about light!"

I say the same thing. If you have vision then you can see light, then you can know yourself.

What you perceive is the truth for you, although it may not necessarily be the only truth. Truth is infinite, yet it is perceptible. Thought is your limit; the senses are your limit—and what you can know through them is limited. To know the limitless you must rise above them.

What you will perceive when you go beyond thought is the infinite, limitless and timeless soul. The soul is known through meditation, through the science of yoga. When the currents of the mind dissolve and your vision perceives the inner light, your life is transformed. Then there is no question as to whether the soul exists or not, for then you know, then you have realized it for yourself. Then you are beyond thought; then you experience knowledge.

The ultimate is achieved through emptiness, and emptiness is attained by remaining an impartial and inactive witness to the processes of thought in your mind. These processes are the life of the mind, the essence of the mind, and you must free yourself from their bondage.

Impartiality, inactivity and thoughtlessness are attained through meditation. You only have to see, to watch; there is nothing to choose, nothing to be decided. But this kind of perception requires great effort. The habit of activity has become so strong in you that the simple task of not doing anything has become tremendously difficult.

If you concentrate your vision on a single point thoughts begin to disappear, just as the drops of dew on the grass evaporate in the warmth of the morning sun. The heat of your concentrated observation is enough to dissipate thought. This is the point where emptiness begins, where man begins to attain vision, where he begins to perceive his soul.

One dark night I was sitting by myself. No one was with me; there were no thoughts within. I was totally passive, simple looking, with no point of focus. My vision was without object, without any reason behind it. I was engaged in experiencing perception itself. Someone passed by and asked me what I was doing. What could I say? I was not doing anything. I was just there, alone. But that is the beginning of emptiness. This is the point where you pass the physical world by and the realization of God begins in you.

I teach emptiness, I teach dissolution, I teach death. I teach this so that you may become perfect, so that you may become immortal. It may come as a surprise to you, but a man gains life through death. Those who cling to life lose it. The man who worries about perfection achieves nothing, but the man who frees himself from worry by becoming empty attains perfection.

A raindrop cannot become the ocean by holding itself aloof from the other drops. Its ego is the hindrance, the obstacle. By standing on its own the drop can never amount to anything; all that can happen is that it will be reduced to nothing. The ocean does not keep it out, its only obstacle is its own desire for individuality. Its walls and its boundaries are its alone. It wants to merge with the ocean but it does not want to lose its own existence, it does not want to cease being a drop. This is the problem. And the problem for man is the same. It is impossible for the drop to remain an entity unto itself and become the ocean at the same time. Man's case is the same. An individual cannot remain an individual and still become one with God.

When the ego dissolves, the soul is attained. The soul is so near, so very close at hand, and yet we are so unnecessarily and foolishly concerned with the ego. The ego has to be destroyed; we have to remove these walls, these boundaries, with our own hands. Then and then alone can we become part of the infinite and limitless truth.

Those who do not possess the courage to do this can never become religious. Becoming religious is the bravest thing possible for a man because it means the annihilation of his ego. Religion is not for cowards. It is not for those who are tempted by heaven or afraid of hell. These enticements and fears belong to the ego alone. The ego must be destroyed. The individual has to die. Only a fearless and courageous man can embrace the infinite realization of truth.

You want to know the truth and yet you allow the dust of thoughts to accumulate in your mind. The mind is like a mirror. Wipe it clean. Then you will see the truth standing in front of you. Then you will see that the truth has always been there, right in front of your eyes.

The tiniest speck of dust in one's eye can hide the biggest mountain, and the closing of a fragile eyelid can shut off the world from one's vision. For sight, for pure sight, there must be no obstacle between the seer and the seen. But when there is an obstruction, the closer it is to one's eye the bigger it looms. And a similar thing happens spiritually. It is something that is very, very close to the seer himself that keeps him from being able to see the truth. And what, you ask, is the closest thing to the seer? It is "I". The sense of "I" is the nearest, closest thing. Is it any wonder it becomes an obstacle between you and the truth?

A man's outward appearance is a reflection of what he is inside. The outer is painted with the colors of the inner. If everything within is blissful, everything is beautiful outside; if there is misery inside, everything outside is ugly. A man only sees himself everywhere he looks. If you are in hell, know that you have caused it to be so—but know too that it is within your power to be in heaven as well.

If you want to know God you have to merge with him, you have to become one with him. This may seem paradoxical to you, because how can you become one with God when you do not know him at all? And how can you ever get to know him if you have to become one with him to know him? The whole thing certainly appears paradoxical indeed! But to unscramble this puzzle is to understand clearly and correctly the entire base of all spiritual practices.

Once I came upon an artist who was painting a sunset. "When you paint," I asked him, "What is the first thing you do?"

"I become one with the scene I am about to paint," he replied.

"How do you do this?" I inquired. "How is it possible to become one with this sunset for example?"

He said, "The moment a man forgets himself he becomes one with everything."

The artist put it very well. God is all that exists; the totality of existence is God. And to become one with existence, there is no other obstruction than yourself, than your "I".

God is only there when the "I" is absent. This is knowing God; this is living in God. To really know something you have to live it. God can only be known from within, never from the outside, and so you have to become one with him, you have to lose yourself in him.

When you are separate from God and look around you, what you see is the world. You may not see it, but that is God too. But when you look at the world from inside that merger, everything you see is a manifestation of God.

The outer vision of truth is the world; the inner vision of truth is God himself.

What is the real proof that God exists? As far as God is concerned the language of proof is completely inapplicable. No thought, no argument, no proof can rise to the level of God. In thought, argument and proof, "I" exists, and wherever "I" is, God is not.

Kabir was right when he said God's street was so narrow that two could not walk along it at the same time. Love is the name of that street. Love is where I live, where I exist, where I am—and that is where there is no ego, where "I" is not.

It is only in this state that the blinders fall away from one's consciousness and the vision of God becomes possible. That vision itself is the proof. What other proof of love do you need than being in love? There is no other proof of God's existence than being in him.

But all kinds of proofs have been put forward in the past and many more will be advanced in the future. Those who are unable to love talk about love and those who have no eyes are the ones who discuss vision. There is only deliberation and discussion about God where there is no sight to see him, where there is no heart to experience him. And it matters not whether the arguments are for God or against him. The pros and cons do not make one iota of difference. The theist and the atheist are just two sides of the same coin. Neither has any vision.

This lack of sight is the central bone of contention. Whether a blind man accepts or does not accept the existence of light makes no difference whatsoever. The only thing that has any significance for him is the realization that he is blind, because it is only through that understanding that he will begin to search for sight. He doesn't have to concern himself with light, it is sight he needs. When sight is present so is light. And if there is no sight, how will you prove to him there is light? If there is no sight there is no proof of God's existence either.

So do not ask for proof that light exists, simply understand that you have no sight. And do not ask for proof of God either. Simply know that what is, is unknown to you and that you are in ignorance. The light may be unknown but your own blindness can be known. God is unknown but your own ignorance can be known.

Now, I ask you, what do you hope to achieve by thinking about the unknown? No thought can move beyond the limits of the known; it only runs on the track of the known, in the groove of the known. The unknown can never be known this way. The unknown only comes when the known gives way and makes room for it. The advent of the unknown is dependent on the removal of the known. Only when the known says farewell does the unknown appear on the threshold of one's consciousness. It does not come through discussion; only when there is no discussion does it come. It only sprouts in a soil that is free of deliberation.

This barren land of discussion and deliberation is your blindness, and busying yourself in its pointless cultivation is your unconsciousness. Only when all discussion and deliberation have vanished and your consciousness is totally alert do you attain the sight that allows you a glimpse of the light called God.

To me, a man shows his earnest desire to know truth not by talking about light but by treating the blindness of his self. Religion is the cure for the blindness of the self.

What is the irrefutable proof of light? Eyes. And what is the irrefutable proof of God? Eyes. What I myself saw when I gained my sight was that only God exists, that nothing else exists. What I thought in my blindness was that everything else existed but that God did not.

The moment you realize the divinity within you, you begin to see visions of God everywhere you look. You only see on the outside what is within you. If you do not see God everywhere, then realize you have not yet sought him within.

In order to dispel one illusion do not create another. It is foolishness to move into a new dream to rid yourself of an old one. Do not try to conceive God; do not create concepts of him. Let all your inventions go and just open your eyes. What you see in front of you is God. That alone is God.

Truth is like the firmament—endless, beginningless, boundless. Is there a door for entering the sky? Then how can there be one for entering truth? But if one's eyes are closed, then there is no sky. And the same is true of truth.

The opening of your eyes is the entrance to truth; closing your eyes is shutting the door.

I do not live in a different world. I live in the same world everyone else lives in. But my way of looking at life has changed totally. And this change is a change in the world itself, because what we see is what we are.

Our vision is our world; our vision is our life. Our vision creates the world around us. If life appears miserable to you, know well that the misery is yours, that it is your creation. Try to alter your vision, not life. Transforming your vision is transforming yourself.

Everything depends on you, on the self within you. Hell and heaven live in the self; worldliness and salvation abide there too. The self is unchangeable, it remains the same forever, but one point of view looks at it as a prison while another sees it as the essence of salvation.

When life is viewed from the standpoint of the ego it becomes hell, because the ego is in opposition to everything, to everybody. I can remain "I" as long as I want to, but only by remaining different from and opposed to the rest of existence. The effort to become "I" is an attempt to fight with the all. And it only results in anxiety and distress. It leads to the fear of destruction, to the dread of death. It is no wonder misery is the only result of achieving this rigid "I", of attaining this stubborn and impossible unreality.

But the word can also be looked at from the viewpoint of egolessness. "I" conflicts with the all; "non-I" is the assimilation of everything. And only that absorption is real because existence is unseverable, undivisible.

All bits and pieces and divisions are only the products of man's fantasy. If "I am", I am only a piece, only a part; if "I am not", I am absorbed into the undivided whole. Being a part is slavery; being whole is freedom. As long as "I am", I am in misery, because the very existence of "I" is an eternal duel with life, a battle to the death. But when "I am not", I am in bliss. Non-being is infinite peace.

When consciousness is liberated from "I" it is released from all traditions, freed from all conditionings. Separating the self from "I" is merging with God.

I do not consider thoughtful meditation, the idea of meditating upon something by thinking about it, as true meditation. True meditation is thoughtless, because thoughtlessness itself is what meditation is. Where there is neither thought nor deliberation there is meditation. There are no thoughts in deep sleep either, so to say that meditation is only the absence of thoughts is not quite accurate. This is a negative approach, and meditation is not the negative aspect of anything. On the contrary, meditation is a positive presence. It is the positive presence of sensitivity, of awareness, of understanding. Only complete wakefulness, only total consciousness is meditation. And perfect, consciousness is only possible when one is completely free of thoughts.

You wish to meditate? Then while you meditate, bear in mind that nothing lies before you and that nothing lies behind you. Let the past perish and let the future go. Empty your memory and empty your imagination. There will be no time; there will only be emptiness. And during this moment of emptiness you will know you are in meditation. This moment of meditation is a moment of eternity as well.

You ask what it is that is known in the ecstasy of *samadhi*? Nothing. As long as something remains to be known you are not in *samadhi*. *Samadhi* is union with existence. Not even a hair's breadth of separation remains to be known.

Truth is one—but splitting existence into two is the most deep-rooted of all mankind's blind beliefs. What exists is one; there is not two. Nature versus God, body versus soul, animate versus inanimate—these differentiations have no place whatsoever in existence.

But it is because of these seeming differences that the arguments of the materialist and the spiritualist carry weight. Existence is one, yet its manifestations are many. In its diversity, it is also one. In each and every part the undivided whole exists. But discussion and deliberation give rise to differentiation because they only look at the surface and do not plumb the depths. They look at things from the outside; they do not penetrate within.

In any discussion the personality of the speaker also has to be taken into consideration. When the speaker believes himself to be separate from existence, this very feeling prevents him from entering into existence. To enter into existence the ability to merge is essential; to penetrate deeply, oneness is needed. But he can never attain this unless he loses himself. And he cannot lose himself unless he gives up all his thoughts and all his ideas, because he is only the shadow of his thoughts. He has no existence of his own; he is only a collection of thoughts. But what he wants to do is preserve his identity, not lose it. And he can only do this by diving into more thoughts, into more discussion. And as he deliberates on truth he moves further and further away from truth itself.

It is this discussing of truth, this deliberating on truth that creates the chasm between truth and one's self. In that perception that comes when the mind is empty of thoughts neither the soul exists, nor the body, nor God, nor nature—but there is something that cannot be given a name. For the sake of convenience, let me call it the universal soul. That unknown, nameless, undivided entity is truth. When you try to think about it, it appears in different pieces—but when you are free of thoughts it manifests in its undivided form. That is its original form; that is its real face. Deliberation breaks it asunder to look at it.

Deliberation is an analytical process and the nature of analysis requires that something be dissected, that something be broken into pieces before it can be looked at.

The man who is integrated, synthesized, simply looks at it as it is. There is no action involved in his looking; he is just looking. His gaze is a perfect mirror and truth is reflected in it exactly as it is. In the mirror of a synthesized consciousness there is no one single trace of duality.

That unknown entity that I have called the universal soul is body *and* soul, both God and nature. There are all just notes of a single melody. All is life. Nothing is dead; nothing is inanimate. Death is nowhere to be found. The waves surge up in the ocean of life and then they fall back, and then they merge. They are there when they crest and there when they ebb. In both conditions they exist, because the ocean exists.

Individuals die because there really is no such entity as an individual. Theism perishes because it really does not exist. Whatever has no real existence perishes, but what exists, exists always. This is not just my idea; this is not just my thought—this is what I see. And anyone who avoids thoughts and opinions, who remains aloof from discussion, who simply remains silent and calm and empty and aware will have exactly the same vision.

If you look at the world through analytical eyes you will see duality, you will see division, but if you look at it directly and clearly, with nothing in your eyes but pure sight, you will see that it is one.

A consciousness that is empty of thoughts is in meditation, and meditation is the doorway to truth. This is my invitation to you, an invitation to move into the miraculous world of meditation.

You ask me what to do to meditate. I say not to do anything at all. Just be quiet and be aware of your breathing.

Consciously watch your breath. Witness the incoming and the outgoing of your breath. Don't make it a strenuous activity, just watch it in quiet, peaceful, restful awareness. Then in a totally natural way and without knowing how, you will find you are experiencing a sensation that is tremendously pleasant. You will not be aware of how or when you entered that state, but suddenly you will be somewhere you have never been before. This, in fact, is the very place your consciousness has been forever.

There are two ways to investigate truth. One way is by thinking; the other, by realization.

The path of thought is a circular one. You go round and round, but you never come to the end. This is a false, illusory direction; it only leads to division, to sectarianism. A thought, an ideology, is nothing more than an intellectual proposition, whereas the realization of truth is the experience of the whole vital force of life itself. All sects depend on logic and that is why they have no stability at all. Truth is unchanging, and the attainment of truth establishes a man once and for all in existence, in the eternal, in God.

The path of thought is a borrowed one; you proceed along a road paved with the ideas of others. Through argument and through different combinations of these second-hand thoughts you create the illusion of originality. Realization alone is original because realization is born within one's self. The known cannot lead to the unknown. Truth is unknown, and so familiar thoughts can never become stepping-stones to truth. Only by leaving thought behind can you pass through the doorway of truth. The perception of truth cannot happen in thought, it can happen only in the clear stream of thoughtless consciousness.

Man collects experiences through his senses. All of these experiences belong to the outer world, because the senses only know that which is external. The senses have no access to one's inner being. It is these outer experiences that give rise to thought. On the level of scientific exploration thought can be very constructive, tremendously helpful, but in the search for inner truth thought is totally useless. Thought is bound to the senses; it cannot touch the consciousness at one's inner core.

It is of great importance to remember that thoughts are external. They cover the self rather than help reveal it. And the greater a man's accumulation of ideas is, the more difficult it will be for him to attain to his self.

A man who does not know the self can never know truth. To reach the truth there is no other way, there is no other alternative. Being caught up in intellectual speculation about truth is like being a blind man and constantly thinking about light. His thinking will lead nowhere; light is something to be seen, not thought about. He needs medical treatment, not the ideas of some philosopher. Thought is the malady; realization is the medicine. The question is not one of light, but rather of vision.

This is exactly how thinking and meditation stand in relation to one another. Thought is the pondering and analysis of light by a blind man; meditation is attaining the sight to see the truth. And yoga is the science of meditation.

As I see it, meditation is a state of mind, a state of emptiness and of perfect wakefulness and awareness. When the mind is empty of objects and fully awakened to the seer himself, one has attained to the state of meditation.

Meditation is the ability to see the truth. Our minds are generally cluttered with objects—with thoughts about things, with reactions to outer stimuli—and this creates a wall that shuts us out, that separates us from our selves. The consciousness of man is hidden by his intellect, just as the clouds obscure the light of the sun.

Man is free to close the door to his own inner being if he so desires. But someone who is capable of chaining himself can also free himself. There are two sides to freedom, just as the power to create always hides the power to destroy. It is important to keep this truth in mind.

The man who aspires to attain the truth, to know the self, must attack on two fronts. He must mount an offensive for wakefulness; he must launch a drive for emptiness. When the two fronts meet he is in meditation.

To awaken, one must discard not only unconsciousness but also personal pride in one's thoughts and in one's deeds. All thinking and all activity must take place in a totally conscious state. And through constant practice the witness is eventually born within the self. One's latent wisdom begins to stir, and with it, the consciousness of true knowledge. This comes from a steady and continuous battle against the lethargy of the mind. And finally, even in sleep, awareness is ever present. This is the first line of attack.

The second thrust is for emptiness. The inherent peace of the mind must be protected from the restlessness and agitation caused by the constant flow of thoughts and ideas. One must become like a man walking in the night, protecting his candle from the wind.

Each of these onslaughts complements the other; the launching of one assists the other. The birth of consciousness helps lead to emptiness; the beginning of emptiness helps the growth of one's consciousness. It is difficult to say which of the two is the more important.

When both consciousness and emptiness ripen, when they both reach fruition, the mind passes through a revolution that is virtually impossible to imagine or to describe. No other change in a man's life is greater than this one. This revolution is so basic, so fundamental, that his whole life is transformed. The closest I can come to putting it into words is to say that it is like a blind man's sudden achievement of sight. Through this incredible experience of indescribable light a man becomes established within his self.

Through this revolution a man comes to realize the bliss, the consciousness and the reality of his existence. Death dissolves; he perceives immortality. Darkness disappears; he realizes truth. Only after this experience does real life begin. Up to this point a man experiences life only in a very limited way.

A friend said to me "Wouldn't it be wonderful if we could transform the world?"
I replied, "It would be very nice, but where is this world? I look for it but cannot find it. I seek the world and only see the reflection of myself. Leave the world alone. Let us transform ourselves instead. When we do that, the world will be transformed. What else is the world but that deep inner connection we are all a part of, that we all share?"

The realization of truth is a difficult process because it has to be sought and it has to be lived. But it is very easy to accept what the scriptures say about truth; the scriptures only have to be believed. To realize truth you need open-eyed discrimination; for the other, blind belief will do quite nicely. It is for this reason that the scriptures are obstacles that stand in the way of realizing truth.

Where blind belief exists there can never be any sort of discrimination whatsoever. And remember well, all beliefs are blind. How can blind eyes perceive the truth? Blind eyes are the closed doors of consciousness and truth only knocks at that door where an impartial and unbiased mind stands ready to bid it welcome.

Are you ready to become impartial? Are you brave enough to free yourself of beliefs? Are the doors of your heart open to truth? If you answer "yes", I tell you that nothing will be easier for you than the realization of truth. It is only in your mind that it seems difficult. Your beliefs, your convictions, the values you have accepted have complicated everything.

The man who is able to sweep away the web of these complications will find truth standing before him. It has always been there. Your eyes were just too cloudy to see it.

Every house is full of mirrors. But have you noticed that a little bit of truth, a little bit of love or a kind act brings a fresh beauty to your eyes, to your face, to your whole being? If not, you are as blind as a bat. You have been wasting your time in front of the mirror. Smash all your mirrors to smithereens then; you have no idea how to use a mirror at all.

Man is suffering. Our whole age is suffering. What is the reason for this? You don't have to look very far for the answer. We know so very much, but we have no direct experience at all. Only the brain is intact; the heart has dwindled into nothing. And no true realization ever comes by knowledge alone; it comes through experience. The eyes that light the path of life are not connected to the brain, their link is to the heart. And if your heart is blind, then darkness is all you can expect in life.

Is this disappointment I see in your eyes? Do you know that when disappointment shows in one's eyes it means the fire in one's heart has gone out, that one has become stagnant and dull. Disappointment is a great sin; it restrains the energy of life, it keeps it from moving upwards. Not only is it sin, it is suicide, because the man who is not striving for a better life is moving like an automaton towards death. It is an eternal law that one who does not rise falls back, that one who does not move ahead is pushed backwards.

Whenever I see someone falling I know he has stopped trying to scale the peaks of life. Rising to the summit of life is a positive action; falling back, plunging into the dark valleys, is the negative aspect of not striving onwards and upwards. When I see such disappointment in your eyes it is only natural my heart fills with sorrow, love and compassion, because this kind of disillusionment with life is the beginning of the descent into the valley of death.

Like a sunflower, hope turns towards the sun. Disappointment lives in darkness. The disillusioned man is unaware of the great potential that is latent within him; he forgets what he is, what he can become. Like a seed that lies in the earth, unaware of what life has in store for it, the situation of the man who is engrossed in his disappointment with life is the same. Today, everyone is in this same predicament.

Nietzsche has said "God is dead", but I do not find this as disturbing as the death of hope, for as long as hope exists there is a possibility for men to find God. If hope does not exist, whether there is a God or not is irrelevant. It is the impetus of hope that sets a man off on his journey into the unknown, and it is hope alone that gives him the inspiration that can awaken his sleeping energies and activate his dormant consciousness.

What should I say about hope? Should I say that hope is theism? Should I say that hope is the source of all growth? But more important, where is hope to be found? I look for the fires of hope everywhere; all I find are the ashes of disillusionment. If you have no hope how can you live? Without it you are not really alive at all.

Pardon me for saying so, but you are all dead. You have not lived yet. You may have been born but you are not yet up to life. Birth is not life. You may have been born, but you have to attain life personally. You have to achieve it on your own.

Birth may be cancelled out by death, but death cannot destroy life. Life is neither birth nor death. Life exists before birth; life exists beyond death. Only the man who knows this will be able to rise above his fear and misery. But how can someone who is cloaked in disillusionment realize this?

Such a man simply perishes from the tensions of birth and death.

Life is just a possibility; it requires effort, a spiritual *sadhana* to transform it into a reality. And one's *sadhana*, one's journey to truth, is not born out of disappointment. Disappointment is barren; nothing whatsoever is born out of it. This is why I say it is suicidal. It is incapable of manifesting any sort of creative power whatsoever.

All you have to do is stand up. Just get up on your feet and throw off this mantle of disillusionment. You have allowed it to envelop you all by yourself. You only have to decide to be rid of it and then throw it off. You and only you are responsible for its existence.

A man becomes his thought. What he thinks creates him. Man is the architect of his own fate. The constant repetition of some thought or idea will eventually consolidate into an actual situation, so remember, whatever you are is what you have wanted to be. You have thought about it; you have hankered after it. Search your memory and you will see the truth of what I am saying to you. When you see the truth you will also find the key to changing yourself. Once you have this key it will not be difficult to throw away the thoughts and ideas you have borrowed. It will even be easier than taking off your clothes, because these ideas you have accumulated are illusory, they only exist in your own imagination.

We imprison ourselves in our own ideas. And we do this all by ourselves. But what exists deep inside you has always been free. It has been free since time immemorial. And can you conceive of any greater prison than that of disillusionment? I cannot. What stone walls cannot accomplish, disappointment can. It is possible to break down walls of stone, but disillusionment even destroys a man's desire to be free.

Break these chains! They can be broken; that is why I am asking you to smash them. They are not real, and all it takes is your resolve to shatter them forever. Just as darkness disappears the moment you light a lamp; the unreal in you dissolves as soon as determination awakens in you. The light that pervades one's consciousness when the shackles of disillusionment have been cast off is what I mean by hope.

Disillusionment is a self-imposed condition; hope is the innate nature of the self. Disillusionment is a veil over one's mind; hope is a manifestation of one's spirit. If it were not, then the constant movement of life towards development and growth would not exist at all. A seed is anxious to sprout because somewhere in it hope exists. All of life wants to flower; whatever exists contains within it the desire for its own fruit.

Without hope how can there be any desire for perfection in the imperfect? Without hope how is the journey to God possible at all? When I see rivers rushing towards the sea I recognize hope in them. When I see a bonfire reaching towards the heavens I see hope in the flames. The light of hope shines in the eyes of children, in the eyes of animals, in the songs of birds. Whatever lives, lives in hope; whatever is dead has died in disillusionment.

If you observe young children who have not yet been spoiled by society, education and civilization, you will see three distinct threads of the life force in them. You will find hope; you will find curiosity; you find faith. These qualities are natural; they have not been acquired. These things exist within us, but they can be lost. Yet you cannot really lose them entirely because the essence of nature can never be destroyed. Nature can only be hidden, veiled. Whatever is unnatural can be nothing more than a cover, it can never be the inner essence itself.

This is why I urge you to throw off your clothes and see who you are in your nakedness. Clothes are bondage, and one thing is for certain—God is not swaddled in tight-fitting clothes. How wonderful it would be if you would remove your clothes! But remember, I am not speaking of clothes that are fashioned from threads of cotton, I am talking of clothes woven from the iron chains of negative ideas. These are your bondage. Whoever discards them can attain to that pure nakedness in which Mahavira lived and of which he spoke.

You have to become naked to know the truth, to know your self, to become established in the very nature of your self. But you will have to discard the mantle of disillusionment first. Your other clothes can only be removed after you have shed this heavy cloak.

If you falter or hesitate at the idea of attaining God then you had better realize that the poison of disillusionment exists somewhere within you. This is what makes you negligent and lethargic. Negligence may cost you the final goal of life.

Before God and other than God there can be no goal to life. Let this understanding resound throughout your entire being. Let it sink deeply into you that there is no peace in life except in God, that perfection is to be found in God alone. The man who drops out of life before reaching God has insulted himself. He has given up before becoming what he could have been.

The greater your sense of determination, the higher your sights, the deeper is the awakening of the energies latent within the self. The height of your achievement is in proportion to the power of your energies. Look at the trees that touch the sky. Their roots go deep into the ground. If you are bestirred by hope and by the desire to touch the sky then the dormant powers lying in the innermost recesses of your being are awakened.

The height of your aspiration is the depth of your power. Setting your sights low is demeaning your self—but if you must beg, at least beg for God. What you ultimately wish to become must be your dictate from the very beginning, because the beginning itself is part and parcel of the final attainment.

I know that you are constantly surrounded by situations

that go against you, that prevent you from rising to God—but remember, all those who have ever attained to God were also encircled by similar circumstances. Do not use situations as excuses, because the excuse, not the situation, is the real hindrance.

No matter how unfavorable circumstances may be, they cannot be real obstacles between you and God. It is impossible. It is like saying it is too dark to light a lamp. The darkness is never that black nor are conditions that unfavorable that they can prevent you from reaching the light. The only obstacle is your own disillusionment. Really, there is no obstacle but you.

Do not attach too much importance to what is here today. It will be gone tomorrow. Something that changes from moment to moment is of very little value. The flow of situations is like the current of a river.

Concentrate on something solid, like a rock in the middle of the stream. That is your consciousness; that is your soul. That is you in your natural state. Everything else changes but that is unchangeable. Catch hold of that point of immobility because you are drifting in the winds, you are being tossed about by the waves.

You must locate the solid base of your being. Focus on it; zero in on it in your mind. As soon as you focus on this firm foundation your disappointment turns to hope and the darkness is transformed into light. Remember, whosoever knocks at the door of the soul with a heart full of hope and confidence, with strength and determination, with love and prayer, is never unsuccessful. He is never turned away. Such a man cannot help but find God.

On the road to sin, success is as impossible as failure is on the path to God. If sin brings you success it is only an illusion; if you seem to fail on your way to God it is only a test. God's door is never closed. Your eyes may be closed—but you have only closed them in your disappointment. Throw away this disappointment, this disillusionment, and see what stands before you. Isn't it the sun you have been searching for? Isn't it the beloved you have always longed for?

Christ has said, "Ask and you shall receive. Knock, and the door shall be opened unto you." This was true before Christ as well. And it will be true in the future. Most men stand at God's door with their eyes closed. Blessed are those who open their eyes and knock.

Open your eyes and look around you carefully. Don't you see constant change wherever you look? Whatever your eyes behold is part of the perpetual current of life. The man who wants to build a storehouse for his treasures in the midst of a rushing river is not in his right senses.

Truth is not something you create. It cannot be created at all. The only thing you can create is untruth. It is possible to see the truth, but not to create it. Truth is always present. You only need eyes to see it.

5
LIFE AND DEATH

Wherever I look I see the thrill of life, the pulse of life. Everything is throbbing with life. Even the tiniest atom vibrates with the love of life. All around you the dance of life goes on; everywhere the symphony of existence is playing. Even if you can neither see it nor hear it, the delightful, exhilarating rhythm of life is there!

Isn't this life we see around us God himself? Any God that is aloof from life, that is apart from life, is dead, unreal. Life is the only truth.

God does not indulge himself in the play of creation sitting somewhere far off in the distance. Life is one perpetual process of evolution, and this continuing creation of life is God himself.

Even for life's longest journey you only need the courage to take one step. No one can take more than one step at a time. Even a journey of thousands and thousands of miles begins with one step and ends with one step.

Life is here, now, today. Tomorrow is far off. Tomorrow is infinitely far away. And that is why it never comes. Live today. The man who really lives always lives today. Today is life and tomorrow is death. If you want to live, then live today—but if you only want to die, then you will find tomorrow very useful.

You only live life when you touch your ultimate depths. Otherwise, you simply exist. The difference between just existing and living life is as great as the difference between living and dying.

I wish everyone would live as if the eyes of the world were upon him. Whether we know it or not, nothing is hidden, no matter how deep it may be. No man can ever really be aloof or apart from the whole. The echo of everything that arises in him reaches everyone else. His life is part and parcel of the life that flows around him.

I love beauty—the beauty that lies deep beneath the body. The body, with its beautiful thoughts and its beautiful sensations, is only the protective frontier, but there is also the deep and perfect beauty of inner emptiness, free of thought, free of sensation. So do not stop at the body. Stopping is death. Wade through the deep water. You will only find pebbles and shells on the shore. You have to go far out to sea to dive for pearls.

The attainment of knowledge is not an end to the mystery of life. In fact, it is only when one has acquired knowledge that the true mystery is revealed. And then, only mystery remains. Knowledge is the understanding of mystery, the acceptance of mystery, the communion with mystery; knowledge is the bliss of a life with mystery, of a life in mystery, of a life through mystery. When the self has dissolved and only mystery remains you have entered into the sacred precincts of the universal soul. There is no greater mystery than this dissolution of the self, because when the individual self disappears the pure existence of the absolute self is manifest in its indescribable glory and total grandeur.

What should I say to you today? Should I talk to you about life? Perhaps I will. Perhaps it would be appropriate, because although you are alive you have no relation with life whatsoever. This may appear to be a contradictory statement, but not only is it possible to say this to you, this is really the way things are. You are alive but you have forgotten about life. Perhaps you are too involved in living to remember life.

Whenever I look at a tree I wonder if it is aware of its roots. But even man knows nothing of his roots. And unless he does, unless a man possesses this knowledge, how can he have any real relation to life? Life exists in roots, in invisible roots; the essence of the visible is rooted in the invisible. In every living thing, the source of the visible is in the invisible. And unless you are aware of this you will go through your life without any relation to its true essence whatsoever.

To be related to life the simple fact that you have been born is not enough. Birth is nothing more than a platform, a stage upon which the experience of life that is latent within you can unfold. Birth is only the beginning. But there are many, many people who stop here, who never progress beyond the starting point. They mistake it for the target itself. This is what generally happens.

There are only very few people who are able to distinguish the difference between the starting point and the finish line. Others, perhaps, may be able to differentiate between the two but do not live their lives accordingly. Their differentiation is purely intellectual, and it must be remembered that intellectual perception is not pure perception at all. It is only when perception comes out of a deeper understanding, out of a great sensitivity to life that it is fruitful. This understanding comes from an intense feeling for life and from the depths of one's heart. It transforms a man; it renews him.

The intellect labors under the illusion it possesses knowledge, but this so-called knowledge is nothing more than the borrowed thoughts of others. Intellectual perception is basically quite superficial. It is like the waves that ride the ocean— fickle, changeable, without stability or endurance. They come and they go, but in the depths the ocean is unchanged, unaffected by them. The intellect is to understanding as waves are to the ocean.

Awareness of the self, awareness of the difference between being born and living life, must come from the heart rather than from the intellect. Birth is simply the beginning; it is not the be-all, not the end-all. And the man who mistakes birth for life will automatically accept death as the culmination point of life as well. This is an illusion, just a natural outgrowth of having accepted the initial misconception. And those who misunderstand birth will also be afraid of death.

What we know as life is really a living death. The man who is not aware that he is separate from his body is not alive in the real sense of the word. The man who does not know that he existed before the birth of his body and will exist after its death is not alive at all. The phenomenon of life is an unbroken one, yet such a man will not even be able to experience fully the life that is his between this birth and this death.

Birth is an external event; life is inner. Birth is the world; life is God. Birth is only the gateway to life. But unless a man makes an effort to realize this, birth, for him, becomes the gateway to death and nothing more. Death is just a development of birth.

Only consciousness and awareness lead to life. This is what *sadhana* is; this is what the journey to self-realization is. This is what religion is.

I look at old people and I look at young people. From

the standpoint of birth and death there is a difference between them, but as far as life is concerned there is none whatsoever. Life is outside the realm of time. Birth and death occur within time and the advancement of age happens within time, but they are not developments of life itself. Age and life are two totally different things.

To attain to life it is necessary to move outside time. Do you know what time is? Time is change. In the material world nothing is static. Not one single atom in the physical world is stable. Only the self is stable. There is something in the self that is beyond change. And the existence of the self is also beyond time. Entering into this unchanging existence is awakening to life.

Search for life. If you don't, death will claim you. Every moment it comes nearer and nearer. After birth, each moment brings you closer to death's victory. And no matter what you do, unless you decide to live a real life this victory is already decided. Property, power, fame—all these count for nothing in the wake of death's triumph. The realization of the existence of the self is the only thing that is outside death, because the self alone exists outside time. Living in the realm of time is rushing towards death.

I see everyone running towards the jaws of death. Stop and think about the direction you are moving in. Someone dies every day and yet each of you still remains a disinterested spectator. If you were aware of the truth you would recognize your own death in his. The same thing is going to happen to you. Really, it is already happening. What you have mistaken for life is actually a gradual death. But the process of dying is so slow that you do not recognize it until you are face to face with it.

A subtle insight is required to see this slow motion advance of death and to recognize the situation of the self in the scheme of things. And the desire to attain to life is born only when a man realizes the precarious position his self is in. When he sees the self being enveloped by the fires of death he is like a man who wants to escape from a burning house. Then he develops an intense and acute thirst to live. This wish to live is the greatest fortune that can befall a man because this desire leads to his penetration of the deeper layers of life.

Do you have this desire in you? Does your heart want to reach the unknown, to move beyond the known? If not, then know well that your eyes are closed and that your blindness will lead you nowhere but into the hands of death.

Awaken while there is still time. Open your eyes. Look. Death is all around you. But in your self, outside the world and outside time, there is nectar to be found. The man who reaches to that divine nectar will not encounter death anywhere. To him death is just an illusion and only life is real.

Christ said, "Man cannot live by bread alone." He spoke truly; bread is not enough. This does not mean that a man is able to live without bread. He cannot. But he cannot live on bread and on nothing else. It is impossible to live without bread, but to live solely on bread is equally impossible.

Bread is to man as roots are to plants. The roots do not exist for themselves; they are for producing fruit, for creating flowers. If fruit and flowers do not grow then the existence of the roots has been in vain. And although fruit and flowers cannot be produced without the roots, the fruit and the flowers are not produced for the roots. The lowly is needed to create the lofty. The lowly serves its purpose through the very evolution that creates the higher form.

Man needs bread in order that he many live and satisfy his hunger for truth, for the beauty of life. Bread is needed to satisfy hungers even greater than the hunger for bread. But if there is no greater hunger the bread has existed in vain. Bread does not exist for bread alone. On its own it has no value. Its purpose is served when it transcends its own existence. Its purpose lies in those values of life that are far above and beyond it.

A *sadhu* used to come to see me and would always tell me he was thinking about immortality. I used to tell him it was just not possible to think about immortality, because whatsoever falls within the sphere of thinking simply cannot be immortal. Thought is mortal. How can it have any contact with immortality? I used to tell him he would be better off to think about mortality, to search for death and to come to know it.

Facing death squarely is what leads the soul to immortality. But we are frightened of death; we prefer to ponder immortality. Doesn't all this thinking and talk about immortality come out of our fear of death? And how can a mind that is terrified of death succeed in attaining immortality?

If the truth be known, there is no fear of death—death is in fear. Death is unknown and unfamiliar, and I find it difficult to understand where the fear comes from. You need to be familiar with something to be afraid of it. It is not possible to fear the unknown, but fear of losing the known, of losing the familiar is possible. Fear of death is not really fearing death, it is fearing the loss of what you know as life. And when this fear solidifies it is transformed into death.

That is why I advised the *sadhu* to search for death, why I tell everyone the same thing. And this is the only quest that bears fruit. At the end of that search it is not death that is achieved, but immortality itself.

Why is there so much misery in man's life? It is because man's life is a medley of notes, but there is no noteless medley. It is because there is always the pandemonium of thoughts, but never any thoughtless silence. It is because there is the constant turmoil of emotions, but no simple affection, free of fantasies. It is because man is always racing hither and thither in countless directions, but there is never any pause with no wish to go anywhere at all. It is because his life is an open market place of activity, but there is never any isolation, never any being alone, never any inactivity. And lastly, it is because his ego is always predominant and his soul is completely suppressed.

Learn how to surrender yourself to truth. Unless you surrender yourself the truth cannot be realized. The seed has to crumble and disintegrate before it can become a seedling, green and full of life. Learn to die if you want to live.

I had a dream in which I saw some of my dead acquaintances once again. They were all wearing the same clothes they had died in, they were all obsessed with the same thoughts, opinions and prejudices with which they had died. Since they had died everything in life had changed, but they had not changed one bit. I mentioned this to them and they laughed. "The dead never change," they said. "We remain fixed in our beliefs. There is no change whatsoever in the world of the dead. Our principles are eternal. It is only life that is affected by and afflicted with the disease of change."

"There are people who never change in life as well," I said. "Their principles are also eternal and they shut their eyes to change as well. But aren't there at least a few here who change too?"

In one voice they answered, "No. No. No. How can that happen here? No one is alive here. Such a thing may happen in life because many people are already dead long before they actually die."

Did I hear you say life is miserable? No, my friend, life is only what you make it. As long as you do not make it blissful, life will never be blissful for you. Life is an opportunity; it is a blank check. You fill it in by living it; you make it full by living fully. Life is not handed to man. He builds his life by living it day by day. Life is a self-creation. No man is responsible for anyone but himself.

We were seated beside a mountain stream and just below us was a pool in which fish swam about. There was a sandbar nearby, full of shells and conches. I took some of these in my hand and said to those with me, "Look. There are many unborn creatures in these shells. When they are strong enough to break out of these shells they will be born. Are there not similar unborn creatures within us? Are we not covered with hard coatings, just like these shells? Aren't our egoistic selves just like these shells? And can't we too give birth to that unborn existence within us by breaking out of the shell of the ego?

"It is the 'I' that is against the birth of that new life," I said, "and it knows only too well how to protect itself. It protects itself by worldly possessions, by status, position and fame. And in more subtle forms it protects itself by religion, society, ideals, values and the like. It will do anything to survive, to flourish and prosper. But remember, the stronger it grows the less chance that yet-unborn life hidden inside has.

"The ruthlessness and hardness of the ego can kill the unborn soul that is there, in the womb of your self. The ego has to die for the soul to be born."

Life is frustrating because we ourselves have imprisoned it within the ego. If life is liberated from the four walls of the ego it transforms itself into bliss. Life does not exist in "I"; nor does it exist in "you". It is a never ending current that flows between the two.

One's life is a conversation with the whole. But we have turned it into a debate. And that is why there is so much misery, so much affliction; that is why there is anxiety and death. All of this is the result of imprisoning our consciousness within the confines of the ego. Because of this, life has been retarded. It has been rendered insensitive, deathlike, without ups or downs. It has become our bondage, our prison.

We are like the germinating sprout trapped within the hard casing of the seed. As soon as the outer shell breaks open the sprout stirs and begins its upward journey from its dark underground prison towards the sun. The voyage for which it exists begins.

Man is the sprout that is imprisoned within the shell of the ego. This shell is very hard to break through; it affords us the solace of security. But instead of trying to crack it open we go on strengthening it, nourishing it. And the stronger and more solid it becomes the more the inner sprout becomes weak and lifeless. So under the illusion we are making our life safer, more secure, we are losing life itself.

I have heard about an emperor who, in his desire to protect himself, built a palace that had no doors. He installed himself inside and had the passage he used to enter sealed off. Hidden within, he was completely safe from any enemy; in his doorless palace he was totally secure. But the moment he was completely closed within he realized that it offered him no security at all, but certain death. The palace itself became his tomb.

Out of his concern for his security a man turns his ego into a house without doors. And it eventually becomes his own tomb as well.

Life is not separating oneself from existence, life is merging with it. This is why I tell you that if you want to realize life, that if you aspire to the bliss of freedom you have to drop this madness for security. That alone is the basis of the vicious circle that, under the pretence of protecting life, eventually kills it. Life is insecure. Life only exists in insecurity. Security is sluggishness. And what more can security bring you than death?

The man who is ready to live in insecurity can break

through the shell of egoism, and then the sprout that is his life can make its way to God.

Life leads us into deep waters—not to drown us, but to cleanse us. But those who are frightened of being drowned simply sink in life's ocean in vain. Who has ever drowned in life? I know of no one at all. It is those who huddle on the shore in fear who drown.

To create beauty you have to lose yourself in beauty, you have to become one with beauty. Only then can beauty be known. If you heard an artist say, "I don't know beauty but I create it," you would say he was mad. Is this not true in regard to good conduct as well?

How can you live a life of truth, how can you practice truth without knowing it, without becoming one with truth? Our actions only reflect what goes on in our consciousness. Isn't that so? If an artist who does not know beauty but dreams of painting beauty is considered mad, then that person who does not know truth but tries to put it into practice in his life is equally mad.

The creation of beauty is the outcome of the experience of beauty and a truthful life is an outgrowth of the experience of truth. Living a truthful life is not a stairway to the experience of truth, a truthful life is the manifestation of the experience of truth. A so-called life of truth that a man leads without the actual experience of truth is not only untrue, it is worse than untrue because it creates a false idea of truth, it allows him a fantasy of truth. And that is fatal.

What do you live for? If you can tell me this I will know what you are all about. Your life is determined by the direction in which you move. Your life is your own creation. You build your own life; what you build is you. You are the stone, the sculptor and the chisel. No art is as complex as the art of life, and it is to escape from the work and discipline necessary to mold it that some people deny life completely. Their lives are like rocks, blindly shaped by the shocks and tremors and steady erosion of the current of life. And they never feel anything at all. This is a life of misery; this is a life of affliction and pain. This is a living death.

I was staying with some friends and their children were getting ready to take part in a race. They asked me, "Babaji, what is the secret of winning a race?" "Courage," I answered. And then I quickly added, "Be sure to remember this even in life's race. In the race of life there is no greater secret than courage."

Once I stayed in a house that had no windows. It was quite an old building. I said to the landlord, "Your house is like man's mind. There are no windows in it either. You have made no arrangements for fresh air, for the light of the open sky."

He replied, "This building is very old."

I said, "Man's mind is pretty old too."

Being old seems to mean the end of openess to life. Being closed is death. It is a preparation for being entombed forever. But couldn't you just tear down a wall and let the light in? Is what is within the walls not supposed to be in touch with what is outside them? Are the walls so precious that it is too costly to pull them down to reach the sky? The person who is encircled by walls will never know the real panorama of life.

What a terrible fate, being cut off from the sky by these old walls! How self-destructive it is, being isolated from the soul by this old mind!

The physical body grows old naturally, but be careful your mind does not grow old along with it. It is a sure sign that you have successfully completed life's pilgrimage if your mind has kept the perfect simplicity of a newborn child when your body has arrived at the threshold of death.

Do not seek *nirvana* as opposed to life. Rather, make life itself *nirvana.* This is what those who know do. Do not strive for salvation but let all your actions bring salvation to you. I assure you this is possible. I speak from my own experience. The day this becomes possible for you, your life will become as rich as the most beautiful flower—and as filled with fragrance.

Life is not a problem to be solved from outside. The solution to life is only found by living it.

What a wondrous world this is! Those who appear to live are not alive at all. A life that is entangled in dreams of passion is not a real life at all. I also see that those they say are dead are not dead at all. The soul knows no death.

What do my eyes tell me? They tell me that all men are asleep, whether it is night or whether it is day. Those who are presumed to be awake are really asleep. For a real awakening, man's inner consciousness must be activated. Only then will man's sleep, both physical and spiritual, come to an end.

Consciousness is life; sleep is a form of death. Consciousness is the light of awareness that fills the heart; sleep is the darkness that is ridden with misery, pain and remorse. If this is how you feel, know well that you are in darkness. But you must understand that you are asleep, you must understand this state before you can awaken from it. To appreciate the desire for freedom you must first experience imprisonment.

I ask everyone to look inside, to be introspective. If you have any inclination whatsoever to escape from your inner mind, from your inner feelings, it is just an attempt to flee from the darkness you have encountered there. I meet people every day and have the opportunity to study many of them at length. One thing is common to them all, and that is suffering. Everyone is caught in a net of deep misery, entangled in a web of intense anxiety. Everyone seems to be choked by a sense of suffocation. Is it the same with you? Do you have the same feeling of claustrophobia as well?

Everywhere I look I see a lack of purpose; there is an atmosphere of boredom and of frustration all around. Is this what life is about? Are you satisfied with this? Have you not had enough yet? Is this life? Or is this death?

Life is a totally different proposition altogether. It is a whole other experience—one you are not familiar with at all. I tell you this for a reason, because I too once mistook this so-called life for the real thing. This is a natural mistake, because unless you are aware that there is an alternative you will accept what you know as life. This is not a conscious mistake, it is an error of ignorance. But the tiniest thought about the self, the most minute attention to one's inner being can eradicate this ignorance. You should not accept whatsoever is presented to you, for this is blind, unconscious reacting. Thought is conscious, and so it can destroy all illusions.

Thought is diametrically opposed to belief, which is completely unconscious. So to attain to a life that is real it is necessary to follow the path of thinking, not the cul de sac of belief. Belief is blind acceptance; thought is alert investigation. Acceptance is detrimental to the growth of knowledge and belief is an obstacle to investigation. Those who accept everything blindly have no incentive whatsoever to move ahead. The greatest hurdle on the path to knowledge is this tendency to believe. Belief is the only real barrier that stands in the way of freedom of thought. The chains of belief impede progress. Do not get caught in this trap. You will only attain to a life that is authentic through your own investigation

Do not be satisfied with life as it is. It is not real. It has no meaning, no validity. It is only an episode, just a part of the overall evolution of life.

I have heard a story of an old man who wanted to choose an heir before his death, and so he decided to put his two sons to a test. He gave each of them some wheat seeds, said he would be away for a while on a pilgrimage and told them to look after the seeds carefully. The first son stored the seeds in an underground cellar; the second son planted them. Some years later, when the old man returned, he found that the seeds he had given the first son had rotted away while the second son's seeds had increased a thousandfold.

Life is also like this. Life is like a seed; its potential is latent, hidden within it. Only the man who realizes this potential can become the master of his inner being.

Each of us has the opportunity to grow. And reaching the greatest level of attainment possible, reaching the highest peak there is, is becoming real.

Have you ever noticed flowers? One morning, in a garden full of beautiful flowers, I said to some friends who were with me, "These flowers are so lovely, so healthy and fragrant, because they have become what they were meant to be." The flowers had attained their intrinsic perfection; their potential had been fulfilled.

This is possible for man too.

Life is like a flute—hollow and empty within, but possessing infinite slumbering possibilities for beautiful music. The music that poors from the flute depends on how you play it.

Do not center your life around the future. Life exists here, in the now. The future is hidden in the present, and the man who loses today loses all his tomorrows. Aren't all tomorrow's flowers hidden in the seeds you plant today?

A friend died at a very young age. He was just a youth.

but his life had been pure and beautiful, quiet and harmonious. Someone remarked, "What a tragic shame! Dying at such a young age!"

I said, "No, do not say this. It is quite possible that a long life may not be a worthwhile one at all, but a life that has been pure is profound and long and vast. In terms of hours and minutes you may not be able to agree, but this simply proves the inefficiency and limitations of our yardsticks."

I die every day. In fact, I die every moment. This is the secret of life, of a long life. The man who carries the weight of the past dies from bearing the burden of the dead.

Have you ever seen good men dying or bad men living? Just as bad men never truly live, good men never really die.

Haven't you invented God because the fear of death perplexes you so? Nothing is more untrue than a concept of God based on fear.

Light travels in a straight line. Truth and religion also travel in straight lines. If your life does not travel in a straight line then be aware your life is traveling the path of darkness, evil and untruth.

Where does this mad race after wealth, fame, knowledge or renunciation take a man? Where does the headlong rush of the ambitious mind lead? When I think about this I am reminded of a dream I have never been able to forget.

In this dream, which came to me a number of times, there was a long ladder with its upper rungs completely lost in the clouds. It seemed to be a ladder that led to the sky. Urged by an irrepressible desire to reach the sky, I began to climb. But it was very difficult; each rung required great effort. My breathing grew strained and perspiration poured from my forehead. But my desire to reach the sky was so great that I went on climbing. Soon there was a feeling of suffocation and it seemed as if my heart would give out. But all at once I realized that I was not the only climber, that mine was not the only ladder. There was an infinite number of ladders and endless numbers of people were climbing upwards. I experienced a surge of great rivalry and I began to climb even faster. This mad race, this using of all our strength to keep climbing continued until it eventually faded into the end of the dream.

That is always the same.

I finally reached the last rung. There is no rung beyond, and turning around, I see that there is no ladder either. And then the fall, the descent from that great height begins. It is even more painful than the climb. Death seems inevitable. And sure enough, it is my death. And the shock of that death invariably awakens me.

But that dream shows me a great truth, and since the first time I have had it life has seemed nothing more to me than an extension of that dream. In every dream is there not some kind of vision of the mad rush in which mankind is involved? Doesn't every mad scramble end in death? But then, ask yourself what "death" means. Doesn't it just mean there is no higher rung on the ladder? Death is the end of rushing. It is an end to the future; it is the impossibility of any further possibilities. The rushing, racing mind leads a man to great heights, and what is death but the fall from those heights?

Whenever there is a mad race of any kind, death invariable steps in. It makes no difference whether the goal is wealth or religion or enjoyment or renunciation. Wherever there is rushing there is dreaming, but where there is no rushing, racing mind, there is truth. And there is life too—the life that has no death.

There was a time when death was stalking me. Because I was afraid it was always lying in ambush for me. But the day I stepped forward to embrace it, it was not there at all. Death is in the fear of death; accepting the fact of death is salvation from its jaws. Fear is death; fearlessness is freedom from death. Like a shadow, death pursues those who flee it, but if you turn and face it, it vanishes. To welcome death before it comes to you is to escape from death forever.

It is not up to me how I will die. It is not left to me to choose. But how I live is certainly my decision. Death is the completion of life and, precisely for that reason, by choosing how to live I also choose how to die. One's death is an indication of one's life. The seeds a man sows in his life come into flower during his death.

Life is only for those who know how to die in a fight for life.

If a man does not feel the existence of the self at a time of crisis, then he is not alive at all. Somehow he manages to live and somehow he manages to die, but he has not yet begun to ponder the existence of his self. Thinking about life is what eventually awakens a man to the truth of death. One's death becomes a real possibility at a time of crisis. A crisis ushers in the search for the self. It marks the beginning of a man's quest in the direction of truth. It is the moment of transition from death to immortality.

This is why I ask if you have ever had a crisis in your life. If you haven't, then how do you hope to set out on the search for truth? It is necessary for a man's consciousness to meet with a crisis. A crisis is a face to face encounter with the possibility of the end of your self. It is out of this that the desire to attain immortality is generated and the campaign to achieve it is set into motion. No one has ever set out in search of life unless he has first looked into the eyes of death. Nor can he ever do so.

Life is a quest, but until death is faced this pursuit does not become a quest for life. Unless this happens a man goes on chasing insignificant things and simply dies in vain. He is completely caught up in trivialities and so death comes in search of him. But the moment he has a glimpse of death it is such an unprecedented crisis for him that the race after inanities comes to an abrupt halt. This shock shakes him out of his dreams, out of his drowsiness. It becomes impossible for him to sleep any longer. This hour, this hour of crisis awakens him to life. And then his consciousness becomes engaged in surmounting death.

This is why I tell you to seek out death. Go find it. It is better you go in search of it than to have death come looking for you. Nothing is of more everlasting importance than this.

You ask me what the greatest virtue in life is—and I say it is courage. Without courage there is no freedom; without freedom there is no truth; without truth there is no virtue. Courage is to the edifice of life what the cornerstone is to a building.

You have to wade through death to conquer death. The man who becomes conscious of death defeats it and attains immortality.

I would like to ask you what you are living for. Is there a goal or an ideal for which you are prepared to lay down your life? If your answer is negative then know for certain that you are already dead. The tremendous and powerful energy of a life of purpose is only awakened and kept alive by an ideal for which you are prepared to court death with a smile. You only win life by staking your life.

Man is all caught up in problems. And as a result, society is also entangled in problems. The problems of the world are the same as those of the individual.

How is it that man is always faced with some sort of problem? It is not that the individual has a problem, the individual himself is the problem. His individualistic consciousness itself is the problem. His egoistic consciousness itself is the problem. But if, from "I am" you remove the "I" and are left with the experience of "am" then the problem vanishes, then the solution is knocking at the door.

In reality, life is simply existence; it is just the natural flow of the current of existence. "I" is an attempt to halt that flow; "I" is a man-made dam impending that natural current.

Look for the "I" in yourself. It is nowhere to be found. There is life, there is being, but there is no "I". And yet we build our entire lives on this "I". No wonder we are unable to find any peace in life. Our religions, our civilizations—all are built on the foundation of "I". Isn't it natural then that religion and civilization only generate worry, tension, bewilderment and madness? No matter what is erected on the foundation of "I" it is unsound, unsafe.

It is only the life built on "I" that transmigrates, that is reborn. It is only "I" that is born and dies. Only dreams are born and disappear. What exists cannot have birth or death. It merely exists. It exists and exists and exists.

Forget that "I". Just let it go. Wake up to existence. And live in it.

The "I" will not allow you to awaken to life. It will not allow you to live in existence. It lingers in the past or in the future, but life is the eternal present. Life is always here and now.

The man who shakes off "I" and awakens to the present realizes that the nectar of life, that the truth, beauty and harmony of life surround him from all sides, from all quarters, from within and without—just as a fish is encompassed by the sea.

Man does not know what life is. And if he cannot even

understand life then there is virtually no possibility of his ever knowing death. As long as the meaning of life is unknown, as long as it remains an enigma to us death can never be understood.

The truth is, our ignorance of life causes death. To those who have known the meaning of life the word "death" does not exist at all—because death has never happened, does not happen, can never happen.

Some words in man's language are totally false. In some of them there is not one iota of truth. "Death" falls into this category. It is a totally false word; it is a word that is completely untrue. Death never happens. Yet we see people dying every day. We are surrounded by death on all sides. Every village and every town has its cemetery, and many a corpse must have been burned on the very ground upon which we tread every day. The plots of land upon which we have built our houses must surely have been the cremation grounds of of bygone days. Millions and millions of people are born and die every day, and although it may surprise you I venture to say there is no word more false than "death" in the languages of mankind.

There was once a Mohammedan *fakir* who lived in Tibet. One day a man came to him to ask the meaning of life and death. The *fakir* burst out laughing. He said, "If you wish to ask me about life, then you may certainly do so. But as far as death is concerned, I have never come across it. I am not acquainted with it at all. If you want to ask about death then ask someone who lives a dead kind of life. Or ask someone who is already dead. I am life itself and I can only tell you about life and its meaning. I know nothing at all about death."

There is a similar tale about darkness.

Once darkness complained to God about the sun. He said, "God, your sun persecutes me constantly. I am so fed up with it. From the moment the morning dawns he follows me throughout the day. I admit he leaves me alone in the evening but he even does that reluctantly. What have

I done to deserve this? What offense have I committed that he pursues me like this? He is after me the whole day. And even with a little rest at night I am unable to recover from the exhaustion of the day. Then the first thing I know it is morning again and the sun is knocking at my door, and I have to start running again to escape his persecution. This has been going on since the beginning and now I am worn out, at the end of my tether. Please, Almighty God, take the sun to task. Please grant me this wish!"

God sent for the sun. When the sun appeared before him, God asked, "Why do you chase darkness? What harm has darkness done to you? Do you have a complaint to lodge against him? What is the reason for this hostility."

Unruffled, the sun replied, "Darkness? I have been revolving around the universe since time immemorial and so far I have never run across darkness. I do not know him at all. Who is darkness? If you will call him here I will certainly ask his forgiveness. I will also be able to meet him. Then I will avoid offending him in future and will be able to stay out of his way."

Aeons have passed and this incident is still in God's file, unsolved. God has been unable to bring darkness into the presence of the sun and will never be able to do so. This problem can never be resolved. How can darkness ever be summoned into the presence of the sun? Darkness has no power of its own. Darkness has no individual existence; it has no separate entity of its own. Darkness is just the absence of light—so how can the absence of the sun be called into the presence of the sun? It is not possible. Darkness cannot be brought before the sun.

But forget about the sun, the immense sun, for the moment—it is not even possible to bring darkness into the presence of the tiniest lamp. Darkness can never enter the lamp's circle of light. How can darkness come in where light is present? And how can death exist where there is life? Either life does not exist or there is nothing like death at all. Both cannot exist side by side.

We are alive and yet we do not know what life is. It is because of our lack of knowledge about life that we think death happens. Death is a kind of ignorance. And ignorance about life inevitably results in death. If we could only know the life within us! A single ray of the knowledge of our inner life would remove our everlasting ignorance about death forever. It would dispel our blind belief that we can die, that we have died before, that we will die again. But we do not know the light that we are, the light that is our selves, and we are afraid of the darkness, afraid of something that is totally alien to us. We never encounter the light that is us, that is our very being, our soul, our life, our power—and yet we fear the darkness that is not within us at all.

Man is not death; man is the nectar of the gods. But we do not even lift our eyes to see the cup that is held out to us. We never probe into life, never take a single step towards uncovering its meaning. We remain strangers to life and approach death in terror.

The major question is not one of life and death, it is one of life alone. I was asked to speak on life and death. But this is impossible. There is only life. Death does not exist. If one understands life then there is only life. But if life remains unknown there is only death. Life and death never exist together, like two aspects of a problem. We either know that we are life and then death does not exist, or we do not know that we are life and then only death exists. They cannot exist together. But we are all afraid of death. And this clearly shows we have not understood the meaning of life. Fear of death only betrays one's ignorance of life.

What flows in and out of us every moment, through every pore, though every breath, is completely unknown to us. And this means that man is in a deep slumber, because it is only when one is fast asleep, that it is possible to forget one's self. This means man is in a deep coma. It boils down to the fact that the full power of man's spirit is not awake, but lost in some kind of faint. When he is asleep man is not aware of anything. He does not know who he is, what he is, where he has come from. In the darkness of sleep everything is lost. Man even forgets his own existence. It is only when he has awakened that he knows he has been asleep.

Some kind of hypnotic sleep of the spirit seems to have paralyzed man and has made it impossible for him to grasp the true meaning of life. But we refuse to accept this as a fact. We will even question the sanity of such a theory and will insist that we do know life because we are alive, because we move about, because we stand, sit, sleep. But look, a drunkard also moves about, breaths, sleeps, opens and closes his eyes, speaks. And so does a madman. Both the drunkard and the madman are alive yet you cannot say that the drunkard is in his right senses or that the madman is conscious.

An emperor's procession was moving down a road. At one crossroad a man began hurling stones and insults. The emperor's soldiers immediately took him into custody and threw him into prison. But while the man was throwing rocks and shouting abuses the emperor had simply laughed. His soldiers had been quite surprised and his chief minister had asked, "My Lord, why are you laughing?"

The emperor had replied, "I don't think that man knows what he's doing. He must be drunk. In any case, bring him to me tomorrow morning."

The man was accordingly brought before the monarch the next morning. The emperor inquired, "Why did you insult me and throw stones at me yesterday?"

Very subdued, the man said, "My Lord, what are you saying? Me? Abusing you? Impossible! If I insulted you I could not have been myself. I was drunk and not in my right senses. It was not the real me at all. Really, Your Majesty, I have no idea what I said at all."

We are not ourselves either. We walk, talk, love, hate and wage war—all in sleep. If someone from another planet were to see us he would most certainly conclude that the whole human race was in some kind of trance, in some kind of deep sleep. In three thousand years mankind has fought some fifteen thousand wars. Does this sound like a humanity that is wide awake and aware of itself?

From the moment he is born until he breaths his last the whole story of a man's life is one of death, anxiety, sorrow and pain. Not a single moment of real happiness does he experience. What joy is, what delight is, remains totally unknown to him. A man lives his whole life without a single glimpse of joy. You cannot say such a man is in his right senses. Worry, suffering, sorrow, despair and madness seem to be the story of his life. But we do not notice this because all around us everyone else is asleep too.

Once in a while a conscious, wide-awake man is born, and those who are asleep cannot tolerate him. They lose their tempers and they kill him. We crucified Jesus Christ because he was awake. People in deep sleep cannot bear the presence of such a man. He is a symbol of disrespect to those who are not awake. Such men disturb our sleep, and so we give a cup of poison to a Socrates. We behave toward conscious, awakened men as madmen would were they to find a sane man in their midst.

A friend of mine went insane and was locked up in an asylum. In his madness he drank a whole bottle of a disinfectant he found in a cleaning cupboard. As a result he had such intense attacks of diarrhea and vomiting that within two weeks his whole body was transformed. The madness left him and he became well again. He had been confined to the madhouse for six months, and although his sanity returned at this point—after he had been there only three months—they kept him there the full term.

When he was finally sent home he told me of the incredible agony he had had to bear during the last three months of his stay. He said, "While I was mad myself I noticed nothing. We were all mad, insane. But as soon as I was cured I asked myself where I was. I would be asleep and two huge men would sit on my chest. I would be walking and someone would push me from behind. When I was insane I never noticed things like that at all. In my condition I didn't even realize that everyone around me was mad."

We move among people who are spiritually asleep and so we fail to realize that we ourselves are also asleep. We destroy those who are spiritually awake because such men disturb and plague us. We cannot possibly understand the full meaning of life because all around us everyone is asleep. We only know the physical form of life; we never try to move inside the spiritual.

Knowing only the physical is akin to a man mistaking the outer wall of a palace for the palace itself, like a man who sleeps on the outer parapet and thinks he is sleeping in the *maharajah's* bedroom. Those whose whole understanding of life centers around the body are just like that ignorant man. They bed down on the parapet and think they are guests in the palace. We are the same. We only know the outer aspect of the body; we know nothing of the inner. We only know the outer circle of the body; we know nothing of what is inside, of the spirit. We do not even know the interior of the parapet, let alone the inside of the palace, and we think the outer portion of the wall that surrounds it is the palace itself.

We only know the body from the outside. We have never tried to enter it and to see it from within. If you and I are sitting inside this room we are seeing it from inside but a man who is wandering around outside is only able to see the exterior of this house. Similarly, man is unable to see his body from inside. He only knows it from outside. What we know is just an outer covering, a sort of outer garment draped over the body. It is like the outside wall of a house. The real owner of the house is sitting inside, and unfortunately we have never had the occasion to meet him. We do not even know the inside wall of the house, so there is no question whatsoever of knowing the owner. He is deep inside, at the very center of the house.

This understanding of life from outside is what causes the experience we call death. The day this experience we call life begins to slip from a man's hands and his consciousness begins to shrink away from the body and to move inside, anyone looking on from outside will say the man is dead. And the man himself will feel that he is dying because his consciousness will begin to move inside, to move away from what he has known as life. His consciousness starts to leave behind the surface existence he thought of as life. And this preparation for the new journey makes his spirit cry out because everything he knew as life is being engulfed, swallowed up. People on the outside will take him for dead, and in this moment of supreme transformation even the man himself thinks he is dying or that he is dead and will be gone forever.

This body is not our authentic being. Our true inner being is of an absolutely different nature: our real essence is a complete contradiction of our bodily existence. For example, a seed has a hard outer shell to protect the fragile, living seedling inside. The outer covering is not the living sprout and the man who mistakes the outer wrapping for the inner seed will never come to know the real fountain of life that is encased inside the shell. He will only see the outer shell and the essence of life that is inside will never have the chance to spring forth. The fact is that when the seed sprouts the outer shell has to disappear. It has to break open, to fall apart and vanish into the earth. It is really only when the outer wrapping, when the external wall of the seed is gone that the true nature of the seed manifests itself.

Our physical body is just an outer wrapping. The consciousness of life is inner: the awakening of the spirit is from inside. We perish because we mistake the superficial, outer shell for the seed itself. And so the seed never has the chance to sprout, never has the chance to break through into the light. But when his seed is allowed to crack through its shell a man can grow into a fully developed tree. Until that happens man is just a seed, just a potentiality—but when that does happen, when man experiences the light of spiritual awakening, his seedling rises upward like a tree and man becomes a solid reality. Some call this reality the soul; some call it God.

Man is the seed of God, but how can a seed know the fullness of its realized potential? Only the tree can feel the complete, total experience of full development; only the tree can know the immense joy of that fullfilment. The seed can never know that tender, green leaves will adorn it as a tree. It can never know that the rays of the rising sun will dance on its leaves and that the gentle breezes will sing through its branches. It can never understand how the soul of the tree will swell with the ecstacy of life. How can the seed know that flowers will grace the tree's branches, surpassing even the beauty of the stars that twinkle in the sky? How can the seed understand the joy of birds nesting in the tree's branches, singing their songs of happiness? And the peaceful shade the tree will give to weary travelers, the seed can never know. The seed is unconscious of all this joy, of all this satisfaction. It cannot even dream of these delights. These are only possible when the seed becomes a tree.

Man cannot grasp the meaning of life because he has confined all his efforts to perfecting the seed alone. He can only know life when the tree has risen out of the tiny seed. And quite apart from being ignorant of the tree that grows out of the seed of life, we neither know, remember or are willing to believe that anything separate and distinct from the physical body exists. Man has concentrated all his attempts to perfect himself on the seed alone. He has gone this far and no further. But realizing the true nature of life by experiencing what is inside is a question of the utmost importance.

I asked one tree, "Where is your life?" It replied, "In the roots you cannot see." The life of the tree springs from these invisible roots. The visible tree draws its life from that which is invisible. But man assumes, takes for granted, that the outer manifestations, that the leaves and the flowers are the tree's life, and conveniently disregards the fact that its roots are buried deep in the earth. And it is from these hidden roots that the life of the tree springs forth. In the same way man pays no attention to his inner self, to the spring of his own life. Rather, he deliberately ignores it. He does not remember that what he really is is hidden inside him. Truth, power, all the force all the abilities of his life are there inside. What is apparent on the outside are merely outer manifestations. The authentic being is inside. The soul is the innermost shrine of life.

Those who view life's outer manifestations as life itself are troubled throughout their stay on earth by a continuous fear of death. Even though they live and breathe, they are like corpses. They live in the constant fear that death will confront them at any moment. Such people weep over the passing of others and worry about themselves because every death they witness becomes a harbinger of their own. The death of a dear one is a vivid and painful reminder of their own impending end. Actually their horror is not at the death of others at all but at the thought of their own fast approaching death. And so they shudder. They are stricken with terror and suffer great mental anguish.

It is at such times that a man begins to think great thoughts and makes grand assumptions about the imperishability and immortality of the soul. It is then he sees himself as an infinitesimal part of God. But this is all nonsense, ridiculous prattle by which a man endeavors to deceive himself and to escape from the truth. And terrified by the mere idea of death, such a man tries to console and strengthen his feeble mind by repeating over and over to himself his theories about the immortality of the soul. He falsely tries to convince himself that he will not have to die. After all, he tells himself, the soul is deathless. But on the inside he is still afraid.

One who really knows the soul is immortal does not go on repeating some theory of immortality—he simply knows it to be true. Those who quake in their boots at the thought of death create a dangerous illusion for themselves with their theorizing because they have not really grasped the true meaning of life. But these people keep on talking about the immortality of the soul, and it is really a difficult task to distinguish between those who truly and sincerely believe what they are saying and those who are only trying to console themselves out of their fear of death. Somehow this misfortune only seems to take place in this country.

In India, more than anywhere else in the world, one can find the greatest number of people who honestly believe in the soul's immortality as well as the greatest number who are afraid of death.

For those who know that the soul never perishes, that the soul is an everlasting truth, death has ceased to exist and so their fear of death has ended forever. No one can kill these people; no one can end their lives. And there is another important fact to note—not only can no one kill them, they cannot kill anyone else either. They should not harbor any illusion they can kill, because the existence of death is no longer a reality for them.

But those who preach the immortality of the soul over and over again are nonetheless afraid of death. Not only do they spout the doctrine of the eternal soul, they loudly support the principle of non-violence as well. They do not advocate this because they are not prepared not to kill anyone, but so that no one will step forward and kill them. The world, they say, should follow the principle of non-violence. Outwardly they profess it is bad to kill, but in fact they are afraid they may become someone else's prey. But if they really come to know death does not exist, then there will be no fear of killing or of being killed, and then all this talk will cease to have any meaning or importance whatsoever.

In *Bhagavad Gita*, which Krishna himself expounded to Arjuna on the battlefield of Kurukshetra, he told Arjuna not to be afraid at the prospect of killing his relatives. Krishna explained, "Those who are standing before you have lived many times before. You were there; I was also there. We have all existed before. We have lived many lives and we will live many more lives to come. Nothing in this world perishes and so there need be no fear of dying or of being killed. There is no death and so there can be no destruction. The question is of living one's own life. As far as life is concerned, those who are afraid of dying or of being killed are impotent. Those who can neither kill nor die do not know the truth of immortality—that what is cannot die, cannot be destroyed."

What a world it will be when everyone realizes the soul is eternal, indestructible! That will be the day when the whole fear of death vanishes forever and, with it, the empty threats of destruction that are now so effective. That day wars will disappear. But not before. As long as man thinks he can kill or be killed war will never cease in this world. Until then war will continue, unhampered, whether it is Mahatma Gandhi or Buddha or Mahavira who preaches non-violence. Millions of lessons in non-violence can be taught throughout the world, but they will be ineffectual until mankind realizes in the innermost depths of his being that what he is, is divine and therefore deathless. War will never stop in this world until then.

And do not think that those who carry swords in their hands are brave. A sword may well be evidence of a man's inner cowardice. The status of those holding swords in their hands are monuments to cowards. The truly brave need no swords, because they know talk of death is simply the prattling of a child. Yet how man propagates this marvelous self-deception! Out of his fear he tries to show his defiance of something he does not understand.

In his heart of hearts each man knows he will have to die because death is in the order of things. If he looks inside he sees that his body grows weaker and weaker every day, that youth is fading and giving way to old age. The body is slipping through his fingers, and yet he goes on preaching that the soul is deathless, eternal. He tries to bolster his faith and muster his courage by telling himself again and again not to be nervous, not to be afraid. He knows for certain death exists, but the great saints and sages have confirmed that the soul is immortal, everlasting. People who are afraid of death and hold forth on the soul's immortality are the ones who throng about these sages.

I am not trying to say that the soul is not immortal, but I do wish to assert that this theory of the soul's immortality is just a theory, propounded by those who are afraid of death. To realize the immortality of the soul for yourself is quite a different thing from simply putting a theory into words. Only those who have experimented with dying, who have sacrificed themselves during their lifetimes can fathom the depths of the soul's immortality. This is the only way to know the eternity of the soul.

This statement needs further explanation.

What actually happens in death? At death the spirit, that glow of life that spreads over the external form, begins to shrink away from the outer shell and to move back to its origin, to its source.

If we slowly and gradually lower the wick of a lamp, the light that has spread throughout the room will diminish and it will become darker. If we continue to lower the wick still more the flame will become smaller and smaller and will move closer to the lamp itself and we will finally be enveloped in total darkness.

In the same way, the light of life, the spirit of life which has permeated every nook and cranny of the physical body, begins to shrink, slowly and imperceptibly, until it finally returns to its origin. And then it becomes the seed, the atom for its journey into a new and fresh life.

It is shrinking that makes a man realize that death is approaching, that he is dying, that what he thought was life is slipping away from him. His hands and feet grow numb, his breathing becomes difficult, his eyes no longer see and his ears no longer hear the sounds of life. His limbs, his senses, his entire body functioned because of this unseen but potent connection with the spirit. And now the spirit is returning to its origin. The body is only a physical entity and now that the spirit has departed, it becomes dead, lifeless.

The Master of the house is preparing to leave his abode, and so the house is becoming forlorn and gloomy. At this crucial moment of death a man feels himself going. He feels he is drowning, that he is finished forever. This sense of drowning; of dying, of everything ending, brings on such a flood of nervousness, anxiety and anguish that in his suffering he deprives himself of the experience of death.

It requires great peace of mind to know death, to acknowledge it. We have died so many times. So many times we have left this mortal frame, but every time we suffer this mental agony and so miss the experience. And the ultimate knowledge eludes us, remains inaccessible to us.

Every time death has ever knocked at our door, every time we have ever encountered it we have not been able to see it. At the time of death it is not possible to know it, but there can be a planned death, through yoga. What happens in meditation is that what automatically and naturally occurs in death is precipitated by certain activities and efforts of the meditator. He shrinks his whole life-force and directs it inside. Since the effort is his own and only an experiment, he suffers no anxiety. He simply endeavors to redirect his life-force inside. And he accomplishes this in a tranquil frame of mind. Then he is able to understand that the body and the spirit are two different things.

The electric bulb is quite distinct from the electricity that illuminates it. The bulb is lifeless, a piece of matter, and when the electric current is withdrawn there is no spark, no light, no current flowing through it. The human body is nothing more than a light bulb. Life is the electricity, the energy which keeps the physical body alive, glowing with vitality.

In the culmination of meditation, in *samadhi*, the meditator dies of his own accord. And because he has embraced death of his own free will he realizes the truth—that his inner self is separate from his physical body. Once this ultimate truth dawns on him, death ends for him and then he understands life. The real experience of life and the end of death happen together, because as soon as death ends for a man he understands the fullness of life. This is really saying the same thing in two different ways.

This is why I look upon religion as the art of dying. But you may say you have also heard me call it the art of living. Yes, I do say both things. And I say them in the same breath because only one who knows how to die knows how to live life as it should be lived. And so, religion is both the art of dying and the art of living.

If you really want to understand the true meaning of life and death, then you must, by your own effort, learn the art of withdrawing your life-force from the exterior body and focusing it on your inner self. Only then will you be able to grasp the true meaning, the real significance of life and death. And remember, this energy can be controlled and redirected quite easily. It is not a difficult task at all. This energy is motivated by your own will and can move outwards or inwards as you direct it. This energy is the offspring of your will.

Make up your mind to do this and for half an hour every day concentrate on diverting your life-force to your inner being. If you make up your mind to dive, to drown in yourself, and you withdraw your energies from the outside you will achieve what you wish. But this requires consistent, daily practice. Then you will find that your energy, your life-force has begun to move inward. You will feel that the physical body has relinquished its hold on you and that it is quite separate from you.

If you follow this technique continuously for three months, you will find one day that your body is lying outside of you, separate from you. This you can see. At first this is perceived from inside, but after more practice, after the application of more courage you can bring the inner spirit out and from outside you can see your own body lying outside you, quite separate from you.

Let me tell you about a remarkable experience that happened to me. Up to now I have never mentioned it anywhere. I have suddenly recalled it, so please listen carefully.

Some twelve or thirteen years ago I had the habit of meditating at night while sitting in a tree. Whenever I meditated on the ground I felt that my body was the more powerful, that it had the upper hand. This is perhaps because the body is made of earth. The fact that yogis go to mountain peaks or high up in the Himalayas to meditate is certainly not without reason. It is definitely based on scientific principles. The greater the distance between the body and the earth, the less the force of the physical body is and the greater the power of the inner force becomes. That is why I used to climb a tall tree to meditate for hours every night.

One particular night I became so lost in deep meditation that I did not notice when my body fell out of the tree. I looked around me with mistrust when I finally noticed my body lying on the ground. I was quite surprised. How it had happened that I was still sitting in a tree and my body was lying on the ground I could not comprehend at all. It was a very strange experience. A bright line, a glittering silver cord running from the navel of my body was joined to me where I was perched in the tree above. I was at a loss to understand this or to foresee what would happen next. I was worried how I would return to the body.

How long this experience lasted I do not know. But nothing like this had ever happened to me before. That day, for the first time, I saw my own body from outside and since then the idea that my life was merely the physical existence of my body has finished for me. From that day on death also ceased to exist for me. That day I experienced that the body and the spirit are two different things, quite separate from each other. This was the most important moment in my realization of the spirit that dwells within every human body. It is really very difficult to say how long that experience lasted.

As morning dawned two women carrying milk cans from some nearby village passed by and noticed my body lying there. From the top of the tree where I was sitting I saw them looking at my body. They approached the body and sat down beside it. They touched my forehead with the palms of their hands and in a moment, as if by some tremendous force of attraction, I returned to my body and opened my eyes.

After that experience I had another.

I began to see that a woman could create an electrical charge in a man's body and that a man could do the same thing in the body of a woman. I pondered over the touch of the woman on my forehead and my instantaneous return to the body—how and why had this happened.

Many more experiences of this sort happened to me and then I understood why those Indian yogis who experiment in the realms of *samadhi* and death enlist the aid of women. If, in deep and profound *samadhi,* the spiritual self has left the man's physical body it cannot return without the help and cooperation of a woman. In the same way, if it has left a woman's body it cannot return without the assistance of a man. As soon as the bodies of a man and a woman come into contact a current is established, an electric circle is completed, and at that very instant the departed spirit returns.

I experienced this phenomenon six times within the next six months. And during that eventful half year I felt my life span lessen by ten years. That is to say, if I had been supposed to live seventy years I would now, because of those experiences, live only sixty. And the experiences of these six months were extraordinary! The hair on my chest even turned white! Yet I failed to grasp the full meaning of what had happened.

After much thought I finally realized that whatever connection or link there is between the physical body and the spiritual being had been interrupted, that the natural adjustment between them had been broken. And then I understood why Shankaracharya died at the age of thirty-three and Swami Vivekananda at thirty-six. Their deaths took on a different meaning for me. If there is a disruption between the two, between the visible body and the invisible spirit, it is difficult for the body to remain alive. I also understood Ramakrishna Paramahansa's being afflicted with so many diseases, and saw that Shree Ramana Maharshi's dying of cancer was not due to physical causes but this break in the adjustment between body and spirit.

People seem to think yogis and sages are hale and hearty but the opposite is true. In fact most yogis die young, and when they are alive they are usually unwell because the adjustment has been disturbed and a discord has been created as a result. Once the spirit escapes the body and leaves it, it can never re-enter the body properly, never as fully as before. Of course then there is no need, no reason for a proper re-entry of the spirit into the yogi's physical body.

Determination—strong and unfailing determination—can force the energy to turn in, to direct itself inside. The thought, the desire to go in, to return to the center can definitely enable you to reach to the source. The urge must be so intense that it permeates every fiber of your being, every breath you take. And then it may happen any time. One day, in a flash, you may reach your innermost core and perceive your body from within.

What they say in yoga about veins and arteries is not in agreement with the science of physiology because it has no connection with this science. If you study physiology you will find that the veins and arteries yoga talks about have nothing to do with this science at all. They are perceived from inside. And where are the seven *chakras* they describe in yoga? They are not to be found in the body because we try to locate them from outside.

There exists a specific science that deals with the body from inside—an inner physiology. It is a very subtle science and it acquaints you with a number of separate and distinct circuits and centers which cannot be found when the body is viewed from outside. These centers are fields of energy formed where the body contacts the inner soul.

The most important of these fields of contact is the navel. If you are driving a car and there is about to be an accident—or even if you are nervous—you will notice that first thing to be affected is your navel. In the upheaval precipated by an impending disaster the navel becomes very perturbed because it is the most intimate contact between the physical body and the inner soul. The prospect of approaching death will even throw the circuits out of balance and they will lose their harmony with the centers of the entire body.

There is an internal arrangement by which the inner body and the outer physical body retain their mutual contact. The *chakras*, talked about so much in yoga, are the energyfields of these points of contact.

To get to know your body from within is like getting to know an entirely different world, a world about which we have never before had knowledge or information. Medical science knows nothing of this inner body at all, nor will it ever be able to fathom it.

Once the complete realization that the inner self is distinct and different from the outer body happens, death ceases to exist. When there is no death one can very easily leave the shell of the body and view things as a disinterested spectator.

The way to probe into the facts of life and death is not by thinking about philosophy or the scriptures—and those who pursue these avenues will uncover nothing worthwhile. My approach is existential, because this way you can really understand that you are life and that you have no death. This truth can be entered into, experienced as fact, lived. But those who use thinking in their attempt to unravel the meaning of life and death will never achieve anything, will never arrive at any kind of result—even if they spend their whole lives immersed in such thoughts.

We can only think about what we know. You will be utterly lost trying to think about something that is unknown to you. How can you think about something which you have no idea, no knowledge whatsoever? How is it possible? You only know life. You do not know death. So what is there to think about as far as death is concerned? How can you formulate ideas about something you do not know at all? How can you even imagine it?

Whatever theories the philosophers have evolved about life and death have no value at all. Whatever is written in the books of philosophy about life and death is only indulgence in thoughts, mere theorizing—and totally worthless. Only what yoga says about life and death holds true, and all other theories are just word games.

Yoga approached the mystery of life and death from the existential point of view, with an experimentalist's eye. The immortality of the soul is not just a theory, not an ideology—it is the real experience of certain people. And only actual experience can solve the riddle of life and death. As soon as one achieves this experience, it clearly dawns upon one's consciousness that only life exists, that there is no such thing as death at all.

All the same, you will say, death does happen in this world. But the crux of the whole matter is that we only leave behind the house in which we have dwelt and proceed to another. We simply move to another house. Each house has its limitations as well as its strengths. It is like a machine that wears out and so we have to leave it behind.

If science succeeds in the experiments it has undertaken the human body can be made to survive for one hundred, two hundred, even three hundred years—but the mere continuance of the physical body will not be proof there is no soul. The soul must change residences frequently, and this will only show that science has been able to repair the old house. No scientist should indulge in the fantasy that because he can preserve the human body for five hundred or a thousand years that there is no soul, no eternal flame in man. This prolonging of life through advanced scientific research will only go to prove that this machine, this body which the soul must abandon because it has become worn out, can be repaired and so need not be discarded.

If the heart can be replaced, if new limbs can be supplied, if new eyes can be provided, then there is no need for the soul to change bodies. If a new heart can be implanted, new hands and feet substituted, then the soul need not relinquish the old body. Now the old house will do. But by no stretch of the imagination does this prove the soul does not exist.

Science may also produce a test tube baby, but then scientists will be under illusion that they have created life itself. I would like to clear up this misconception here and now. Even the existence of a test tube baby would prove nothing of the sort. Such an assumption on the part of the scientist would be completely erroneous.

What happens when a man and woman meet? They do not give birth to the soul. They simply create a situation, an opportunity for the soul to enter. The mingling together of the mother's and father's seeds allow the soul to find a suitable abode. Test tube conception may well furnish such an occasion but it will provide no proof that the soul can also be created in the laboratory. The mother's womb is also a mechanism, but it is a natural mechanism and not a mechanical contrivance.

In its laboratories science may succeed in reproducing, in a test tube, the same chemical combination that comes about when the sperm of the man mixes with ovum of a woman at the time of the conception of a child. Through research into the chemical essences which prepare the sperm and the ovum for the entrance of the soul in the natural process, they may be successful. And just as soul enters the woman as soon as the opportunity has been created in the womb, the soul will enter the test tube if the correct conditions are fulfilled. This will not mean science has created a soul, it will simply mean the soul has found a suitable opportunity for its entry into life.

Birth consists of two stages—the physical preparation of the infant's body in the mother's womb and the descent of the soul into it. But the future must seem very dark and gloomy for the soul because scientific research keeps trying to convince mankind it does not exist at all. This will not disprove the existence of the soul, it will only weaken man's determination to go inside himself. If test tube babies are created and man comes to doubt the existence of the soul because of them, he will stop all attempts to explore the depths of his inner being. This will be a great tragedy that will come to pass in the next fifty years. During the past fifty years of scientific research the groundwork for this catastrophe has already been laid.

Up to the present, disease, suffering, privation and poverty have populated the earth. People have had no food to eat, no proper clothes to wear and their life spans have been much shorter than they are now. From all points of view, people have been poor, very poor indeed. But as far as belief in the existence of the soul is concerned there has never been such a multitude of poor and totally destitute people as there are today. And this can be attributed to the growing disbelief in the soul, to the idea that there is nothing inside man. If this becomes the general conviction, there will never be any question of man moving inside himself. The future may well be one that is black and full of pitfalls.

Some people must come forth, from every corner of the world, to gain this inner experience for themselves. They must step forward to declare to the world that man is not a mere physical being, but something much more, much more valuable, much more lasting. But these declarations cannot simply be the repetition of the principles expounded in the Gita, the Koran or the Bible, they must be emphatic declarations of life. They must be ringing statements saying that whatever man may be he is not just his physical form, not just his bodily existence. Such affirmations must be spontaneous; they must come from a man's own direct experience of the soul that dwells inside the human body, the soul that gives it the spark of life, the soul without which the body is useless. Then perhaps we may be able to save mankind from impending ruin.

Otherwise, as it becomes more advanced, science will undoubtedly reduce the living, breathing human being to a mere robot. And when the day comes that mankind has become totally and utterly convinced that there is nothing inside him and that there is no such thing as a soul, then all the accesses, all the approaches to the inner soul will be closed. And what will happen then is anyone's guess!

Even today most people's inner doors are locked, but every once in a while a courageous person breaks through the solid inner walls and rushes inside—a person like Mahavira, Gautam Buddha, Christ or Lao Tzu. These men penetrated their inner beings and gained first-hand experience of the soul. But the possibility of this kind of happening decreases day by day.

Perhaps after two thousand years or so man may be able to state with complete conviction that there is nothing like life, but only death—and this will be absolutely contradictory to what I say today: that there is no death, that there is only life. The seeds of that which will be believed two thousand years hence have already been sown in the minds of the general populace today. After all what does Marx preach? He says there is matter but no soul, that there is matter but no God. And that what we think of as God is only a byproduct of matter. God, Marx says, is born out of matter. He puts forth the hypothesis that only death exists, and not life. He says the soul does not exist, that matter only matter exists and therefore there is no such thing as life. You may not know it, but the preachings of Marx have influenced many many people.

There have always been people who have denied the existence of the soul or God or whatsoever you choose to call it, but until now there has been no religion or cult of these non-believers. Marx has given the world its first cult of this nature. There have been world famous atheists like Charvak, Brihaspati and Epicurus, but there has never been a distinct organization or church. Marx is the first atheist who has an organized religion, and surprisingly enough, half of the world stands within its precincts today. And in the coming fifty years the remaining half of the world will follow in their footsteps.

That the soul exists is an indisputable fact, but the doors to it are closing more and more and so we are neither able to know it nor to attain to it. Life also exists, but the possibilities of realizing it are slowly becoming less and less. We are therefore unable to know life as it really is. But before the doors are locked tight those who have even a little amount of courage and a little bit of enterprise should begin to experiment upon themselves.They should try to enter their inner beings, to experience the inner flame, the true light for themselves. If only a hundred or so persons with this experience existed, they would be able to drive away the darkness of ignorance from millions of people. A small lamp is able to provide light for many.

If only one man in a village has known the immortality and eternity of the soul, the whole atmosphere, the whole life of the village will be completely transformed. The villagers will come to view life with a new perspective. A tiny flower blossoms and spreads its fragrance far and wide. In the same way, a man who has gained the true knowledge of the soul's existence can guide and purify the souls of his fellow villagers.

But our country is overflowing with *sadhus* and others who shout at the top of their lungs about the immortality of the soul. They preach their belief in the soul and profess their experiences of its existence. Believe me, there is a huge crowd, a very long queue of such *sadhus*! But then why is there so much baseness and immorality in our nation? This is all fake, all a thorough deception, the *sadhu* circus! *Sadhus* and so-called holy men are spread over the entire length and breadth of this country, but they are just performing, simply deceiving the public. It is just not possible that the moral and spiritual life of this country could sink as low as it has if the vast host who claim the soul exists eternally really knew what they were saying.

And those who say that it is the common man who has lowered the moral character of the world are absolutely wrong. The ordinary man has always been the same as he is today. At one point the level of morality in the world was high but only because a few great men had attained to spiritual realization. The man in the street has not changed at all. A few were able to pull themselves out of the mass and raised the general social conscience along with them. Such men gave others the incentive to elevate their own standards. And if the world has fallen to its present state morally and spiritually, these *sadhus* and *mahatmas*, these hypocrites who profess to know religion and who preach so-called religion, are entirely responsible. The ordinary man is not responsible at all. The responsibility has never been his. He wasn't at fault before; he isn't to blame now.

If you want to change the world for the better then stop all this meaningless talk and moral sermonizing about reforming each and every individual. If the world is truly to be transformed, a small number of people will have to undergo very intensive spiritual ordeals and exercises. Many are not required. If only one hundred persons in a country attain to self-realization, the spiritual life of that country will be automatically uplifted.

I agreed to speak on this subject in the earnest hope that some courageous man might step forward and ask for initiation into this inner journey. I would have extended my heartiest welcome to him. I would have told him that I am always ready to help a man to go inside and to give him a glimpse of the eternal soul that resides in his body. If you are ready, come forward and I will show you what life is, what death is.

The ultimate experience is of God. The ordinary man's experience is confined to the physical body, the yogi's to the invisible body and the experience of the self-realized man is of God himself.

God is one; physical bodies are many. The invisible body is the causal body, and energy that is invisible to the mortal eye is constantly flowing from it into the physical body.

Electric current can illuminate many light bulbs. The light, the electricity is one, but it spreads its power throughout many bulbs. The physical appearance of the bulbs may differ, but the current is one—just as the spirit is one.

The consciousness, the spirit within us is one, but it has two facets—one is the invisible body, and the other is the outer physical body. Man's experience is centered around the exterior body alone, and as a result of this imbalance he suffers. He is in agony, in pain; his life is full of darkness, full of utter darkness.

Some men are able to reach only as far as the invisible body, and then they believe there are a number of souls, as many as there are individuals. But those who transcend the invisible body confirm out of their own experience and without a shadow of a doubt that God is one, that the soul is one, that *Brahman* is one.

As such, there is no contradiction in either of my statements although they may look contrary to each other on the surface.

When I speak about the entry of the soul I mean that particular soul whose invisible body has not yet been discarded. This is the main basis for the assertion that the soul, which is destined for the glory of ultimate liberty, is not bound by the shackles of birth and death, that it is completely free from the cycle of birth and death. The soul experiences neither birth nor death because it is never born and it never dies.

When the invisible body perishes there is no longer any birth or any death because it is this invisible body that is the cause of each death and each resulting new birth. The invisible body is the sum total, in seed form, of all our thoughts, desires and aspirations, of all our longings and cravings, of all our knowledge and study, of all our experiments and experiences. It is this invisible body which leads us on new travels, to fresh births. But the man whose thoughts and dreams have ended, whose desires and yearnings have finished, whose emotions and feelings have vanished has no place to go. There is no longer any reason for him to go anywhere. And so no cause remains for him to be reborn.

There is a very strange and puzzling incident that occurred in the life of Shree Ramakrishna Paramahansa. Those who knew him well, who knew him as a man who had attained to the highest pinnacle of *samadhi*, were astonished by his great love for good food. He would often get very excited and become quite anxious about his food and many a time he walked straight into the kitchen and asked his wife, Sharada, "What's the matter? It's getting very late. Are you cooking any special delicacy today?"

Sharada Devi would only look at him in consternation. In her innermost heart she did not approve of this habit of his at all. He even went to the extreme of walking out in the middle of spiritual discussions to go to the kitchen to find out what was being prepared especially for him and to see what kind of snacks he could lay his hands on. Sharada would ask, "What are you doing here? What will people think? You have left a serious conversation about *Brahman* to come down to the kitchen to ask about something as mundane as food!"

Ramakrishna would just smile and say nothing.

At times even his disciples would point out that people were saying all sorts of things about him because of this particular idiosyncrasy of his. They said people would lose faith in him, that they would wonder how a man who was so attached to a worldly thing like food and so devoted to eating could impart knowledge, could show the path to light.

One day Sharada lost her temper and told him off. She said the way she saw it, his love for food was such a compulsion that it was beyond his power to control it. In a very calm and quiet tone he explained, "Sharada, you don't understand. One day I will lose interest in food. Remember that day and mark it well. I will die exactly three days after."

Totally puzzled, Sharada asked, "What do you mean?"

Ramakrishna answered, "All my desires are gone. All my longings, all my cravings have vanished. All my thoughts have been destroyed. But I wish to remain in this world a little longer, for the good of humanity. And that is why I am consciously holding on to one straw, to desire. When all the chains that moor a boat have been broken loose but one—the one that keeps the boat attached to the dock—the ship will sail off into the limitless ocean towards its ultimate destination if even that last chain breaks. I am holding on purposely. That is the main reason I take so much interest in food."

No one grasped the full of significance of his explanation. But three days before his death Sharada entered his room with a plate of food in her hand. When he saw the plate he closed his eyes and turned his back on his wife. That very moment Sharada remembered what he had said to her several days before. The plate dropped from her hands and she began to weep loudly at her husband's impending death, the death he had predicted would take place exactly three days after he lost interest in food. Ramakrishna consoled her, but exactly three days later he died and his soul was liberated from its physical bonds, from its mundane desires.

Ramakrishna Paramahansa stayed alive by holding on to one very small desire, and as soon as that desire also vanished no chain remained to hold him in the world. When that small desire vanished, the insignificant support which caused his physical body to survive also vanished.

Those *Teerthankaras* we regard as living incarnations of God, those we look up to as sons of God also remain alive on the basis of one desire alone. They want that desire to persist so they can survive in their physical bodies for the good of mankind. The day that last desire vanishes, their worldly existence ends and their journey to eternity begins. After that there is no life and no death for them, nothing more to be counted, nothing more to be enumerated. That is why those who know and have experienced the reality of the soul say that God is one, that *Brahman* is one.

But it is really pointless to use the number "one" unless at least two exist. If the numbers two and three do not exist, then the number one cannot exist either. To speak of the number one is only helpful if we know two, three, four. Then there is a link between the numbers. Therefore, those who have gained true knowledge do not say that *Brahman* is one. They say that *Brahman* is not two, that he is not dual. It is an amazing statement. They say that God is not dual and cannot be counted in numbers. No measure exists to evaluate God. Even when we say "God is one" we make the mistake of stating his existence with a number. And this is completely erroneous.

Forget about reaching God for a moment. At present you are only conscious of your physical body, and it is many-sided, with endless facets. If you try to enter your physical body you will come upon another body, an invisible one. If you succeed in going beyond this invisible body you will find yourself face to face with something that is not a body, that is nothing physical, that is something you can only feel, sense. This is the soul.

Nothing I have said today contains any contradictions whatsoever.

A friend has asked me if the soul, when it leaves one body, can enter another that is dead. Yes, it can—but there is no point, no sense to its entering a corpse. That body died because the soul that resided in it could not remain in that particular body any longer. And since that body has become useless for the soul that was in it, then what is the point in a soul leaving another body to occupy this dead one?

Yes, it is possible for the soul to enter another body. But the question of how to enter another's body is of no importance at all when you do not even know how the soul that resides in your own body came there. What is the earthly good of wasting our precious time in a futile discussion about entering the body of another when you do not even know how your soul has entered your own? You do not even know your soul lives in your body. You cannot even see your soul. You have no idea how to separate your soul from your body.

Although there is no reason for entering another's body, yet from a scientific point of view it can be said that it is possible for the soul to enter another body—because your body is not really yours and neither is anyone else's body his. All bodies are alien to the soul.

When the soul enters the mother's womb it enters a

body. That body is very tiny, just an atom, but it is a physical body all the same. That tiny atom in the mother's womb is hiding the physical body which will become fully grown in time. After fifty years, your hair will begin to grey—and this potentiality is also hidden in that minute atom. In seed form, that atom contains the color of your eyes, whether your hair will be curly or straight, whether your hands will be long or not, whether you will be healthy or prone to illness, and all the other aspects of your physical appearance. That atom is a tiny body and it is into that atom in the womb of the mother that the soul enters. The soul enters that atom according to the particular condition or construction of that atom in that particular situation.

The main reason for the deterioration of mankind is that married couples do not create opportunities for higher souls to be born. The situations that are being created invite the entry of lower souls.

It is not necessary that the soul should find an opportunity to take birth in a new body immediately after the death of the old one. In general, most of the souls which are neither very high nor very low seek out new bodies to enter within thirteen days. The lower souls have to wait longer because low bodies are difficult to find. These lower souls are known as ghosts and demons. Very high souls also have to wait because they do not often get the right opportunity to enter proper bodies. These high souls are known to us as godly spirits.

In olden days the number of ghosts was much smaller and the number of godly spirits was much greater. In the modern world the number of ghosts is increasing and the number of divine spirits is decreasing. The opportunities for the birth of divine souls lessen every day. And it isn't possible to see ghosts today, because those who have been waiting to enter bodies have already done so. It isn't necessary to see them either. Look at the common man and you get an idea of what these ghostly souls are like.

In his actions and behavior man resembles the lower spirits and ghosts so much these days. And our faith in God is slowly vanishing. How can we believe in godliness, in divinity, when we never encounter godly men in this world?

There were times when gods were as much a reality as anything else in our lives. The saints who recorded the Vedas speak of divine, heavenly spirits, and I do not feel they only spoke out of their imaginations. They spoke of godly spirits who talked to them, who sang songs to them, who laughed with them, who walked with them upon this earth, and whose presence they felt close by, all around them. Our contact with such divine spirits has been totally destroyed. And the cause of the destruction is that there are no men among us who can form a bridge between men and the gods. There are no men who can declare their existence to the world, who can describe their form and appearance to mankind. And the responsibility for the disappearance of such men can chiefly be laid at the door of our matrimonial system. It has become incredibly ugly and grossly perverted.

The first and foremost reason for this is that we have discouraged marriage for love in India for hundreds of years. All our marriages are finalized without taking the factor of love into account. A marriage that deliberately ignores the importance of love cannot possibly result in a mutual inner bond, in an harmonious blending of the hearts of husband and wife. This is only possible through mutual love.

Neither harmony, nor oneness, nor heavenly music can exist between two people who are bound together in a purely material marriage. And out of such a marriage there is no opportunity created for the birth of a higher soul. Whatever love there is, is just the result of staying together and is nothing more than worldly attachment. The love of such a couple is not from the innermost depths. It does not touch the tender cords of their inner hearts, the ties that unite the two into one. And so children that are born out of such marriages can never be the children of love. The children themselves can never have the higher qualities, the attributes of love, kindness or understanding. On the contrary, they are more like ghosts and demons. Contrary to divine or godly lives, they will lead lives of sin, contempt and violence.

One small thing changes the whole picture, however. If the foundation of the union is based on personalities that live in harmony and beauty, amazing changes take place.

You probably have no idea why the woman is more beautiful than the man, why there is a shapeliness, a roundness to her person. Why isn't this to be found in a man? Perhaps you do not know that there is a music, an inner dance in the personality of a woman that is not evident in a man. The reason is so small, so minute, so insignificant you will never guess it. And this tiny reason accounts for such great differences in their personalities.

When the child is conceived in the mother's womb there are twenty-four female atoms and twenty-four male atoms present. If all of these masculine and feminine atoms mix together then the first cell that develops is composed of these forty-eight atoms. The life that evolves out of these forty-eight atoms is that of a baby girl and after birth she will grow into a woman. Each side of this body consists of twenty-four atoms. In this body there is perfect balance.

The male cell consists of forty-seven atoms, twenty-four on one side and twenty-three on the other. And so there is imbalance. Because of this there is also discord in the masculine personality. The harmony is broken.

The atoms in the feminine personality are in complete balance and therefore she is beautiful and shapely, full of art and poetry, aglow with a sense of and an appreciation for the aesthetic. In the body of a man there is one less atom.

The atoms a baby boy receives from the mother number twenty-four; those he receives from his father, twenty-three.

This slight imbalance in the number of atoms causes him to remain discontented throughout his life. His discontent is always intense. What to do, what not to do, why to do this, why not to do that, this worry, that dissatisfaction—these are the things that plague a man all his life. And this discontent comes from this imbalance in his atomic structure. One atom less results in this personality imbalance.

Contrary to this, a woman's personality is in complete harmony, and so there is concord, a continuous music to her life. This had given women beauty but has not allowed them to progress, not permitted them to develop themselves significantly. The reason for this is that a personality that is in balance does not develop, but stagnates.

The imbalance in man's personality is why he is so active, why he is able to progress. He climbs Mount Everest, he forges rivers, he scales mountains, he reaches the moon, he yearns for the planets, he becomes involved in research, in scientific discoveries, he writes important books, he creates poetry. And it is man who gives religion to the world.

A woman will not achieve any of these things. She will not reach the moon and the planets, she will not write profound books or present religious principles to the world. The balance that exists in her personality does not give her that intense desire, that deep urge to achieve things beyond the ordinary routine of life. The absence of one tiny atom in man's personality has enabled him to develop all of science, all of culture for the benefit of mankind, but the balance in a woman's personality has proven to be a handicap and stagnated her progress.

I am saying these things to you because they are biological facts and the scientists will have to agree with me. And if such a small difference in the makeup of men and women can have such repercussions, how much more difference will the bigger discrepancies cause?

The characteristics of the child who is conceived when a man and woman meet depends on the mutual love and respect that exist between the father and mother, on the sacredness of the feelings they hold for one another and on the oneness of their hearts and spirits. How high and how divine the soul is that is attracted to them depends on their approach to each other during their joining. If they come together in a holy and prayerful attitude a divine soul will choose to enter the womb. Higher consciousnesses will be pleased to house themselves in such bodies.

With the passing of time humanity is becoming poorer, growing weaker and more and more unhappy. And the main cause of this deterioration in the human race is the ugliness that prevails in marriage. Unless we accept the sanctity of the marital state and begin to look upon it from a spiritual point of view there will be no future change in mankind.

To a very great extent, the blame for the frailty and misery of humanity, especially here in India, can be laid at the feet of those who condemn the institutions of marriage and family life in favor of lives of asceticism. They have condemned family life and have paid no more attention to it. But I would like to state that the path of asceticism does not necessarily lead to God. Very few ordinary people reach God this way. Most men reach their goal through happy marriages and family lives. This is a much easier way than that of asceticism—and enough thought has been given to this way of reaching God.

Up to the present, religion, for the most part, has praised this path and looked down on family life. But religion has unfortunately not provided proper direction as far as marriage and family life are concerned. If religion had fully grasped the true meaning and importance of the role of the family in the development of mankind, we would have already given ample consideration to the process of birth and to the quality of the soul being invited to enter the body of the child that is destined to see the light of the world. If real religion can be properly preached, if everyone is given the opportunity to learn the true meaning, the underlying truths, the noble thought and deep feelings of religious principles, then in the next twenty years a whole new generation will have a completely fresh and new perspective on life.

The man who indulges in sex without considering the life to be born out of that physical union, without extending a loving invitation to a spirit to enter the body of his child, is really committing a great sin. That man is guilty of sin even if his children are born within the state of matrimony. If he has not, with a prayerful and devotional attitude to God, invited a spirit to enter the child he and his wife are conceiving, he is guilty, a condemned man. The type of soul that enters the woman's body ultimately decides the future.

We pay great attention to our children's clothes, to their fads, to their education, to their health—but we totally ignore their souls. This will never result in the creation of a sound race of humans on this planet.

So, it is of much more importance to discover how your soul has entered your body, rather than how a soul can enter someone else's.

In somewhat the same vein, another friend has asked whether we can know anything of our previous births. Yes, it is certainly possible to know about one's previous births, but when you know nothing about this life it is very difficult to know about past ones. It is possible to be conscious of previous births because whatever has happened to you, whatever has been imprinted on your unconscious cannot be easily erased. Deep down in your unconscious mind whatever has happened to you is always present. Whatever you have known you do not forget.

If I ask you what you did on January 1, 1950, you may not be able to recall anything. You will say you cannot remember anything and you will be very definite about it. But if you are hypnotized—and this can be done very easily—you will be able to relate the detailed happenings of January 1, 1950, as if that whole day were passing before your eyes. You will be able to recall that the cup of tea you had that morning had a little less sugar in it than usual, and you will also be able to tell me who served you that tea. You would also be able to say the man stank of sweat. You would even be able to remember the smallest things like the fact that a shoe you wore on that day was pinching your foot. In a hypnotized state your memories can be brought to the surface.

I have done a lot of research into these things and those who want to know about their past lives can be taken back to them. But first you will have to go back in this life, to the moment you were conceived in the womb of your mother. Only after this can you be taken back to the memories of a previous life.

But remember, nature has arranged things this way, has arranged for these memories to be lost in oblivion. Quite apart from the memories of past lives, if you even recall the detailed happenings of one month in your life they will haunt you and you will go mad. If during the night you remembered everything that happened to you throughout the day, you would go insane. And so nature has arranged it so that you are only allowed as much memory as your mind can easily digest without any strain. All remaining memories are buried in the dark valley of the past.

Just as you have a place in your house where you store unwanted things, the memory also has a hidden, unconscious storehouse where things that are not necessary for you to remember are stored. In the memory's storeroom recollections of countless lives are to be found. They have been collecting there for ages and ages. But if anyone, without proper understanding, unknowingly enters that storeroom of memories he will go mad that very moment. The collection of memories is that stupendous!

One woman I know wanted to probe into her past lives and began experimenting at my place. I explained to her she had to be fully prepared to shoulder the responsibility for anything that might happen. I told her that the knowledge of her past lives would shatter her peace of mind and leave her worried and anxious. But she said she would not get upset at all. She said that the past was over and couldn't see why knowledge of it should create problems for her in the present. And so she continued her experiments.

She was a learned and courageous college professor, and with my guidance she went into very deep meditation. Gradually the curtain of her memory began to lift and the day she entered a past life she came running to me. She was trembling from head to toe and tears poured down her cheeks. She cried and shouted that she wanted to forget what she had seen about her past life. She also refused to go back any further into the past.

I calmly asked her why she now wanted to close her eyes to her past when she had been so interested before, when she had meditated so much for this very reason. She became very upset and said it would be better if I knew nothing about it at all. Finally she admitted that in her past life she had been a prostitute, a *devadasi* in a temple in the southern part of the country. "I enjoyed sex with countless men," she said, "I gave my body to them. I was prey to their desire and lust. I thought I was loyal to my husband, true to him in body and soul, but knowing my past has thoroughly disillusioned me. I don't want to remember that awful past of mine at all!"

I told her that it is easy to remember, but not so easy to forget. To forget the past is very, very difficult indeed.

To enter one's past is possible, but those who want to do it must follow certain methods. The greatest contribution of Mahavira and Gautam Buddha to humanity is not their principle of non-violence, but the knowledge of the art of entering past lives. They are the first men who stressed that anyone who wants to know reality of his soul must also explore the past.

When a man learns the truth about his past he will know when he is repeating the same thoughts and actions as he has done in past lives and will then realize the futility of those thoughts and actions. Then he will be a completely changed man. Then he will realize his madness, his foolishness, because he will come to know that in past lives he has earned millions, built palaces, attained to high posts, attained knowledge, reached honored positions in society and many times has sat on the thrones of Delhi. And how many times, how many hundreds and hundreds of times has he done the same things again and again in his present life! Every life has been a story of failure and this life will be just the same, just as unsuccessful. As soon as this realization dawns upon him fully, his quest for wealth, power and position will cease.

In this way, knowledge of his past lives can stop a man's insane pursuit of wealth and status. Men will know how many women they have taken to bed in their past lives and women will know how many men they have slept with, and both will know they are doing the same things again—living lives of lust and enjoyment once more. But even with all this past indulgence in physical and material pleasures neither men nor women have found satisfaction or contentment.

The irony of it all is that in this life they want to do the same things—indulge in sensual pleasures, think about sleeping with this woman, about sleeping with that man. And this has happened millions of times in the past. But once the futility of all this has been understood through knowledge of past lives, the same things will not be repeated. If after all of this repetition, failure is the only outcome, then doing them again in this life makes no sense whatsoever.

To remember their past lives, both Mahavira and Buddha engaged in deep meditation. And once any man passes through the scenes of his past lives and remembers his behavior and actions in those lives he is thoroughly changed, completely transformed.

And so I can reply to my friend's question by saying that it is both easy and possible to recall the memories of past lives. But how can a man have the courage and boldness to face his past lives when he drinks wine to forget the worries and anxieties of this one! He drinks, he plays cards, he goes to the cinema, he gambles—only to forget the present. He drinks wine at night so that the worries of the day can be lost in the oblivion of forgetfulness. How can a man who doesn't have the guts to remember the happenings of the day, who seeks forgetfulness in wine and women, have the daring to review his countless past lives and expect to find the courage to bear that knowledge?

All the religions have condemned wine and spirits. Our ignorant leaders state that the religions prohibit liquor because it debases the individual's character, because money that is needed for the family is squandered on liquor and because when a man is drunk he quarrels and fights with his friends. This is wrong. This argument in favor of prohibition is simply superficial. Religions have forbidden the drinking of spirits because the man who drinks in only trying to forget himself. And the man who tries to forget himself in alcohol can never know his soul. To know one's soul one has to try to understand oneself. This is the main reason wine and meditation are opposed to each other.

It is generally taken for granted that drunkards are bad people. I know some drunkards and I also know people who never touch alcohol. Through thousands of my own experiences I say that the drunkard is a better human being than the one who does not drink. I have found a deep sense of kindness and humanity in drunkards that is missing in the man who abstains from drink. I have found that those whom the world brands as drunkards are more humble in their behavior, kinder in their attitude to their fellow men than those who do not drink. Those who do not drink definitely are more conceited and more full of self-pride than those who do.

But these are not the grounds upon which religions have based their condemnation of liquor, and the preaching of our present day leaders that this is the basis of religion's attitude is absolutely untrue.

Religion has supported the prohibition of alcohol on the grounds that those who drink forget themselves and lose the necessary courage to recall the past. Setting memories aside for a moment, there is also the fact that the haphazard way of life of the man who drinks ultimately dulls his senses. But in any case, how can one who is trying to forget the present ever have the courage to probe into his past? And if one does not recall the events of his past life, how can he hope to remold the present one in a proper manner? Then it will just be the same old story of blind repetitiveness that has gone on and on through countless lives.

The same thoughts and actions recur again and again, endlessly. You will be reborn again and again and will repeat the same foolish things you have done so many times before. And there will be no end to these recurrences unless you are able to dive into your past lives. This tedious chain of events is pointless, because you will be reborn again and do exactly the same things you have done before. It will be a never ending circle. This is why human life is compared to a revolving wheel, going around and around over and over again.

God knows what the thinkers and ideologists of our country had in their minds when they embossed the wheel on our national flag! Perhaps they did not realize the full significance of what they are doing. Ashoka the Great had the wheel carved on his pillars and *stupas* with the express purpose of helping mankind realize that life is like a wheel that keeps revolving around itself. In the wheel of life everything returns to the same point and from that point begins circling again. The wheel represents life, revolving, circling again and again. It is nothing but a dreary repetition. But every time we forget and so we go on repeating the same old things with fresh desire and new enthusiasm.

A young man who approaches a young girl to show his love, to show his longing, does not know how many times and to how many young women he has made the same kind of approaches in his past lives. And when he gives expression to his tender feelings in this life he thinks he is doing it for the first time, and that it is the most important event in his life. But if he becomes conscious that this seemingly important incident of first love has happened countless times before in countless lives he will see the futility of it. He will feel just like a man who has seen the same movie thirty or forty times.

If you see a film today you enjoy it. If you are made to go see it again tomorrow you may tolerate it. If you are asked to see it again on the third day you will want to avoid it because it will be boring for you. But if you are forced, say by the police, to see the same film for fifteen days running, on the sixteenth day you will want to kill yourself. You will have reached a point where you cannot tolerate the repetition of the film one more time.

But, if you are given opium after seeing the film each time you will forget what you have seen before and you will be able to watch the same movie again and again. Not only would you be able to watch it, you would enjoy it every time you saw it.

When a man discards this body after he dies, the door to all the memories connected with this body and contained in it is permanently shut—and a whole new drama begins all over in the new body. Although it is a new drama it is the same old plot. It is a repetition of the same old story, of the same happenings, of the same goings-on. If the past is remembered somehow, you will realize that it is the same tiresome film you have seen so many times before, that the dialogue is the same, that you have heard the songs sung countless times before—and then it will be beyond your powers of endurance to put up with the repetitiveness any more. So after the memories of past lives parade before you in a passing panorama a wish to discard all that is of this world arises in you. It is because of this that the remembrance of past lives generates a sense of the futility of worldly things.

Nowadays this sense of futility does not happen to many people, because no one has the desire to probe into the secret memories of past lives. If any of my friends wish to carry on experiments of this nature I am willing to guide them. I give my word that at a signal from any of them I am ready for such experimentation. If anyone comes forward it will make me very happy.

Only yesterday I received a few letters from friends saying they were ready, that they were waiting to be called. Now that the call has come I trust they are prepared to come forward. I am ready to guide them on the path of exploration into the past. I will accompany them as far as they want to go. At this stage of the world's progress and development, we badly need people who possess this ability. If only a few men can attain to this knowledge I am certain we can remove the darkness that is so quickly enveloping the whole world.

Two experiments, totally different from each other, have been carried on in India during the last fifty years. One experiment was Gandhi's; the other, Shree Aurobindo's.

Gandhi tried to elevate the personal character and integrity of each individual, of every human being. And it seemed for a while that Gandhi was succeeding—but he failed completely. Those whom Gandhi thought he had uplifted proved to be no more than images painted on clay, pictures that lose their luster and color if a little rain falls on them. The past twenty years have shown that the light of Gandhi's vision has faded into nothingness.

His followers stand naked in Delhi with none of the coloring or intensity Gandhi endeavored to impart to them.

Before the honors of high office rained down on them their faces showed dignity and conviction. Their snow-white hand-woven *khadi* garments were dazzling in their purity; their *khadi* caps seemed as if they could lift an empire out of the dust and turn it into something solid, into something beneficial for a suffering people. But today those same *khadi* caps, once regarded as symbols of purity, have fallen so low into the dust that they deserve to be burned in the public squares. Now they are totally bourgeois; now they are emblems of red-tapism and corruption. Gandhi's experiment failed miserably. But experiments like this have been carried on in our country many many times. Even long before Gandhi.

Shree Aurobindo conducted an experiment in which he achieved almost no success and ultimately failed—but the direction he pursued was quite right and correct. His aim was to uplift a few souls so that they would be able to beckon others to their level, so that their very presence on earth would be a sublime invitation to other men. He felt that if it were possible to elevate even one man's soul on high that the souls of all humanity would rise along with it; his conviction was that the level of all souls would be raised in this way. He felt this is possible, but only because he saw no other alternative.

Mankind has sunk so low at present that if one man cares enough to try to change the entire human race it is likely he himself will be corrupted. You know quite well that public benefactors can turn into public pickpockets within a few days, and instead of benefiting the common man they harm him. They want to improve the lot of the people, they want to serve them, but within a few days they themselves turn out to be the ones who need improving! No, Aurobindo's idea was impossible. It could not happen.

Perhaps you are not aware that the history of spirituality shows that during certain time periods the spiritual level of man reaches unimaginable heights. Twenty five hundred years ago Gautam Buddha was born in India; Prabuddha

Katyayana, Makkhali Goshal and Sanjaya Vittaliputra were also born in this country. Socrates, Plato and Aristotle were born in Greece and Lao Tzu, Confucius and Chuang Tzu were born in China. Twenty-five hundred years ago some ten or fifteen men out of the entire population of the world, some ten or fifteen men of towering stature appeared on the scene and in that century the spiritual standard on this planet rose so high it almost touched the sky. It seemed as if the golden age of the world had come. Never had there been such powerful, enlightened and sublime souls before.

Fifty thousand people followed Mahavira and thousands of Buddha's *bhikkhus* showed the path of righteousness and enlightenment to a suffering humanity. The very dust was transformed whenever Buddha and his retinue of ten thousand *bhikkhus* appeared in a village. In whatever village those ten thousand performed their collective prayers it seemed as if darkness had been driven away and the whole village was illumined with a spiritual, celestial glow. At every stopping place they left an awakening of spirituality in their path. It was as if all the flowers bloomed at once. Nothing like this had ever happened before. Some rose on high, and following them, others looked up and responded to their summons.

Unless there is some cause to turn one's vision on high, no one ever raises his eyes. If there is nothing to attract your vision upwards you will never look at all. Yet there seems to be so much to look downwards for!

When a man focuses downwards he keeps going lower and lower until he has a big safe to keep his money in and owns a Cadillac. By looking downwards, you achieve material prosperity. See how low Delhi is! It is almost in hell. And whosoever wants to go to Delhi will have to stoop lower and lower! There is nothing to be seen above, but there is so much below to attract your attention.

Even if you want to raise you vision upwards you cannot see anyone there because there is no one to be seen.

What a misfortune there are no souls on high to whom we can look for guidance! What a pity there are no souls above to whom you could be attracted! What a shame there is no one to call on you with insistence, no one whose presence makes you feel ashamed and generates an urge in your heart to be like him!

You could be that light, that nectar yourself. You could sing a song of purity and freedom yourself. You could be Buddha, you could be Mahavira, you could be Krishna, you could be Christ. Once this idea enters your mind, once the thought is planted in you that you could be like them, the upward journey of your soul commences. But there must be higher souls to whom you can turn for inspiration. Remember, the soul is never stagnant. It is always moving—up or down, higher or lower. Spiritual consciousness does not make rest stops. Life is one continuous flux. And spiritually, man *must* move upwards!

I want a revolution in the world—not of many people but of a few who are courageous enough to experiment with themselves. If only one hundred people, prepared to elevate their souls to the heights that are possible, would come forward, within twenty years the entire face of India could be totally changed, completely transformed.

In his last moments Vivekananda said he had been calling for one hundred people to come forward to work with him, but that they had not come and that he was dying a very unhappy and disappointed man. Vivekananda was convinced that he could have changed the world if those hundred men had come forward. But they never came. And Vivekananda died.

I have decided not to call but to go to the villages and search out those hundred men. I will look deep into their eyes to fathom the depths of their souls. And if they do not heed my call I will bring them forward by force, by compulsion. If I am able to bring together one hundred such men I assure you that the souls of those hundred men will stand out like Mount Everest, casting their brilliance on an erring mankind and leading it to the right path.

Those who accept my challenge and have the strength and courage to walk that difficult path with me must remember that the path is not only difficult, it is also unknown. It is like a tremendously vast sea, and we have no map, no chart of its depths. But the man who has the courage to enter the deep water should realize that he only has that strength and power because God himself has called on him. Otherwise he would never be so brave. In Egypt it was believed that when a man called on God for strength and guidance it was because God has already called on him and that there would have been no call otherwise.

Those who have this inner urge have a responsibility towards mankind. And today it is of the utmost urgency to go to the four corners of the world, to sound the call for men to step forward to sacrifice their whole lives to reaching the heights of spirituality and enlightenment.

All life's truths, all the experiences which were real at one time are now turning into blatant lies. All the heights that were once reached are now becoming myth, fantasy. They are becoming legends, fairy tales. After another hundred or two hundred years, people will not even know that Buddha or Christ were actually born and really lived in this world. They will think that tales of their lives are only made-up stories from the past.

Someone has already written a book in the West wherein he has openly stated that Christ never existed, that the story of his life is nothing but a drama. In his book he also says that people eventually forgot that it was a drama and began to believe in it as a real historical fact.

At present in India we enact the *Ram-leela* pageant because we believe Ram lived and walked upon this earth—but future generations will say that *Ram-leela* was really just written by someone and that the idea was eventually created amongst the people that Ram actually existed. They will think that Ram was just a character in a drama. And it is only natural that people of the future will think like this, that *Ram-leela* was nothing but a pageant, nothing but a drama enacted generation after generation. When personalities like Buddha, Christ or Ram are nowhere to be found, how can people ever believe that men of such outstanding knowledge and wisdom and stupendous spirituality ever lived, ever walked in this ordinary, mundane world?

The workings of man's mind are rather odd. He can never believe that anyone higher than him can exist. He can never readjust his thinking to accept the idea that a higher being than himself can live and breathe on this earth. On the contrary, his mind is always bent upon looking on himself as the highest and loftiest of all.

A man will only accept the existence of a being superior to himself under great pressure, and even then he will seek loop-holes in the other's character so that he can prove to himself the other man is really of a very low level of consciousness. Whether the defects he imagines he sees in the other give him any inner satisfaction is doubtful, but outwardly he will try very hard to prove the other is lower than him. And as soon as he is able to find the slightest flaw he will immediately shout to the world that his former idol has fallen, that the man no longer holds the same place in his heart because he has uncovered failings in his character. The search is always for shortcomings. And if he is unable to find such a flaw then he will either make one up or take for granted that one must exist; then he can have the false satisfaction of feeling he has been right.

And so, with the passage of time, mankind will gradually refuse to accept the possibility of the existence of superior beings, because there will be no signs of their ever having lived. After all, how long can idols of stone declare to the world that Buddha and Mahavira actually existed and lived wonderful lives of utter simplicity and lofty spirituality? How long can the words of the Bible bear witness to the fact that Christ really existed and walked this earth in all his glory? How many years can the *Bhagavad Gita* go on telling the world that Krishna was born as a human being and that in human voice he expounded the Gita to Arjuna on the battlefield of Kurukshetra? No, it is not possible for too many years!

It is just not possible for future generations to maintain their faith through words alone, through scriptures alone. We need something substantial to support our faith. We need men like Christ, like Krishna, like Buddha, like Mahavira. If we are unable to have such men among us, mankind will have to face the calamity of a very dark age indeed, one full of ignorance and misery. And so there is hardly any prospect at all for the future.

I am throwing out a great challenge to those who feel they have something good to offer humanity. I intend to wander through as many villages as necessary, and if I encounter eyes that can serve as lights for others, or eyes in which I feel I can kindle the burning flame of conviction, I will take those people with me and I will work on them. I will make them able. I will impart to them all the faculties necessary to enable them to hold high the torch and illumine the dark path men tread to a brighter future, to a future full of knowledge and light.

As for myself, I am fully prepared. I do not intend to die like Vivekananda saying I spent my life searching for a hundred men and could not find them.

How can I speak when the mountains are silent? How can I talk to you when the sky says nothing? How can I say anything when God himself does not speak? Still I speak to you, but it is only so that you may hear their silence.

An artist will use a black background to heighten the effect of a bright blue—and I am using the same device.

I am speaking to enable you to understand the language of silence. Words are only meaningful because they represent the gestures of silence. Speech is only meaningful when it leads to tranquility, and life is only significant if it prepares you to face death.

6
LOVE AND HAPPINESS

When I roam the lofty mountains I feel like my soul is raised on high and covered like the peaks in never melting caps of snow. And when I descend into the valleys I feel deep and profound like them and my heart fills with mysterious shadows. The same thing happens at the edge of the sea. There I merge with the surging waves: they pound and roar within me. When I gaze at the sky I expand. I become boundless, unlimited. When I look at the stars, silence permeates me; when I see a flower the ecstasy of beauty overwhelms me. When I hear a bird singing, its song is an echo of my own inner voice, and when I look into the eyes of an animal I see no difference between them and my own. Gradually my separate existence has been effaced and only God remains. So where shall I look for God now? How shall I seek him? Only he is; I am not.

I was in the hills, and what they wanted to tell me was transmitted through their silence. The trees, the lakes, the rivers, the brooks, the moon and the stars were all speaking to me in the language of silence. And I understood. The words of God were clear to me. I could only hear him when I became silent. Not before.

What shall I say to you? Listen to the stars in the sky. I wish to say the same thing their silent, dancing lights are saying. I wish to say that whatever is, is beyond the power of speech, beyond the reach of hearing.

Creation springs from love. It is nourished by love. It moves towards love and eventually merges with love. And you ask me why I say love is God! This is why.

I watch mankind moving from one perversion to another. It is as if some fiber essential to life has been destroyed within him—and within his civilization as well. Not only the individual, all the society is living within a framework that has become perverted and twisted. Its discordant notes echo throughout the world and the harmony that a sound culture creates is nowhere to be heard.

No instrument is as out of tune as man. And just as a stone causes ripples across the surface of a lake, the perversity of one man can agitate the whole of humanity. A man may be an individual but his roots are in the corporate body of mankind. Each man's infection is tremendously contagious.

What is the disease that afflicts our century? Many diseases have been isolated, but I wish to point to one in particular that, in my opinion, is at the root of all other afflictions. Whenever a man is overcome by this fundamental illness he turns to suicidal destruction. What name shall I give this disease? It is not easy to name it. The best I can do is to call it the drying up of the well of love in the human heart.

Everyone is afflicted with this absence of love. Our hearts are not functioning at all. There can be no greater misfortune in a man's life than the absence of love, because without love his relationship with life is severed. It is love that connects us to the whole.

Without love a man stands alone, separated from the core of existence. Without love everyone is a lone entity, lacking any connection with others of his kind. Today, man finds himself totally alone. We are all shut off from each other, trapped within ourselves. This is like being in the grave. Even though he is alive, man is a corpse.

Do you see the truth in what I am saying? Are you alive? Do you feel the flow of love in your veins? If you do not feel that flow, if the throbbing of love in your heart has ceased, then you should understand well that you are not really alive at all.

Once I was on a journey and someone asked me which word in a man's vocabulary was the most valuable. My reply was, "Love". The man was surprised. He said he had expected me to answer "soul" or "God". I laughed and said, "Love *is* God."

That which comes from beyond the body, from beyond the mind, is the ray of love. Love is beyond the material world. Love is unique.

All religion, all poetry and all philosophy are inspired by love. Whatsoever is good and beautiful in life is born out of love, lives in love.

And so I say, "Love is God."

Rising on the ray of love one can enter the enlightened kingdom of God. It is better to say that love is God than to say that truth is God, because the harmony, the beauty, the vitality and the bliss that are part of love are not part of truth. Truth is to be known; love is to be felt as well as known. The growth and perfection of love lead to the ultimate merger with God.

The greatest poverty of all is the absence of love. The man who has not developed the capacity to love lives in a private hell of his own. A man who is filled with love is in heaven. You can look at man as a wonderful and unique plant, a plant that is capable of producing both nectar and poison. If a man lives by hate he reaps a harvest of poison; if he lives by love he gathers blossoms laden with nectar.

If I mold my life and live it with the well-being of all men in mind, that is love. Love results from the awareness that you are not separate, not different from anything else in existence. I am in you; you are in me. This love is religious.

The doors of love only open for the person who is prepared to let his ego go. To surrender one's ego for someone else is love; to surrender one's ego for all is divine love.

Love is not sexual passion. Those who mistake sex for love remain empty of love. Sex is only a passing manifestation of love. It is part of nature's mechanism, a method of procreation. Love exists on a higher plane, and as love grows, sex dissipates. The energy that has been manifested in sex is transformed into love.

Love is the creative refinement of sex energy. And so, when love reaches perfection, the absence of sex automatically follows. A life of love, of abstinence from physical pleasures is called *brahmacharya*, and anyone who wishes to be free from sex must develop his capacity to love. Freedom from sex cannot be achieved through suppression. Liberation from sex is only possible through love.

I have said that love is God. This is the ultimate truth. But let me say as well that love also exists within the family unit. This is the first step on the journey to love, and the ultimate can never happen if the beginning has been absent. Love is responsible for the existence of the family and when the family unit moves apart and its members spread out into society, love increases and grows. When a man's family has finally grown to incorporate all of mankind, his love becomes one with God.

Without love man is an individual, an ego. He has no family; he has no link with other people. This is gradual death. Life, on the other hand, is interrelation.

Love surpasses the duality of the ego. This alone is truth. The man who thirsts for truth must first develop his capacity to love—to the point where the difference between the lover and the beloved disappears and only love remains.

When the light of love is freed from the duality of lover and beloved, when it is freed from the haze of seer and seen, when only the light of pure love shines brightly, that is freedom and liberation.

I urge all men to strive for that supreme freedom.

Do not say that you have been in prayer because that indicates you can also be out of prayer. The man who is out of prayer at any point can never have been in prayer at all. Prayer is not an activity you can move in and out of. Prayer is the perfection and the fullness of love.

To live is to live in God. To live in truth is also to live in love. But those who remember God have forgotten about truth, and those who remember truth have overlooked love. It would be better if they had forgotten God and remembered truth—but it would be even better if they had forgotten about truth and were prepared to live lives of love. Wherever love is to be found, truth steps in of its own accord. And where truth is, God is too.

Every day I watch you going to the temples. I see you poring over the scriptures, day in and day out. And this worries me. I have never seen you show any appreciation of nature. If you cannot see God in nature, how can you possibly see him somewhere else? Open yourself to nature and let its beauty fill your eyes. Open your heart and let nature's sweet music resound within you. Welcome nature; enthrone nature in your heart of hearts. Before long you will recognize that your guest is God himself.

It is utter foolishness to oppose nature. You will never attain God by opposing nature. God is hidden in nature.

You must never fight with nature: you must learn to allow its mysteries to unfold for you. Nature is a veil to be lifted. Nature is part of God: it is his manifestation. He is deeply embedded in nature: it is his home.

If you quarrel with nature you will never move close to God: rather, you will move further and further away from him. But we have always been taught to fight with nature: we have always been told that God is against nature. The spiritual poverty of man is the result of this conflict.

Man has been told to seek God by fighting his nature—but God is in his nature and his nature is in God. There is no God separate or aloof from nature. God and nature intermingle.

In their antagonistic attitude to nature educational systems have stolen from man the ladder that leads him to God. Nature is the bridge. You don't stop on a bridge, you use a bridge to cross over. You don't quarrel with a bridge: it is there to help you. Nature is the bridge that leads to your destination. And there is no other route.

You have to love nature: you have to love it with all your heart. Love is the only force that can throw open the gates to God. But you have been told that nature is a bondage, a prison, sinful. These terrible and wrong teachings have infested man's mind with poison, spoiling any love for nature, preventing any possibility for perfect knowledge. And this has widened the gulf between man and God.

It is essential a man bring nature back into his life before he attempts to invite God into it. A love of nature eventually transforms itself into a prayer unto God. Man is not to free himself from nature, he is to find his own freedom in nature itself.

"Does God exist?" you ask. It is not at all proper to ask a question like this because you don't even know what the word "God" means. "God" means "whole". The whole of existence itself is God. God is not a separate entity; he is not some individual, some power. What exists is God. And even this is not the proper way to say it. It is more accurate to say that existence itself is God. Even in saying "God exists" there is redundance.

Questioning the existence of God is questioning the existence of existence. The existence of all other things is obvious, but this is not the case with God. And this is because he is existence himself. The power, the energy that exists in all things may also be apparent, but this is not so with God. He himself is that power.

How can the totality be known in the same way the component parts can? God cannot be something I can know, because I am in him too.

Yet it is possible to be one with God, to sink into him. In fact, we already are one with him; we have already drowned in him. You realize this when you lose your "I". Knowing this is knowing him.

This is why I say that love itself is knowing God. God can only be known in love because in love the "I" disappears. You will never find love where "I" exists. Love is only there when "I" is not.

There is a parable about a lump of salt who went to visit the sea. It met the sea and it came to know the sea, but it did not return. To know the sea it became the sea itself. The only way it could know the sea was by becoming the sea.

The only way a man can know God is by becoming God.

A friend of mine was very unhappy. When I saw him weeping I led him outside and said, "Look at the stars!" At first the tears kept welling up in his eyes, sparkling like the stars themselves but his misery soon subsided.

"How is it," he asked me, "that my heart threw off its burden when I looked at the stars? How is it my misery vanished when I looked at the sky?"

"It is misery to be removed from God," I replied. "It is sorrow to be alienated from nature. It is anguish to be separated from the soul."

That same evening someone asked me, "What is the greatest pleasure in the world?"

I answered, "To be in the world and yet not of the world. The only way to guarantee happiness in your life is to have your feet firmly planted on the earth and your heart firmly planted in God."

Don't we eventually get tired of our pleasures? And doesn't a pleasure we are tired of become a bore, a pain? But have you ever noticed a man tiring of those pleasures he gives to other people? No, such a thing has never happened. Let me tell you a secret: only the pleasure we give to others becomes bliss. And there is no end to bliss. Bliss is the nectar of life. It is eternal, endless.

I remember the days when my mind was in darkness, when nothing was clear inside me at all. One thing in particular I recall about those days was that I did not feel love for anyone. I did not even love myself.

But when I came to the experience of meditation I felt as though a million dormant springs of love had suddenly begun to bubble up in me. This love was not focused, not directed to anyone in particular, it was just a flow, fluid and forceful. It flowed from me as light streams from a lamp, as fragrance pours from flowers. In the wonderful moment of my awakening I realized that love was the real manifestation of my nature, of man's nature.

Love has no direction; it is not aimed at anyone. Love is a manifestation of the soul, of one's self.

Before this experience happened to me I believed love meant being attached to someone. Now I realize that love and attachment are two completely different things. Attachment is the absence of love. Attachment is the opposite of hatred, and hatred it can easily become. They are a pair, attachment and hatred. They are mutually interchangeable.

The opposite of hatred is not love. Not at all. And love is quite different from attachment too. Love is a completely new dimension. It is the absence of both attachment and hatred, yet it is not negative. Love is the positive existence of some higher power. This power, this energy, flows from the self towards all things—not because it is attracted by them, but because love is emitted by the self, because love is the perfume of the self.

When I came to know love I also came to understand non-violence. And my understanding came from my experience of the self and not from any scriptures. This realization of my self provided the answer to everything. If love is a relationship it is attachment; if love is unrelated, uninspired, unattached, it is non-violence.

An ascetic once asked me how he could attain the love I talked about so much. I told him, "Love cannot be attained directly. First attain wisdom, and then love will come of its own accord." Wisdom is the important thing. Love follows automatically.

It is impossible to achieve knowledge without attaining non-violence at the same time. And so non-violence is the real test of a man's knowledge. Non-violence is the ultimate accountability; it is the ultimate criterion. A man's religion can be called pure only after it has been forged in this furnace. The individual man's search for wisdom is the same as the basic inquiry of religion.

When knowledge is freed from attachments it is transformed into wisdom. When all objects, when all points of focus disappear, knowledge knows itself. Knowledge of the self by the self is wisdom. No duality exists in this awakening; there is only pure knowledge. And this illumination of knowledge by itself is the greatest revolution possible in human consciousness. A man becomes truly related to himself, to his being, only through this revolution. Then and only then is the real purpose and meaning of life revealed to him.

This revolution is attained through meditation. Meditation is the way to attain wisdom. Meditation is the means; wisdom, the end. And love is the result of having successfully achieved that goal.

Man's mind is constantly filled with objective things, with outer objects. And one's knowledge is always surrounded by objects, by ideas, by one thing and another. You have to free knowledge from this bondage to objects. Meditation is the way to attain this freedom.

When one is asleep one is free, but one is also unconsciousness. The mind is absorbed within itself. This state is its nature. The Hindi word for this state is *supti.* It comes from *swa* meaning "the self" and *apti,* "to enter". In deep sleep one enters into the self.

The states of deep sleep and of meditation are similar to one another except in one important respect. Meditation is a state of perfect consciousness and awareness, whereas sleep is a state of unconsciousness. In deep sleep one has a feeling of harmony with the world; in meditation there is complete oneness and identification with the universal consciousness.

Remember, sleep is not a state of meditation. Many psychologists think that when the mind is empty, that when there is no object in the consciousness, that one is in the state of sleep. This is a mistake; this is the result of thinking without experimentation. When the consciousness is asleep it may be free from attachment to objects, but this does not necessarily mean it is empty of them. To set one's consciousness free requires so much work and such conscious effort that it becomes impossible to sleep afterwards. Then, only pure consciousness remains.

There are three stages in the process of meditation: detachment from the objects in the mind, awareness of the thought currents of the mind and finally, retention of the understanding of the mind. With detachment from the objects of the mind, their impressions stop forming; with awareness of the currents of the mind there is gradual slowing down of their development. Only when these two stages have been achieved and one is able to retain the understanding of the mind is there the possibility of self-realization.

The point of origin of a thing is also its point of dissolution. No matter what something's origins are, its dissolution is innate within it. It is inherent in its very nature. Meditation is the dissolved state of mind. Just as the waves ultimately disappear into the ocean, the mind dissolves into the universal consciousness.

The center of the mind is the ego. When the mind dissolves the ego is released and what remains, what is experienced, is the soul.

People ask me what non-violence is every day. My answer is that non-violence is knowledge of the self. If you come to know yourself you will know the essence of man. This awareness gives birth to love, and it is impossible for love to inflict pain. This is non-violence.

The ego is at the core of one's ignorance of the self. All violence is born there; it is born within the ego. A man feels that he is everything and that the rest of the world exists for him alone. He sees himself as the center, as the focal point for all existence. The exploitation that is born of this egoism is what violence is.

Love is the center of self-knowledge. And when the ego dissolves, love is perfected.

There are only two states of consciousness that exist—the state of the ego and the state of love. The ego is the narrow state, the seed-form, the atomic stage; love is all encompassing, love is God. The center of the ego is I; the ego exists for itself. The center of love is the universe. Love exists for all.

The ego is exploitation; love is service. And the service that flows from love, freely and spontaneously, is non-violence.

Begin to meditate. Practice it faithfully so that your life can be filled with the light of wisdom. And when there is light within you, love will flow from you and spread itself far and wide. Love is the highest flowering of spiritual growth, of spiritual attainment. Those who die without experiencing love have perished without experiencing life.

If you have not known love, you have not known anything at all—because love is God.

It is unnecessary to go in search of God. Just live a life of godliness; just show your godliness in every action. In fact, godlines must become your very breath, for only then will you realize God.

Once I stood by the sea and asked myself why all the rivers flowed into the ocean. But I knew the answer; even a child does. It is because the ocean is lower than the land through which the rivers flow. The thought filled my mind with dancing beams of light. Blessed is the man who is lowly, who is humble, because God showers down on him the riches of his glory.

You wish to serve? Remember, a man who is drowning in a vast ocean cannot save another who is floundering in the same sea.

I was standing by the bank of a river. It was a small stream and in the gathering dusk the young girls from the village were hurrying home with their earthen jars filled with water. I had observed that they had to stoop down to fill their jars from the river. One also has to know the art of stooping to fill one's jar at the fountain of life.

But how to bend is something man seems to keep forgetting. His ego will not let him bend. And so all love, all prayer, is slowly vanishing from life. In fact, anything of any real significance seems to be disappearing. Life has become a kind of struggle instead of the beauty and harmony it ought to be. But strife is the only thing that can endure where the mysterious art of bending has been lost. It should not be considered at all surprising if rigid and unbounded egoism cause unbearable pain in a world where the warm hearted art of yielding to each other is unknown and unrecognized.

Yielding links the individual to the group. Being unable to yield separates a man from the universal existence. Of course this giving way must be natural and spontaneous or else it only serves to puff up the ego. Any yielding that is done deliberately is not real and behind it, in some recess of the mind, an element of resistance persists. When it springs from the intellect it is not genuine; it is not vital, not complete. And furthermore, this kind of giving way ends up causing remorse because the ego is wounded. It is an action that has gone against the ego and, in revenge, the ego indulges itself in self-pity.

Only when the human heart is devoid of egoism can it yield naturally and perfectly. And this yielding will be as natural and as complete in every detail as the bending of the tiny blades of grass in the wind. They have no hostility towards the breeze; they have no egos. The day a man is able to assimilate this natural bending, this spontaneous yielding into his being, the mysterious secrets of God will be revealed to him.

A certain young man once said to a *fakir*, "In the past there were people who saw God with their own eyes. How is it such people do not exist today?"

The venerable gentleman replied, "Because nowadays no one is prepared to stoop so low!" To drink one's fill at God's fountain you must stoop down. How can those who stand on the bank with their noses held haughtily in the air ever fill their jars with water?

I know that you are in search of bliss, but how can you find bliss by searching for it? Bliss is available to those who distribute bliss, to those who spread bliss around. If you wish for bliss then give bliss. Do not desire; give. Only by giving will it come to you; only by sharing will you receive it; only by scattering it lavishly will it shower on you. God's ways are strange. Do not stand at the threshold of bliss like a beggar; go there like an emperor. Haven't you noticed that all doors are closed to a beggar. And who is a beggar anyway? A beggar is a man who begs, who pleads, who supplicates. And who is an emperor? An emperor is a man who gives. So I urge you—give, give, give. Give with no strings attached. Then you will see that what you have given is returned to you a thousand times over. Everything comes back to you. Your only asset is the echo of your own liberal gift. Do you ever recall receiving anything without having given something first?

A relative of a friend of mine was ill and he took her a bouquet of fresh flowers from his garden. When he returned from the hospital I noticed the fragrance of the flowers still lingered on his hands. I observed the same thing in many other ways. Whatever we give, its perfume or its foul odor always lingers on. Those who wish to live in fragrance only give fragrance.

Whenever I think of mankind I am reminded of the thousands of eyes into which I have looked. It pains me to think of them because I remember what I have seen in them. What I hoped to see was never what I saw. I was looking for happiness and found misery: I was looking for light and found darkness; I was looking for God and I found corruption. What has happened to man?

Man's life is not real. Where there is neither peace nor harmony, nor energy nor bliss, how can we call it life? How can we call chaos life? This cannot be called life at all. A more apt description would be to call it an agonizing dream, an unconscious hallucination, an endless chain of misery. It only ends in death. And most people die before they have ever lived at all. It is one thing to be born—all men are born—but very, very few attain life.

The only man who really attains life is the man who experiences God in himself and in all of humanity. Without this realization we are but lifeless bodies, unaware of the timeless beginnings of life, unaware of the vital currents of life. Without this consciousness one's life can never be blissful. Man's ignorance of himself, of his self, is his misery.

When a man has achieved self-knowledge his heart is filled with light. And unless this happens, his being is in total darkness. When a man reaches to his self, to his soul, ne becomes divine, but if he does not, he becomes less than the animals. Those who are unable to feel any truth in themselves apart from the animals, those who are unable to feel any truth in themselves apart from that of the body can never attain this godly existence, this divine life. When a man experiences the light of life beyond the physical body, only then does his upward path to God begin. And then everything he has seen or experienced in nature becomes transformed into God.

If restlessness, misery, agony, darkness or unconsciousness exist within us, the infection spreads from the inner to the outer and envelops us completely. One's interior condition governs one's outer conduct; it is but a reflection of the inner. Whatever we are on the inside pervades all of our external relationships. In one's thoughts, one's speech, one's behavior, the inner being is externalized.

In this very way, the inner feelings of each and every individual ultimately add up to and create the society in which we live. If you find poison in a society, the seeds of this poison are hidden in the individuals who comprise it. If a society wishes for nectar, then these are the seeds that will have to be sown in the hearts of its citizens. If men's hearts are filled with happiness, then society, the result of their mutual relations, will reflect this love, friendship and compassion. If its members are in misery, then a society will be filled with violence, envy and hatred.

If there is harmony within a man, this symmetry will be apparent on the outside—and the melody of his inner symphony will spread far and wide. But if there is misery within, if there is weeping and wailing, then the same discord will echo in his conduct. This is only natural. The only man who is full of love is the man who has attained happiness within himself.

Love is moral; the absence of love is immoral. The deeper a man goes into love, the higher he reaches to God. The less a man loves, the lower his spiritual state is. Love is the basis of a pure and moral life. As Christ said, "Love is God."

Someone once asked St. Augustine, "What should I do, how can I live so that I commit no sin?" St. Augustine replied, "Love. Just love. And then whatever you do will be right and moral."

Love. In this one word everything that enables man to rise to God is contained. But it is important to remember that you can only love when you are happy inside. Love cannot be tacked on from the outside. It is not a garment you can wear. Love is your soul. It has to be discovered, uncovered. It is not imposed, it is manifested.

Love is not an action. It is a state of consciousness. It is only real when it has become your nature, and only then can it become the basis for a divine life, for a life in God.

You must also remember that a moral life, in the absence of this spontaneous inner manifestation of love, is not capable of leading you to God. This kind of morality lacks validity. It is always based on one thing or another, like fear or attraction, and it makes no difference whether the foundation of this morality is spiritual or material.

A man who leads a pure or a moral life because he is attracted to heaven or afraid of hell is neither moral nor pure. He is not really moral at all. Morality is unconditional; there is no question of loss or of gain. Moral behavior grows out of the combination of happiness and love. If it springs from any other source it is false. Just as light streams from the sun, purity and morality flow from inner happiness.

A strange incident comes to mind. One day Rabiya was seen running through the bazaar carrying a torch in one hand and a pitcher of water in the other. People stopped her and asked, "Where are you running with these things in your hands? She answered, "I am going to burn heaven and douse the flames of hell. I am going to destroy the obstacles that block your path to God."

I agree with Rabiya. I would like to eradicate both heaven and hell as well.

A truly moral life has never been based on fear or on allurement. Nor can it ever be. If it is, it is an illusion of morality. And this leads to self-deception, not to self-development. The evolution of mankind's knowledge to date has shown the falsity of lives based on this so-called morality. And as a result, the immorality of mankind has been exposed in all its nakedness.

The old concepts of heaven and hell are now disappearing, and along with them, the attraction and fear men once had for them. A great responsibility now rests on the shoulders of the present generation, on our shoulders. We have to find a new basis for moral living. This foundation has always been there but it is up to us to reveal it, to uncover it.

The inner beings of Mahavira, of Buddha, of Christ and of Krishna were not based on false ethics, on a pseudo morality. They lived in love, knowledge and happiness, but not through fear or because of enticements. We must revive the morality that is grounded in love. Without this, there is no possibility for a moral man in the future. Morality based on fear is dead. And if the flame of love is not rekindled, man will have no choice but to become immoral. You cannot force a man to be moral, just as you cannot force an intelligent man to accept some belief blindly.

The only path for man to follow is the path of love. It is through love that purity and morality will be reborn. But love in man will only happen when happiness is born in the self.

And so the real question is of attaining the experience of inner happiness. If there is happiness within, if there is self-realization, love will grow. One who does not have the total experience of the self cannot achieve happiness. Happiness comes from being established in the self. And so self-knowledge is the real path to morality.

As soon as a man knows his self, happiness flowers in him and the perfume of knowledge spreads from his being. What a man has seen within his self he then sees in all. As soon as one knows the self one knows the whole of existence, the totality of all. And when one sees oneself in every living thing, love is born.

There is no greater revolution than the revolution of love. There is no greater purity, no greater attainment. The man who attains love attains life.

I had a bath in the Ganges and washed the dust from my body. I said to the friends who were with me, "You know, there is another Ganges. If you bathe in it your soul will be cleansed."

"Which Ganges is that?" they asked.

I answered, "The Ganges of love."

I saw you worshipping God and heard you praying to him, and now you tell me I must say something to you about God. What shall I say to you? I will say this much: a prayer that comes from the heart, without sound and words, is better than a prayer that is all sound and words but has no heart in it. But prayers are always just words, and it is precisely for this reason prayers never become love and worship is always lifeless.

How can you reach God with this deathlike worship? How can God's doors be thrown open in answer to these loveless prayers? If God were a stone perhaps these prayers would reach him. I grant you that God is present in stones, but he is not a stone himself. Only those who approach him with love and vitality are able to meet him face to face.

If you nurture the poison of hatred within your heart you can never expect the flowers of bliss to bloom in your life. They need love to blossom. When the nectar of love is sprinkled in profusion, the flowers of bliss grow tall, spreading their fragrance on the four winds.

If the task you are engaged in neither thrills you nor pleases others, would you like to know why? You evidently feel it is a burden that has been imposed on you. Only a job that is undertaken and carried out with joy will bring you pleasure.

Give. Give. Give. Spread kindness all around. Render service wherever it is needed. And give love in abundance. He who gives will receive.

So you are in search of bliss? Then get ready to shower bliss on everyone you meet. The world is just an echo—whatever you do comes back to you. The man who rains well-being on others finds himself drenched in blessings that pour down on him from everywhere. And words of abuse are repaid with still viler insults. Never expect love from those at whom you throw stones, and if you stick thorns in others expect nothing more than a rich harvest of nettles. It is an eternal law that hatred begets hatred and love begets love.

There are friends who hurl insults at me and then go away. My heart is genuinely grateful to them for through the abuses I can feel my love flowing towards them, and it spreads a peace that is not of this world throughout my entire being.

I used to think a great deal about non-violence, but everything I ever heard about it seemed so superficial. It touched my intellect but not my heart. And slowly I understood why. The non-violence everyone talked about was negative. The negative can never go deeper than the intellect; to touch life something positive is needed. If by non-violence one means nothing more than the renunciation of violence then it can never have any relation to real life. To relate to life, one needs achievement as well as renunciation, something positive as well as something negative.

It is the negative character of the term "non-violence" that has made it so deceptive. The word is negative, but the experience to which it refers is a positive one. Non-violence is an experience of pure love, of a love that is not attached to anything at all. A love that is free of attachment is not focused; it is not directed to someone in particular, but to anyone and everyone. In fact, it is not really directed at all; it simply is. Unattached love is non-violence.

The aim of non-violence is to transform man's nature through love. Being non-violent is not renouncing violence, it is expressing love. And when love is there, violence automatically drops away with no effort at all. If a man feels he loves and yet has to make an effort to rid himself of violence then his love is not real at all. Darkness disappears at the advent of light; if it doesn't then you can be sure it isn't light which has come. Love is enough. The very existence of love is the non-existence of violence.

What is love anyway? Generally, what is known as love is really attachment. It is a way to forget oneself. It is a means of escaping oneself through someone else. This kind of love acts as an intoxicant. It does not free someone from misery, it merely stupefies him, makes it bearable. This kind of love I call the relationship form. It is not really love at all. It is an illusion of love that grows out of one's own wretchedness.

Misery can lead the consciousness of man in two directions—he can try to forget about it or he can do something to relieve it. Through the first approach a man may feel some happiness, some pleasure, but it is transitory because it is not possible to forget about the underlying unhappiness for long. What is popularly known as love is exactly this sort of thing—a state of intoxication, of infatuation, of forgetfulness. It springs out of one's misery and is nothing more than a way to forget it.

The love I speak of as non-violence is the outcome of real happiness. It does not alleviate one's misery, it only happens when one's misery is gone. It is not intoxication, but wakefulness.

The consciousness which chooses the second direction, relief from misery, moves towards the essence of authentic love. When a man is happy inside, love flowers in him. In fact happiness on the inside becomes love on the outside. They are two aspects of the same feeling. Happiness is an experience of the self, and those who approach a happy man can feel the emanations of his love. Happiness is at the center; love is on the circumference.

This love does not require a relationship for its expression, it is the innate nature of the self. As light pours from the sun, love flows from the self. It has no relation with the outside world at all, nor does it aspire to any. It is totally free. This love I call non-violence.

If a man is in misery he is in a violent state; if he is happy he is non-violent. No one ever commits non-violence. It is not an action. It is existential; it refers to being. It is not a change in one's conduct, it is a change in one's self. The important question is not what I do, it is what I am.

Everyone must ask himself whether he is miserable or happy. Everything depends on one's answer to this basic inquiry. But we have to look beyond outward appearances. One must strip oneself naked to perceive the reality, to look clearly, to see without self-deception. But when a man lifts the veils that covers his self he only sees darkness and misery. He becomes afraid. He wants to run, to hide. But those who mask their misery out of fear will never attain happiness. Misery is to be removed, not hidden. And to remove misery, it has to be exposed. This perception is penance; this insight is atonement. Disguising one's misery leads to the world; perceiving one's misery leads to the soul.

What we know as life is nothing more than an illusion, an hallucination. Success is our measure for life. We say a man has made a success of his life when he has succeeded in forgetting his underlying misery through the intoxication of wealth, of fame or of position. But the real truth of the matter is something totally different. These kinds of people have not attained to life at all, they have lost it. By forgetting their misery they are committing suicide.

Becoming aware of one's misery is planting the seed of understanding in the soul. Misery contains the essence of awakening within it. One who does not try to escape from himself will awaken into a new consciousness, fresh and unprecedented. He will become the witness to an inner revolution that will transform him entirely. Within himself he will see the darkness dissolving and he will discover that light pervades his entire consciousness. In this light he will come to know himself for the first time. Then he will realize, for the first time, who he is.

When a man can feel the urge for awareness beginning to pierce through his misery, his self-awakening has begun. Only those who face the extremes of their misery finally transcend it. To know the truth requires this kind of courage.

Knowing who I am is knowing the truth. And then all the pain is gone. Misery is nothing but ignorance of one's self. When the self is discovered, one lives in consciousness and bliss. This is *Brahman;* this is God. To know the self, to know God, is to know the truth. To know the truth is to attain happiness. When truth is attained, love and happiness flower in one's inner being. Happiness within becomes non-violence without.

Non-violence is a result of the experience of truth. And then the fragrance of non-violence spreads from one's being on the four winds.

Love is freedom. Even the bonds of love are freedom. The man who binds himself with the infinite bonds of infinite love becomes free. So I say, don't seek freedom—seek love.

More times than not the search for freedom leads to the chain of egoism, but the search for love cannot even begin before the ego has been destroyed. The search for love means the death of the ego, and the annihilation of the ego is freedom itself.

The ego dreams of possessing the world. It is afraid of death so it even begins to dream of triumphing over salvation. The ego exists in the race for worldly things and it will also continue to exist in the race for spiritual salvation. The man who does not understand this will fall into the valley of self-deception.

The slavery and bondage of this world coexist with the ego. Isn't the ego slavery itself? Isn't the ego the birthplace of all bondage? I ask, how can the seeds of salvation root in that soil?

What can be more absurd, more stupid, than the desire of the egoist for salvation? For salvation, it is not the ego that has to be liberated, it is we ourselves who have to be freed from the ego. That is why egoists are not afraid of renunciation, of self-sacrifice, of religion, of perfect knowledge, of salvation—but are afraid of love.

The ego can escape in renunciation, in self-sacrifice or in the hope of salvation, but it cannot escape in love. Love is not the ego's salvation. It can never be. Love is complete and total liberation from the ego. Forever.

Somewhere Dostoevsky has a character say, "I wish to assure you that my love for mankind is increasing every day, but at the same time my love for my associates is decreasing."

How easy it is to love mankind but how difficult it is to love men! And perhaps the less a man loves his fellow men the more he loves mankind! We do not love ourselves and so this attitude suits us quite well. This is how we escape our duty to love ourselves and how we avoid any remorse that could rise out of this self-deception. This is the selfsame reason those who profess to love humanity are always so hard-hearted, so ruthless and cruel. Mass murder can be carried out with no compunction whatsoever in the name of this love and concern for humanity.

I have no wish to placate you with false, hollow and worthless words exhorting you to love mankind. The so-called religions have said these things to you for generations. I am here to urge you to love real men, to love your fellow beings—not mankind but the men who live and work around you. Humanity is just a word; mankind is just a label. You cannot find humanity or mankind anywhere. And so humanity is easy to love because the only thing you have to do is mouth a few platitudes.

The problem centers around real men, around men like you, around men who walk on the earth beside you. To love them is nothing short of penance; it is a great atonement. To love them is a great spiritual discipline; it is a noble task indeed. To love them you have to go through a revolution that shakes you to your very roots. It is to such a love that I call you. This alone is what real religion is all about.

I once said somewhere that I was an emperor and someone asked, "Where is your crown?"

I replied, "It is not on my head but in my heart. It is not made of precious stones but of virtuous thoughts and deeds. It does not glitter with diamonds and emeralds but sparkles with the lights of knowledge, peace and love. Any emperor who wants to wear this crown has to become a beggar first."

Haven't you noticed how often we search in far off places for what is really close at hand? This is the case with happiness. Understand where happiness exists. That is where you will find it, not where you are seeking it.

A pair of travelers took shelter for a few days in a very squalid hut. One of them grumbled and complained about the dirt and the mess, while the other man immediately set about cleaning the place. He found immense satisfaction in this labor of love. The same hut made one man quite miserable and another very happy.

Is there a greater satisfaction to be found in life than undertaking a task with love? Is anything more gratifying than serving others? No, nothing at all.

If you seek lasting pleasure in life try to make your worldly abode as clean and tidy as possible and leave it more beautiful than you found it for those who come after. You will always find happiness in the creation of beauty.

What has happened to mankind? It always surprises me

how we manage to keep on living despite so much misery, despite such a general sense of futility, despite such utter boredom.

When I look into the soul of man I see only darkness; when I ponder his existence I find nothing but death. Man is alive but has no concept of life at all. Life has become a burden to him. Without beauty, peace, happiness and illumination, life is life in name only. Have we totally forgotten how to live? The animals, birds, and even the plants seem to exist in greater harmony with each other than man is able to do.

Some say the prosperity of mankind is increasing by leaps and bounds. God save us from this kind of prosperity! This is not prosperity, it is just a cover-up for our poverty, for our weaknesses. Prosperity and power are ways to escape from one's self. It fills my heart with sorrow and pain when I see the inner poverty and anguish that lies beneath the mantle of this so-called prosperity.

Anyone who gives this the slightest thought will easily realize that material affluence is only a way to conceal inner poverty. Those who suffer from a sense of inferiority are the ones who hanker after position and wealth. To escape from his inner being, from what he really is, a man tries to project another being, another personality on the outside. What a man pretends to be outwardly is generally the opposite of what he is really like. This is why the proud appear to be humble, the sensual become celibate, the poor seek affluence and the wealthy talk of renunciation. It is foolishness to say the prosperity of mankind has increased; the reverse is what has actually happened.

The richer a man becomes on the outside, the poorer he becomes on the inside. In his race for outer riches he totally forgets about the attainment of inner wealth. A man really grows, really develops when his consciousness rises to the heights of beauty, harmony and truth.

I would like to know whether you are satisfied with

material things or whether you want to develop your consciousness. The man who is satisfied with the outside world will always be basically unhappy. This kind of life is simply one of convenience. Convenience is only the absence of trouble, whereas real satisfaction is the attainment of happiness.

What does your heart say? What is the greatest desire of your life? Have you ever asked yourself these questions? If not, then let me ask you now. If you were to ask me I would reply that I wish to attain to that state where nothing further remains to be attained. Is this not the answer that pulsates in your innermost soul as well? I do not ask this question of you alone, I have also asked it of thousands and thousands of others.

It is my observation that all human hearts are the same and that their ultimate desire is also the same. The soul wants happiness, perfect and pure happiness, because only then will all desires end. As long as desire exists misery exists, because with desire there can be no peace.

The total absence of desire brings happiness. It also brings freedom and liberation, because whenever something is lacking there are both limits and dependency. Only when nothing at all is lacking is there the possibility of total freedom. Freedom brings happiness. And happiness is salvation.

The desire for total happiness and for ultimate freedom lies dormant in everyone. It is in the form of a seed. It is like a seed that contains a tree within it. In the same way, the fulfillment of man's ultimate desire is hidden in his very nature. In its perfectly developed state, it is our nature to be happy, to be free. Our real nature is the only thing that is true, and only perfecting it can bring complete satisfaction.

The man who does not seek to fulfill his own nature mistakenly thinks prosperity will alleviate his misery. But material wealth can never fill his inner emptiness. And so, even when a man attains everything possible in the world he still feels that he has missed out on something. His innermost being remains empty. As Buddha once said, "Desire is difficult to fulfill."

It is strange that no matter what a man may attain he is never satisfied, that even after he has accomplished his goal he yearns for still greater achievements. And so the poverty of beggars and emperors is the same. At this level, there is no difference between them at all.

No matter what gains a man makes in the outer world they are unstable. They can be lost, destroyed at any time, and in the end death claims them. So it is not surprising that one's inner heart is never fulfilled by these sorts of things, by things that can so easily be taken away. This kind of prosperity will never give a man a sense of security, no matter how strenuously he pursues it. What really happens is that a man has to provide security for the things he has acquired.

It must be clearly understood that outward power and prosperity can never eradicate one's sense of want, one's insecurity or one's fear. Self-deception is the only way to camouflage these feelings. Prosperity is an intoxicant; it hides the reality of life. And this type of forgetfulness is far worse than poverty itself because it prevents a man from doing anything to rid himself of his real poverty.

Poverty is not caused by the absence of any material object, nor by the lack of power or prosperity, because even if one becomes rich and powerful it is still there. Do you not see the poverty of those who seem to have everything? Have your burdens ever been lightened by your material possessions?

My friends, there is a great difference between prosperity and the illusion of prosperity. All external wealth, power and security are but shadows of the real riches that exist within you. The basic reason for this feeling of poverty is not the non-attainment of anything external, it comes from having turned away from the self. And so this feeling cannot be eradicated by anything outer, it can only be erased from within.

The nature of the self is bliss. It is not a quality of the self, it is its very essence. Happiness is not a relationship with the self, the self is bliss itself. They are just two names for the same truth.

What we call the self is bliss from the experiential point of view, so be careful not to confuse what you know as happiness with real happiness. Real happiness is the self itself. When this has been attained the search for all else ceases. Achieving a false kind of happiness only intensifies the search, and the fear of losing this so-called happiness disturbs one's peace of mind. Water that increases one's thirst is not really water at all. Christ said, "Come, let me lead you to the well whose water will quench your thirst forever."

We continuously mistake pleasure for happiness. Pleasure is only a shadow, only the reflection of happiness. But most people exist in the illusion that this phantom of happiness is what life is all about. And naturally they are ultimately disillusioned. It is like mistaking the reflection of the moon in a lake for the moon itself and trying to grab hold of it. The deeper a man dives into a lake to find the moon the further and further away he goes from the real moon.

And in the same way, in their search for pleasure, people move further and further away from happiness. This path only leads to misery. Do you see the truth in what I am saying? Surely your own life must bear witness to the fact that the race after pleasure only leads to unhappiness. But this is quite natural. A reflection is outwardly identical to the original, but it is not the real thing at all.

All pleasures hold out the promise of happiness and give one the assurance that they are happiness itself—but pleasure is only the shadow of happiness. Accepting pleasure as happiness can only result in failure and in feelings of remorse. How can I catch you by trying to grab your shadow? And even if I did catch your shadow, what would I have in my hands?

Let me also remind you that a reflection is always opposite to what it is reflecting. If I stand in front of a mirror my reflected image is exactly opposite to the way I am really standing. And this is also true of pleasure. It is just the reflection of happiness. Happiness is an inner quality; pleasure is an outer manifestation, only existing in the material world.

Only happiness is bliss. Continue your pursuit of pleasure and you will discover for yourselves the truth of what I am saying. All pleasure ends in misery.

But what something becomes at the end it was at the beginning as well. Because your vision does not penetrate deeply enough, what you should be able to perceive at the beginning is only apparent to you at the end. It is just not possible that what is revealed at the end of some event was not also present at the outset. The end is but a development of the beginnings. What was hidden in the beginning is manifest at the end.

But you see things in reverse order—if, indeed, you see anything at all. Over and over again you keep on following paths that lead you to misery, pain and remorse. Why does man do the same things over and over again when he ends up in misery every time? Why? Perhaps it is because he sees no other path before him. That is why I say your sight is dim and distorted; that is why I question whether you have any sight at all.

There are very few people who actually use their eyes. Everyone has two eyes, but in spite of them most people are blind. The man who does not see within himself has not yet used his eyes. Only the man who has seen the self can really say he has used his eyes. If a man is not able to see his self, will he ever really be able to see anything?

My friends, your ability to see only begins when you see

the self. When a man has seen his self he begins to move in the direction of happiness. He turns towards pleasure no longer. And others can feel this change in him. The direction of pleasure is from one's self towards the world; the direction of happiness, from the world towards the self.

Virtue is happiness.

One day a friend and I were walking through a field when we noticed some farmers sowing seeds and singing merrily at their work. Their songs delighted me, but the friend with me was very gloomy. He was planning to become a sannyasin.

"Come," I said, "let's go watch the farmers sowing and listen to their songs."

I speak the truth when I tell you that the whole of existence is one vast field. And those who wish to sow the seeds of love, truth and sacrifice must remember that the farmer never sows seeds with tears in his eyes. Only sorrow and misery are sown with tears; and the harvest will also be of tears. The way to sow seeds is to the accompaniment of joyful songs. The attitude with which the seeds are sown permeates them.

Taking sannyas with a downcast heart will only lead to sorrow. Real sannyas is born out of joy and hope.

The young son of a friend of mine asked his father, "When will I be big enough to do what I want to all the time?"

His father replied, "My dear son, I don't know. I have never seen anyone get that big."

I was also there and I said, "I know the secret. I know how it is possible to grow big enough to do what you always want to do. The way to do this is to love whatsoever you do. That is getting big."

I once met a happy man and discovered the secret of

his happiness. He did not worry about finding work that suited his tastes but knew how to love the task that fell to his lot.

What can I give to you? Shall I present you with a precious gem? No, after all it is only a stone. A beautiful flower? No, I won't give you a flower that will fade away. I shall give you the overflowing love from my own heart. It is not hard like stone or transient like a flower. The love from a man's heart is the perfume of God. It is the divine music that thrills the listener to his very core.

The realization of truth, the knowledge of the soul, is not a matter for intellectual discussion or mental deliberation. Only those who remain worthy and receptive through constant effort will be able to comprehend truth.

Our knowledge of the physical world is limited by our capacity to know, but truth is not limited to the extent of our knowledge at all. You must have noticed that no matter what you come to know, something else always remains to be known. The frontiers of truth are always beyond the scope of our knowledge. It does not necessarily follow that what we know is true; truth is much too vast for the reach of our comprehension. It is incomplete, imperfect. The man who thinks the limits of his knowledge and those of truth are the same, gets stuck there; he is not able to move ahead any further.

Even as far as the objective world is concerned our knowledge is restricted. It is limited to what we perceive through our senses. To a blind man there is no such thing as light in his world. You will never find anyone with a true concept of light in a community of blind men. They can never completely understand darkness either, because the experience of light is an essential factor in understanding darkness, in comprehending the absence of light. If a man is deaf, sound is a total stranger to him. The only part of existence that is revealed to us is that which is intelligible to our senses.

Our world is relative to our abilities of perception. But we cannot truly say that this is all the real world is. The frontiers of the world we experience and those of the real world are not the same at all. We restrict our world to ourselves.

Many worlds exist within this one world. There are as many worlds as there are individuals in each of the different species. And on an even more minute level of examination, there are as many worlds as there are living organisms. In this one world the number of individual worlds is countless because the number of beings who know, perceive and experience are countless as well. The universe is subdivided into as many imaginary worlds as there are separate cogs in a wheel. On a lower level than man there are quite a large number of animals whose sense faculties are far inferior to those of men. We know that many of them cannot see or hear. Some cannot taste; some cannot smell. These creatures do not have the total experience of sight, sound, touch, taste and smell that man has. The realm of a man's experience extends only as far as his senses allow, and it would be sheer ignorance to try to restrict the real world to that which our limited knowledge is able to perceive.

Had we been blessed with more senses we would most likely have extended our world of experience still further. This is what the inventions of science have allowed us to do. I only bring this up to illustrate that our knowledge is relative to our capacity to know, to the abilities of our senses to grasp and to understand things.

What is true of the visible world is also true of the invisible one. Whenever people ask me, "Does the soul exist?" I reply with this question, "Do you have the ability to experience the soul, to know God?" The real question is one of your ability, not of the existence or non-existence of God. If you have the capacity, then you will surely experience those truths that are now beyond your reach; as long as you do not possess that ability those truths will always appear false to you. If some unknown fear forces you to accept certain things they are not real truths at all. Real truth only comes from your own experience.

Twenty-five centuries ago a seeker after truth fell at the feet of Buddha, beseeching his guidance. "How do you see truth?" he asked. "What I have seen," Buddha replied, "will not help you much. Your sight is not developed enough to see the truth. Whatsoever I say you will misunderstand, because you cannot realize the reality of what you have not yet experienced.

"Once I was in a village," Buddha continued, "and they brought a blind man to me. They asked me to convince him of the existence of light. I told them their request was utter foolishness since the man lacked the instrument of vision, since he had no sight. I told them they should take him to a doctor who could treat his eyes.

"Where there are eyes to see, there is light."

I say the same thing to you. You need not be concerned with truth; your concern should be with whether or not you have the sight necessary to see beyond the objective world.

You only see matter, and whatever exists beyond the world of matter is outside the range of your experience completely. Its vibrations, its waves, its impulses fail to have any impact on you. When you meet a friend your contact with him is confined to his physical being. You do not come into contact with his soul. When you look at a tree in your yard, your perception stops at its outer physical limits; you have no access to its inner soul. Why is this? It is because a man who has had no close contact with his own soul, who has had no experience of the vital energy that exists within it, cannot hope to recognize or realize the presence of the universal soul that pervades all things.

The question is not one of God, of truth or of light, it

is one of vision. In my view, religion is more a remedy than a subject for deliberation.

If we goad our slumbering energies into action then fresh vistas of experience will open up before us and we will have at our disposal the knowledge of those things that give real meaning, direction and purpose to life. As one's sensitivity becomes finer and one's receptivity grows keener the world of matter recedes into the background, the tangible world falls away. Finally a point is reached when the universe ceases to appear as an object of perception on a gross level and only the pure and unclouded vision of God, of the universal soul remains. But to achieve this you have to ready yourself. The farmer cultivates the soil before he sows the seeds, and those who seek the realization of God must prepare their soil as well. They must tune themselves within to hear the outer symphony that permeates all of existence.

Because our eyes perceive it, the sun is visible to us. The sun makes an impression on us because we have the necessary organ of sight and the necessary capacity for receptivity. When I speak to you my voice enters you and produces a responsive echo because you have a sense organ that enables sound to reach you.

God never ceases to exist, not even for a single moment. Our breath is his; even our limits are his—but you do not realize it because you bar his entrance with your own hands.

There are three stages in the process of keeping this entrance open, three vital keys that can bring about your merger with God. I am going to talk about them now. I shall tell you how to generate that power in yourself by which the gross dissolves and the subtle comes into view, by which material objects vanish and the universal soul becomes visible. The keys I am going to talk about will take you from the visible to the invisible, from the gross to the subtle, from the world to God.

The first key is self-love. You have to love yourself. This

love has to be unhampered and unconditional. The man who cannot love himself is incapable of loving others. Without love it is impossible to move beyond the physical, beyond the world. The power of love is the only power in man that is not of this world. The door to God can only be opened by the key of love.

Let me interject a note of caution here. You may find it strange to hear me advocating love of oneself since the traditional scriptures are so against it. Directly or indirectly, the precepts and injunctions laid down by the scriptures promote self-hostility. I ask, is it possible to suppress the self without being hostile and antagonistic towards it? The temple of righteousness and virtue has been built on this very conflict within oneself, on the struggle between loving one's self and hating one's self. No one should be surprised to find that his life, if he has based it on this kind of thing, has turned out to be grotesque and uninspired.

The beauty that is life will never reach fruition through self-conflict, because such a man is simply draining his energies, simply wasting those powers which could have made his life a success had they been used correctly. Such a man ties his hands behind his back and then tries to make them fight with each other. Who will conquer whom? Neither success nor defeat is possible. All that is possible is struggle, the eventual depletion of one's energies and ultimately, death. And since all of a man's faculties are conspiring together to bring about his self-destruction his life becomes odious to him. He feels lethargic; everything seems futile. Beauty, truth and bliss can only be attained if a man is engaged in the creative cultivation of his self.

And sermons on the suppression of the self will never produce any note of inner harmony either. They only generate discord and lead to misery, to anxiety, to cares and woes.

The person who is fraught with inner conflict, who fights with himself, who splits himself into friend and foe, who makes enemies of some of his faculties and pits others against them, actually creates a living hell for himself. And the saddest thing of all is that this kind of life is what has been considered a religious life, what has been praised as a life of virtue!

In my view, a life of virtue is a totally different state of affairs. It is not a life of inner conflict but one of inner peace, inner harmony, inner music. It is not a life of self-hatred, it is a life of concord, a life of integration. And those who wish to attain to the innate harmony of the soul have to lay the foundation for this at the very beginning. Starting out on a basis of conflict, no one can ever hope to achieve a state of bliss that is devoid of conflict. It is just not possible. In the beginning, the end is already present.

Remember, the first stage is infinitely more important than the final one. God is the perfection of harmony, and if you wish to merge with that divine symphony it is essential you have some semblance of accord, some note of harmony within you to begin with. And how is this note of harmony to be produced? It will certainly never be produced by treating yourself with contempt; it will never be achieved by self-reproach or self-hostility. It can only be produced by loving yourself. The most basic prerequisites for a life of spiritual endeavor are love of oneself and inner harmony.

This will most likely confuse you. You have often been advised to suppress things inside you but I assure you that there is nothing whatsoever in you that requires suppression or uprooting. There are certain drives within every man that should be harnessed—not eradicated; there are certain forces that must be awakened, that must be loved—not suppressed. They only need to be controlled and directed along their proper course. But anyone who looks upon these drives with hostility will never succeed in transforming them. A man of understanding is even able to transform poison into nectar but one who has no understanding will turn nectar into poison for certain. To me, understanding is nectar; the lack of it, poison.

You must have noticed that we use decaying things as fertilizers, things with foul odors. A short while ago someone gave me a bouquet of fresh flowers. How fragrant they are! But when their perfume first stirred my heart I also remembered the source of their fragrance. As it traveled through the seeds and the stems of the plants that produced these exquisite blossoms, the foul smell of manure had been transformed into this enchanting aroma. If you simply heap manure all over your yard the stench will corrupt the whole atmosphere. But if you spread it on your garden the air around your house will smell of sweetness. What you call a foul smell is only the undeveloped form of what you call fragrance. They are not hostile to each other. A discordant bar of music is nothing but the undeveloped and disarranged form of the same notes that can blend so easily and harmoniously into a beautiful piece of music.

Nothing in life deserves to be smashed or annihilated, but there is much in life that should be transformed, that should be purified, that should be elevated.

There are certain energies in man which are neutral by nature. They are neither favorable nor adverse, neither good nor bad. They are simply neutral. The way in which we use them gives them their form.

One's sexual potentiality, the thrust of passion—against which so-called spiritual leaders have waged unending war for aeons—is neutral. It is a potential. It is this energy, when transformed, that evolves into divine energy, into a godly force. It is the primordial creative power.

What happens with your sex energy depends on how you use it. What it can become does not depend on it alone, but on your understanding and on how you live your life. Have you not observed that it becomes *brahmacharya*, the state of celibacy when it is transformed? *Brahmacharya* is not hostile to passion; *brahmacharya* is the purification, the transcendence, the sublimation of passion. In the same way, the energy that manifests itself in violence becomes peace, serenity and tranquility. It is only a question of transformation.

In life, the process of creation is of far greater importance than the process of destruction. If you can comprehend this fact clearly then the notion of struggling with yourself or of being hostile to yourself will almost never arise in you. The creation of an integrated self is only possible in an atmosphere of self-love.

I would also like to add that the physical body should not be excluded from this love. Give the body abundant love and it becomes alive, vital; its slumbering potential is awakened. But please remember I am not speaking of debauchery or of abstinence. Neither the debauchee nor the abstainer loves his body in the way I mean.

The debauchee shows his contempt for his body through his lack of self-restraint. Out of his disdain for his body he is inclined to abuse it. The abstainer has recoiled to the other extreme, but he is equally hostile to the body. Of course, the two have gone in different directions. The abstainer harasses his body in the name of self-control, in the name of renunciation; the other harasses his in the name of licentiousness. But neither feels any thankfulness to the body; neither has any love for the body. One of the characteristic features of a healthy mental equilibrium is a positive and a loving attitude towards the body. Harassing the body in any way is an indication of a mind that is unhealthy, of a mind that is sick.

It all boils down to the fact that there are two kinds of mental infirmities that can plague a man. One is unrestrained enjoyment; the other, thoughtless renunciation. This is why the libertine can so easily make an about-face and dive into renunciation so fully. What a shame he cannot just stop in the middle! It is very unfortunate it is so easy to proceed from one illness to another.

These unbalanced people have taught us much. They have taught us that the body is an enemy, that we have to fight with it. And the religions have become obsessed with the body because of these harmful teachings. But this is to be expected; to be opposed to the body requires focusing a great deal of attention on it.

I say that if you wish to go beyond the body, to rise above the body, do not fight with it, do not allow any hostility towards it to grow in you. Love your body. Seek its friendship. The body is not your enemy; it is an instrument, a wonderful tool to be used. You have to stretch out the hand of friendship to anything you wish to use, and above all else you have to extend a friendly hand towards your own body. It is a marvelous example of God's expertise as a skilled craftsman. It is a ladder laden with secrets that can lead you to God.

Only a madman fights with a ladder instead of climbing its rungs, but unfortunately we live in a world of such madmen. Beware of them. It is very difficult to assess the havoc they have wrought amongst us.

You have no idea of the thousands of secrets that lie hidden in this body that has been naturally bestowed upon you. If you were able to learn the secrets of your own body alone you would possess the key to the endless mystery of the universal soul. This body is so small and yet how many wonderful mysteries it conceals! The mind is hidden in the body. The soul is hidden in the mind. God is hidden in the soul.

A certain sage was about to die. He took his leave of his disciples and devotees and then stood up, folded his hands and said, "Oh, my beloved body, it is you who led me to God. I thank you for it. Without you I would not have accomplished anything, and yet I subjected you to untold sufferings, to pain, to work for which I gave you nothing in return. I am deeply indebted to you, for the help you gave me was endless. At this hour of farewell I beg your pardon. For all my actions against you, for all my forgetfulness towards you, I humbly ask you to excuse me. But for you it would have been impossible for me to reach God!"

You have to see your body in this way. Such an attitude of thankfulness, this kind of loving zeal is necessary. The sage said, "Oh, my beloved body!" And these words bestir a wonderful feeling of bliss within me. Would not the same kind of sympathy and understanding for your body also brighten your life? May I inquire if you have ever looked upon your body with such an overflow of love and sympathy? Have you ever felt blessed by its acts of service? Have you ever told it of your gratitude? If not, what great ingratitude! What an unbecoming oversight! What discourtesy you have shown it!

Your attitude towards the body must be one of deep understanding and sympathy. You must have enough awareness to look upon it with friendliness and to protect it. It is your fellow traveler on a long, uphill journey; it shares your joys and your sorrows. It is an instrument, a means, a ladder. And so to me it is impossible for any man with even a single iota of sense to be cruel to it, to enter into any sort of conflict with it whatsoever.

As ill luck would have it, there have been and still are in the world many men of distorted vision whose high-handedness, violence, unrelenting suppression and harassment of their own bodies have provoked such feelings of sadness and remorse in us that we have eventually sounded the fervent prayer, "Oh, God, save mankind from such spirituality!" Activities of such magnitude, of such seriousness, only go to show the total lack of intelligence in such men. But unfortunately their evil influences still linger on, still haunt mankind even today. Let us all keep away from such sick and perverted sermonizers. These kinds of pulpiteers do not deserve to be revered, they need to be healed. I certainly hope we will be able to cure them one day.

As I have explained before, this hostility to the body is a reaction to the resulting weakness, dissatisfaction and sense of failure that come from unrestrained sensual indulgence. And so you blame your innocent body for your own sinfulness. I appeal to you to remain alert to any kind of pain inflicting self-denials based on this hostility to the physical body. Because you have played havoc with your body, you may find yourself tempted by various forms of self-discipline.

If a man sees another man's wealth and grows jealous or another's beauty and becomes envious and plucks out his eyes because of it, I would call him a madman. Your eyes don't ask you to become jealous or to become passionate; they don't tell you to become anything at all. The eyes are simply ready to carry out your bidding and only in the manner in which you care to use them. The physical body is your slave; it is your full-time servant. Wherever you wish to take it, it will follow you. If you want to go to hell it is ready to go to hell, if you want to go to heaven it is ready to follow you there. The real question is not of the body, it is of your volition.

Don't ever forget that the physical body just tags along in the wake of the will. You would be committing a great mistake if you were to torture and victimize or even to destroy the body instead of modifying your will. Harassment of the body is a form of violence, and I do not approve of violence, either to the self or to the body. I advocate self-love; I know of nothing more foolish than self-violence.

What I mean by self-love has nothing whatsoever to do with being egocentric. An individual who is centered in the ego never loves himself; if he loved himself he would be free of the ego. And nothing is more diabolical, dispiriting or disheartening than egoism. The ego centered man is the type who indulges in self-violence in the garb of a holy man, because there is no better way for the ego to attain such a great measure of nourishment and satisfaction than this. This is why you always find a kind of haughtiness and superiority in so-called models of virtue, self-styled saints and half-blown sages. They are egotistical because they believe they are saints; they believe they are saints because they are egotistical.

In the vast universe God has created it is just not possible for anything to be unfriendly or hostile to you. It is a different matter, however, how you use, do not use or misuse things. A man of understanding will turn a rock lying on the ground into a steppingstone while a man without understanding will make it a stumbling block. It is the way in which you look at things that matters in life. If one's vision is distorted it makes a tremendous difference. And if you start out by looking upon the physical body with hostility do not be surprised if it eventually turns against you and lets you down. Set out with the idea the body is your friend and it will be your friend forever.

If this hostility disappears, if this grudge against the body is dropped a great load is taken off the self. You are relieved of tension; you feel peaceful, at rest. Experiment with this yourselves. Remember that the body is only a medium, only a vehicle. On its own it does not lead you anywhere. Feel no ill will towards it. If you look upon it without bias or prejudice you will find that your heart will be naturally filled with thankful love and gratitude for the countless services it has silently rendered you for so long.

But do not stop with the body. Go deeper still. The physical body is only the starting point of our journey towards love of the self. If you move deeper you will encounter the mind. You have to love it too; you have to seek its friendship as well. Man is normally only aware of these two levels of his being—the body and the mind—but if you wish to rise above them or go deeper than them you have to learn how to use them.

Without a doubt, the campaign against the mind has been carried on with even greater intensity than the one against the body. From spiritual quarters the mind has been the central target for attack. We must free ourselves from this barrage of hostility. The mind is a power, an energy, and like all others is a divine power. It is a highly developed, very subtle energy. Criticizing it, being hostile to it, or abusing it are actions of sheer stupidity, fraught with fatal consequences.

You must realize that even today man is not completely acquainted with all of the mind's mysteries. He really does not know how to use his mental energies at all. At present the mind is more or less in the position electricity once was. There was a time when electricity was only a destructive agent, but today it is being employed in colossal creative projects. When man understands his own mental powers in their entirety, it will usher in the most creative and blessed age in human history.

The mind is a reservoir of limitless potential, but those who oppose the mind are clashing with their own potentialities and seeking annihilation at their own hands. They criticize and oppose the mind, they say, because of its unsteadiness, because of the fickleness of its nature. But fickleness is a sign of life! Only those who are afraid of life and eagerly awaiting death welcome sluggishness and unchangeability. They see peace and quiet in these things. But let me warn you: the peace that grows out of lethargy is quite unreal and sluggishness of mind is very self-destructive. What appears to be peace is nothing but the silence and desolation of the cemetery. The restlessness of life is infinitely preferable to the stillness of the graveyard. It is not the forced quiet that comes from suppressing the mind but the serene peace that evolves on its own out of a total understanding of the mind that is worthwhile, that is worth achieving. Only such a peace leads to greater heights. A deathlike silence leads to the earthly, to the material, and not to God.

You need a lively peacefulness, an active silence. Only something that is vital and alive can be a doorway to a life that is sublime. This is why I do not approve of suppressing the mind or of any effort to subdue its fickleness as a way to attain peace. Never allow yourselves to sink into such a mire of stupidity and stagnation. There is already enough sluggishness in the world. Please be kind enough not to add to it any further.

I am for a mind that is both lively and peaceful at the same time. And as I pointed out earlier, the only peace of mind that can be alive and vital is the one you acquire without losing the mind's fickleness. Perhaps "mobility" would be a better word than fickleness. Nevertheless if you wish to go somewhere a calm lake is useless; a rushing river flowing towards the sea is what you need.

With mobility of mind a man can reach the universal soul, he can reach God himself. So never be sorry your mind is fickle. Never censure it for this; never look upon it as an enemy because of this. Rather, be thankful. But for the mind's fickleness, but for the mind's mobility you would have become a stagnant pool long ago. If your mind were not fickle you would have ended up sitting atop some rubbish heap somewhere absorbed in some intellectual exercise. If the mind were not fickle, the greedy would hanker forever after the objects of their greed, the deluded after the objects of their delusion, the sensual after the objects of their sensuality. And then the path to God would be closed to them forever. It is because the mind is fickle it is able to keep eliminating all its false gods and to keep moving ahead. Since the mind is mobile it does not allow us to remain stationary, to become stale; it goads us on and on.

There is a great and mysterious secret behind this fickleness of the mind and I wish to share it with you: unless and until the mind finds a final resting place that suits it, it will never allow you any peace, any rest. That is why it is fickle. And the mind's final resting place is in God. That is when it sheds its fickleness, never before. See just how kind and benevolent your mind is to you! If it were not so changeable you would get stuck in some kind of worldly trap and would then shelve forever all your attempts to reach God. Do not criticize or abuse your mind for its fickleness. Accept its changeability as a great favor and learn how to utilize it.

Remember, if your mind cannot remain steady, if it fails to stay fixed on something it is due to an error on your part, to a transgression for which you must accept the blame. That is why the mind does not want to remain in that situation, in that space. For example, you try your utmost to concentrate but the mind refuses to cooperate. That is your mistake. By its very nature the mind is inconstant. It is trying to tell you this, to remind you of this. But instead of taking the hint you treat the mind as your enemy!

Let me tell you a tale I have heard.

Once upon a time, when Egypt was ruled by a great pharaoh, an equally great saint lived in a small Egyptian village. He was highly respected, even by the pharaoh himself.

One day, without warning, the pharaoh paid the holy man a visit. He had come to invite the sage to his palace. When the pharaoh arrived at the hut he found that the sage had gone out. Although one of his young disciples was present he did not recognize the pharaoh because of the simple garments he was wearing.

The young man invited the pharaoh to sit down on a ridge at the edge of the field while he went into the village to fetch the holy man. Not only did the pharaoh refuse to sit, he began to pace up and down. Noticing this, the disciple suggested he might prefer to sit under a shady tree. The pharaoh still would not sit down, but continued to pace up and down under the tree. A little puzzled, the disciple then invited the pharaoh to go into the sage's hut and sit there. Still the visitor would not oblige him. He entered the hut but continued pacing back and forth.

The young man went to fetch the holy man in a very

perplexed state of mind. On the way back he told his Master of the very odd behavior of the visitor from the city. "My son," the sage said, "he is our pharaoh. Neither in nor around the hut is there a place to sit that befits his status. That is why he is pacing up and down."

Your mind is restless for exactly the same reason. It cannot find a place worthy enough to be its eternal abode. It is your duty to find it a throne that befits its dignity. But instead of doing this, you fight with it because of its fickleness, you argue with it because it keeps pacing up and down. Have you ever thought about the places to sit you have offered it? Can you really expect it to sit in one of those? My friends, the mind is doing you a favor by its fickleness. You may continue to ask it to sit down in all sorts of places, but it will not sit down. The mind cannot and will not sit anywhere but in God. That is its throne. That is its unlimited generosity to you.

Don't forget that the so-called fickleness of your mind is really of great help to you. Understand well that if you cannot get it to settle in one place it is because that place is unworthy of it. I might also add that any success you may have in pinning it down in a place unworthy of it amounts to nothing at all. No sooner do you succeed in forcing it to sit somewhere than it gets up and runs off somewhere else after a while. This drifting here and there, this fluttering hither and thither, you will continue until it reaches its point of ultimate rest. And that point of ultimate rest is God.

Many people say the ability to concentrate the mind is essential if one aspires to the realization of God, but I say that once God is realized the mind will then have the necessary concentration. People say the mind has to be kept fixed so that God can be realized, but I say that where God is realized is the point where the mind becomes still, where the mind comes to rest.

The mind rushes naturally towards whatever promises

it pleasure and never towards something that may cause it pain, but the moment the prospect of pleasure disappears the mind drops its objective and veers off towards something else. This is why you will never find the mind focused on any one object in particular.

For example, get ten thousand rupees together. At first the mind will figure pleasure awaits it here—but the very next moment it moves on. It has hardly sat down before it is disillusioned. Amass ten *lakhs*, ten times ten thousand rupees, and you will again experience the same disillusionment. Even ten billion rupee notes covering you from head to toe will not make any difference at all.

You cannot curb the mind's rambling tendency to keep rushing, as I said before, towards the place that affords it a hint of pleasure. But as soon as the prospect evaporates it flees. It is only the tiniest bit constant as long as the spell of promised pleasure lasts. But the day it gets a glimpse of real pleasure, of the pleasure that never ends, it drops its wanderlust completely and is filled with absolute peace, with total stillness. Therefore I will never advise you to try to enforce any fixedness of mind whatsoever. A forced steadiness causes sluggishness and leads to stagnation rather than to the attainment of the ultimate goal.

When that final goal is reached, the mind becomes steadfast and remains steadfast on its own. Unfortunately, this fact has been misunderstood. It has given rise to the notion that the ability to keep the mind still is necessary if one is ever to reach the journey's end. This is as silly as putting the cart before the horse. The fact that your eyes remain closed when you are asleep does not necessarily guarantee you will fall asleep every time you close your eyes.

My advice to you is to steer your mind in the direction from which the perfume of real pleasure comes, to lead your mind slowly and lovingly towards the abode of absolute happiness. Set your mind on real bliss and the mind is sure to follow. But use no force, or compulsion—not even out of forgetfulness. Contrary to what you might expect, force will only provoke resistance. What you prohibit becomes inviting; what you forbid becomes attractive. If you show any inclination to refrain from doing something the mind will take to it with added gusto. This is natural; this is the way the mind is. It is your ignorance of this simple fact that involves you in so many things that normally you could easily avoid.

The fundamental thing to remember is that the mind is not your enemy. Don't suppress its tendencies, but understand them and guide them with love, with common sense. Only that which is worthwhile can survive in the light of reason, in the clarity of common sense.

An unforgettable rule of existence is contained in the phrase "*amor vincit omnia*"—love conquers all. Never think for a second you can vanquish anyone by hatred. It never happens. It is impossible to overcome those you hate, those you consider your enemies. You can only conquer those you love. So if you wish to master your mind you must love it. Only the path of love leads to victory. There is no other way.

So the first key, the first golden rule, is to love yourself. Let transformation, not suppression, be your guiding light. Allow no split within yourself. Marshal all you faculties into one single effort—into love.

All unity, all unification, is born out of love. If you are filled with an abundance of love for what you are, good or bad; if all hate and slander disappear from your mind; if you cease opposing yourself; if you stop finding yourself noble or contemptible and fall in love with all that you are, with you in your totality—then one compact and indivisible personality will form within you. This is what the formation of a personality is. Love is a cementing force. It amalgamates all the heterogeneous elements into one.

When all your different faculties have joined together into one unified whole a great and wonderful energy is created within you. The energy that was split, that was divided, that flowed in different directions and was simply wasted away becomes immense. It becomes astronomical in its synthesized form.

The wondrous achievement of this newfound energy, the outcome of this fusion, is that it has the capacity to transform things that you have always been unable to overcome in spite of constant effort, in spite of never ending struggle. The moment you love those insignificant things, be they failings you saw in yourself or whatever, they are transformed. This unification of personality is the foundation of self-transformation.

If you wish to improve yourself, to develop yourself, to uplift yourself, then you must become a single and unified whole. The man who is split into several pieces wastes all his energy pitting one piece against the other. He drains himself trying to control the pieces, trying to maintain the balance of power between them. There is no energy left over for the transformation of the self, for its purification. Only the man who loves himself and who is able to attain and retain this undivided and unsplit unity can build up that surplus energy needed for self-transformation.

Now we come to the second key you need to enable you to fly to God. As we have seen the first key is love of oneself—and the second key is love of others. You will never succeed in your progress towards the love that leads to God unless you have abundant goodwill, unbounded love, overflowing kindness and a heart filled with grace towards all living things.

Jesus Christ said, "When you go into church for your daily prayer and kneel down and raise your hands unto the Lord, if you remember that your neighbor is angry with you, first go to him and show him love. Leave God there and go to your neighbor. Love him and beg his pardon. Make peace with him first. How can he who has not yet succeeded in making peace with men succeed in making peace with himself and with the Lord?"

There is no way the person who refuses to love on the human plane can expect to be able to raise his prayer to the level of God.

A sage living in a certain village was once approached by a devotee who expressed the desire to realize God. He asked the holy man what he should do. Looking him up and down and probably getting a very complete picture of him, the sage said, "Well, my son, tell me first of all whether you love anyone. Then I may be able to give you some assistance."

The devotee, under the impression that earthly love was an automatic disqualification for those seeking God, said that he did not love anyone and that his sole purpose in life was to realize God. The holy man said, "My son, think well. Search your heart. Don't you love your wife, your children, you family or your friends?"

The devotee was emphatic, "No. I don't love anyone at all. I only wish to realize God."

The sage said nothing, but tears began to well up in his eyes. Surprised, the devotee said, "Master, why are you crying? Why don't you say something to me?"

The sage replied, "My son, if only you loved someone I could transform that into the love of God. But there is no love in you. And love leads to God; love is the direct route to heaven."

In the name of religion you have all been taught not to love anyone else! The teachings of these so-called religious people have just been food for your egos. These injunctions not to love anyone but God will never take you to him; love is the power that is closest to God himself.

Why are people afraid of love? Are they afraid it may tie them down? But love is only constricting when you are unable to continue radiating it, when you are unable to keep on giving more and more. It is the inadequacy of your love that is the binding factor, not love itself. A love that is insufficient, that is neither full nor frank and honest, can become a bondage. Only a shrinking love can chain one person to another. A love that is full to the brim, that is always expanding and increasing, breaks through all barriers and begins to overflow. When love really ripens it knows no frontiers; it assumes the unlimited vastness of the sky.

And so I tell you, let your love increase and multiply. Widen the sphere of your love. Place no restrictions on it; make no conditions for it. Let it expand day by day; let it flow over, above and beyond the person you love. Let it stop nowhere; let there be no halting of its course.

It is the fear that love may get stuck somewhere on its journey to God that makes so-called spiritual people wary of love. But if the flow of my love gets stopped somewhere it is my own fault, not that of love. There is no excuse for any hostility towards love whatsoever. If you blame something on love, the fault is really your own. If a man is coarse or narrow-minded his love cannot help but be static, and if he is antagonistic towards love for this reason then he becomes still meaner, even more narrow-minded. What little fullness and richness love possesses is being lost because of these parochial attitudes held by our so-called religious leaders.

As I see it, we have to increase our love, to let ourselves become submerged in it. If you try to hoard love all you will save is your ego, so expand your love, spread it around. When you toss a pebble into a pond it may sink, but the ripples extend in ever-widening circles from shore to shore. Love is the same. Love produces waves of throbbing vibrations until those ripples of love reach the shore where God is. This kind of love is deep and fervent prayer.

I will never be the one to suggest you should hate your parents or your wife and children or anyone or anything at all. In fact, you must love them so much that they will not be able to contain it within themselves, that it is received in overflowing abundance. Let your love spread everywhere, flooding everything, so that nothing can hold it, so that nothing can contain it. Let your aim be to generate so much love that no one but God can tolerate it. Only the unlimited can sustain the unlimited. No finite receptacle can hold the infinite. A love that is unbounded will fill it, flow over it, flow beyond it. It will be given more than its share, but it will be far beyond its expectations, far more than it can hold.

As far as you are concerned love can never become a hindrance. Love can only be an obstacle if it becomes stuck somewhere. A love that has become stuck is not real love; it is lust, sensual attachment. And expanding, growing love, on the other hand, is deep prayer.

Never forget that a love that comes to a standstill somewhere turns into self-deception, lust, enslavement—but the love that rolls on like the waves in the ocean is no less than a fervent prayer, no less than God himself, no less than the benediction of ultimate and absolute salvation. If your love does not halt on its way, but marches on, it sets you free. Let there be no end to its onward march until the last man in the world has been brought into its fold, into that communion with the universal soul.

Let me repeat a few things to impress them upon you. I advocate love of oneself and I advocate love of others. Also never ever think of love as unholy or evil, and take care your love does not get stuck somewhere en route to God. This stopping is unholy; this stopping is unloving.

Those who look upon love as profane and view it in a narrow-minded way never try to understand that the love they are condemning is simply love that has been restricted, that has been impeded on its way to God. But the more love is restricted the shabbier it becomes. And the man who withholds his love from others becomes completely centered in his ego. He gets stuck in the ego—hung up on the I-ness and my-ness of life. In this whole, vast universe the two poles that are the furthest apart are the center of the ego and the abode of God. Stopping, or even pausing at "I" leads to hell.

There is no end to the pain and misery of the egoistic

man, because all the doors to bliss are closed to him. And only love can open them. All the doors to beauty and harmony are closed to him too. And only love can open them as well. Love is the mysterious and secret key to the abode of truth, beauty and goodness. Whatever is fine and good and perfect in life can only be revealed by using this wonderful key. It is the ego that locks the door.

There is one door, however, that egoism can open—the door of hell. That is the only door it can open.

Remember, except for these two there are no other keys. And no man can hold both keys in his hands at the same time. It is a matter of divine law that a man can only have one key in his possession at one time. The man who is willing to let one go is the only man who can have the other.

Not only does the key of love open the hearts of men, it also opens the hearts of everything under the sun—of every rock, of every plant, of every animal, of God himself. Luther Burbank, the celebrated American botanist, is remembered throughout the world for something the profundity of his love wrought in the vegetable kingdom. He was able to make plants accede to his requests.

Once he said to some cacti, "My friends, you need not be afraid of anyone. You don't need these thorns to protect you. Isn't the great love I have for you enough to protect you?"

In the end the cacti listened to him. And as a token of their love those thorny desert plants brought forth a whole new variety totally devoid of thorns. Whenever anyone asked him how he had achieved this impossible feat he would reply, "With love."

I also wish to assure you that even the impossible is possible through love. Man cannot conceive a greater impossibility than God, and yet he too yields to love. Love is never an impossibility. Love is such a very simple thing. Love is present in everyone. It only needs to be developed; it only needs to grow.

Although the seeds of love have been sown in all men it is only the very fortunate who live to enjoy the flowers of love. Why is this? It is because we never allow the seeds of love to germinate. We seek love but are not willing to give it. Love grows when it is offered, not when it is sought.

Remember, love is an unconditional offering. The man who is capable of giving love receives it in abundance. And giving love freely also creates the capacity to accept it. The giving of love is what qualifies a man to receive it. The measure of love a man is given is commensurate with the amount of love he offers. This is the way greater and greater depths of love are achieved until one's very breath is gradually transformed into love—into full, wholesome and perfect love.

The beginning of the perfecting of a man's love can always be traced to his readiness to give love and never to any impassioned demand for it. Dictatorial demands for love will never enable anyone to begin perfecting his love. Love's state is imperial, not beggarly. Those who insist on love never receive it, and this failure, which is so dispiriting to them, gradually renders them incapable of giving love as well. And as this inability to give love increases, love becomes even harder and harder for them to obtain.

Please remember that love means giving without any desire for return, without any desire for getting anything back, without any sort of demand at all. You have to free your love from any expectation of return whatsoever. In the affairs of love there can never be any kind of commercial transaction. The pleasure of love, the bliss of love, the fullness of love lies in giving, and not in obtaining something in exchange. The giving must be so abundant and so spontaneous that the question of receiving something in return does not cross your mind at all. That is why the person who gives his love is always under an obligation to the one who accepts it. It is only through the act of giving love unconditionally, as an all-embracing gift with no strings attached, that you will grow the wings that take you to God.

Let us spread our wings of love and soar upwards into the vast firmament of God. When your wings of love are fully spread the idea that some things belong to you and some things belong to others, the awareness of mine and yours, disappears—and what remains is consciousness, the very being of God himself.

In the absence of love man wanders in the desert of egoism, amidst the thorny shrubs of hatred, violence and anger. Once your wings of love have grown there is no need to remain stuck on this sandy, desolate terrain. Then your flight to the wonderful world of beauty, to the limitless, inexhaustible and perfect beauty becomes so easy. So let us be filled with love, with love towards all, with love unconditional. Standing or sitting, sleeping or walking, be submerged in love. Love is the very breath of our existence; love is the waves that surge in your heart.

Now you have reached the precincts of the sacred temple of God, so there is no longer any need to visit ordinary temples. Temples with idols of stone can neither claim perfection nor reality. And is it surprising that the hearts of those who frequent these temples of stone are hard and rock-like? I do not doubt that sermons and discussions on God take place within these temples, but what is disseminated from them is nothing but hatred—hatred and violence disguised in the gaudy apparel of false love.

I tell you in all truth that you should recognize no other temple than the temple of love. It is God's only temple. I fear these other temples have been designed to prevent men from reaching the temple of love. Satan himself must have had a hand in this!

Love itself is the only temple. And love itself is the most sacred of scriptures. "The man who has a smattering of the language of love," says Kabir, "is the real scholar." Certainly nothing remains to be learned if one has learned all about love. The mastery of love is the mastery of learning. And the man who hasn't learned the art of loving is totally ignorant. No knowledge, no feeling, no experience is superior to that of love. The eye of love reads what is written on leaves, carved on stones or hidden in the waves. The signature, the autograph of God is everywhere!

Of what real use are the works of mortals? What can we gain from the words of ordinary men? Where will they lead us? The words of man cannot take us above and beyond man, that is for certain. To go beyond man we must leave man behind. In fact, man's words, his scriptures, his principles are all obstacles on the path to God. You have to read, to learn, to comprehend what is God's to reach him. And the word of God is written in love. One has to learn the language of man to read what man has written, to read his *shastras*, his scriptures, but to read God's book you have to learn God's language. And God's language is love. If you wish to attain to God's language learn the art of love.

God's entire creation surrounds you. Look at it; your eyes will not fail you. But if there is no love in you, you will neither be able to see it nor to know it. A great and mysterious miracle takes place when you begin to look around with the eye of love. What you saw before fades away and what had escaped your notice comes into view. Then nothing is left but the form of God, nothing but manifestations of the divine.

What the scholar loses, the lover attains; what learning misses, love achieves. For the scholar who has a smattering of love's language, however, it is a different matter. Nevertheless, entering into the depths of life is impossible without love. On its own, knowledge tends to get lost because it always circles things, it always takes the long way around. And it is also a misconception to think that knowledge can annihilate the distance between man and God. Only through love can this distance disappear. Knowledge goes no deeper than the physical body, but love does not stop before it reaches the soul. And knowledge that is divorced from love is incomplete, not really real at all. Only knowledge that is contained in love is real knowledge.

What shall I say about the importance of love? What shall

I say about how to realize it? Is one to repeat the word "love" as a mantra, over and over and over again like some zealots do with the names of Ram and of Krishna? Will repeating the word help you to attain love? Never. Mere repetition of some word will never achieve anything. Love must be lived; it must become part and parcel of your very being. Your life will only be purposeful, meaningful, when the vitality of love throbs through every moment of it.

Be alert to the energy of love; let it awaken within you. Let no opportunity to love ever find it slumbering inside you. Let no call to love ever go unheeded. Let your love provide a fitting reply to every challenge, and even when none comes from any quarter, let your love continue to flow as light streams from a lamp, as perfume pours from a flower. A steady and unbroken current of love should always radiate from your being.

Always keep the fire of love blazing high within and you will find there are no obstacles in your way. By its constant flow even the gentlest little stream erodes the biggest boulder and so clears the path before it. And can anyone deny that there are enormous stumbling blocks on the path of love? There are huge obstacles in love's path for certain, but the power of love is boundless and more than equal to any barriers. Just let the limitless energy of your love flow on unceasingly; let it be always active, always on the move. Love goes about its business slowly and silently but with a quiet efficiency that eventually wears huge rocks down into particles of sand. A lot of fuss is a sign of weakness; powerful forces function silently. And how silent and free from fuss is the creative activity of God!

Give love the chance to transform your very roots. Love's potion can give you a new life, a life that will never end. This is why love is unafraid even in the face of death. Love knows no death at all.

In 1857, when the Indians revolted against their rulers, the English put to the spear a sage who had been silent for years. They took him to be a spy, an agitator. The sage laughed as the spear entered his body and spoke his first words in years. He said, "*Tat-twam-asi*"; he said, "thou too are that." The soldier who speared him was "that" too; he was the universal soul as well. Even at the moment of his death he embraced his murderer with the glow of deep love and profound prayer in his eyes. He had long before discarded words and selfishness and had filled his being with pure love. Otherwise, how could love have gushed from him when the spear penetrated his flesh? During all the years when his heart seemed mute to all outward appearances it was only filling up with love. It had become a veritable fountain of love and it made it impossible for him to look upon his murderer as an enemy. He only saw the beloved in him. Love had transformed an enemy into a friend and death into salvation.

Love can change darkness into light or poison into nectar. Can you conceive of a miracle more stupendous than the miracle of love? Love transforms everything because it transforms one's very vision. Vision is a creative force. What we see is our world; our world is what our eyes perceive. If there is love in one's eyes, love is all around. But if there is no love, then there is not even God. Instead, wherever we look we see only enemies.

Early one morning a traveler approached a village. He ran into an old man on the outskirts and inquired, "Sir, tell me, what sort of people are the villagers who live here? I have left my own village and am considering settling here."

The old man looked the stranger over and said, "First, may I ask you what kind of people lived in the village you have just left?"

As soon as he heard this question the stranger became very red in the face and quite angry. "The very thought of those people fills me with rage," he said. "Please don't mention those wretched people to me at all. It is because of them that I had to leave the village. You won't find such wicked people anywhere else in the world."

The old man said, "Then brother, I am sorry, but the villagers here are no better. You will only find wicked people here as well. Perhaps you had better go and live in some other village."

The first man had hardly left when another stranger approached the old man with the same question. "Sir, what sort of people are the villagers that live here?" he asked. "I think I should like to stay here. I had to leave my own village."

The old man replied, "Before I answer your question I would like to know what kind of people live in the village you have just left."

The man replied, "Although I have never met such nice people anywhere else I had to leave the village for some compelling personal reasons." As he spoke these words, loving tears rolled down his cheeks at the memory of his former home.

The old man quickly said, "You are welcome to live in this village, my son. You will find the people here even nicer than those you have left behind. There are many, many good people here." And after a pause the old man added, "No matter which village you go to you will be warmly welcomed. In every village you will find good people, nice people. The world is what your eyes perceive."

The world is nothing; it is nothing but your eyes. If your eyes are full of love you will see only hearts throbbing with love everywhere you look. And when you see the whole world pulsating with love know well that is the hour of your realization, the hour of your realization of the divine, of God.

Reaching the door of God does not mean that Ram will be waiting for you in cloud-covered splendor, armed with bows and arrows. It does not mean that Krishna will be standing there, piping a tune of celestial welcome on his divine flute. Attaining God does not mean that some elderly gentleman with a long white beard will be sitting there at a switchboard controlling the universe. Approaching God means attaining that experience where the universe ceases to be a separate object and you merge with the universal soul, where the object vanishes and only the energy, the force, the power remains. It means the attainment of supreme bliss. It means the attainment of truth, of beauty, of eternity.

God is not a person; he is an experience. God is bliss, a limitless ocean of bliss. But before you can merge into that ocean you first have to generate a preliminary realization of that ocean within yourself.

Of the three keys that can lead you to God I have already spoken of the first two. The first is self-love; the second, love of others. Let us now talk about the third key, the love of God himself. To attain this third key, you have to go beyond the other two. The second is a step beyond the first, and the third is a step beyond both.

The first step involves admitting "I am". Although it is not a reality, it is nonetheless a fact. And to the ignorant it is a more important fact than anything else. The knowledge of "I am" may be a means to your awakening, but it can never be a means of escape. Those who try to flee from it will always find it close on their heels. Can you ever really run away from your shadow? You know you can't. The more you try to escape it the faster it pursues you.

Simply accept the fact of the ego, the fact of "I am" and get involved in the search for love. As love grows in you egoism first begins to diminish and then it finally fades away completely. If the man accepts that his shadow exists and just steps into the light of the sun he automatically frees himself from his own shadow and from the shadows of all sorts of other things. Egoism is to love as shadows are to light. The impenetrable darkness of egoism disappears in the all-illuminating light of love.

It is the existence of "I" that gives rise to "him"; only

when I am "I" are others "others". In the light of love both the awareness of "I" and the awareness of "the other" disappear. And in the end only love remains; then there is neither "I" nor "you" nor "other"—there is only love. This is the state of love I call the love of God. This love is not directed towards anyone in particular, not from or for or on behalf of anyone or anything in particular. It simply is. This pure and simple love I call the love of God.

What are the implications of this love of God? It means the disappearance of that illusion that has been present for so long, the idea that "I am something", that "I am what I am". This is entirely untrue, totally unreal. You really are not, not at all. You have no personal existence whatsoever.

Consider the phenomenon of breathing, for example. Breath is drawn into your body and then expelled. If you think that it is you who is breathing, you are wrong. One day the air that goes out simply does not come back in—so how can you say you are breathing? If you think you are living, that you are doing this living, you are wrong. The day life withdraws from you, you are unable to remain here even for a single moment. If you think you are born you are wrong; if you think you die, you are wrong. You have never been born, nor will you ever die. Your breath is not yours, nor do you have any control over it.

Neither life nor death are yours. Some mysterious drama is being enacted within you. Someone is at play inside you. Someone speaks through you; someone expresses through you. Someone is born within you; someone dies within you. You are a playground, a playing field where players come and go. You are just a flute through which someone plays beautiful music.

"I am no more than a hollow piece of bamboo," said Kabir, "and the songs of love directed to God are all his." The man who realizes this understands. The man who has used the two keys I have already mentioned will be able to comprehend this easily and will be able to realize that there is no such thing as individuality in this world. Whatsoever exists, exists together—collectively, jointly. Nothing exists in isolation.

The breath you think of as yours has already been the breath of millions and millions of others; this air I am now exhaling will become the breath of millions and millions yet to come into this world. The billions of cells that make up my physical body have once been part and parcel of billions of other bodies. How can I call this body mine? When I leave this body these cells will help formulate the bodies of countless others. Even before you leave the body it undergoes change every moment, discarding old cells, forming new ones. And the new cells that enter your body are the old cells that have come from others. This body of mine has already belonged to thousands of men, to millions of animals, to billions of other living organisms and will, in the future, constitute millions more bodies just the same. How can I say it is mine?

The mind is not separate either. The component parts of the mind come and go just like those of the body. There is nothing that is mine; there nothing that is yours. Adopting this attitude is the first step in developing love for God.

When a man actually realizes that nothing is his, when this attitude goes deep, since nothing is his he begins to feel that he does not exist at all. As long as you have the idea that you possess something the delusion that you are persists and so you begin to want things. You measure your greatness by the size of your house; you measure your greatness by the elevated post you occupy; you measure your greatness by the extent of your property; you measure your greatness by the power you wield. Why? I-ness increases in proportion to one's possessions. I-ness grows right along with my-ness. The frontiers of I-ness and my-ness coincide. And so if the illusion of my-ness is eliminated, the basis for I-ness disappears. If nothing is mine, if I have nothing, what am "I" left with then? Then where is "I"? With my-ness gone, I-ness is left empty-handed.

People often ask me whether I am suggesting they simply drop everything and run away to rid themselves of I-ness, of the illusion of "I". My usual reply is that it is not a question of renouncing or of not renouncing what one possesses, but that the crux of the matter lies in one's attitude towards one's possessions. Even if you lay aside everything you own, the attitude of my-ness can easily continue. That is why so-called renouncers keep a careful account of what they have renounced and measure the worth of their renunciation by the value of the things they have given up.

One holy man once told me, "I have thrown away hundreds of thousands of rupees." I asked him when he had done this. He replied, "About thirty years ago." When I heard this I was quite amused and said, "You don't seem to have gained much by your action; otherwise, in thirty years you should have forgotten about all those *lakhs* of rupees."

The question is not one of renunciation, but one of realization. Unless realization has happened to you, even your renunciation may feed your ego, may puff it up even more. It is the assumption that things are yours that is wrong; there is nothing wrong with using things that exist.

There are two types of misguided approaches as far as this question is concerned. One way of looking at things is that of the hedonist. He says, "These are mine. I will enjoy them." The other viewpoint is that of the renouncer. He says, "These are mine. I will let them go." But both approaches begin with "These are mine." The man of real knowledge takes a third stance. He says, "Whatever is, is God's." Things are neither yours nor mine. Even we ourselves are not ours. I really am not; you really are not. The ego is illusion. Everything is simply happening, and I am only part of that process."

If one can achieve and maintain this third attitude then life becomes as natural and as easily accessible as water and air. Such a life is a life of love. And such a life is a life of sacrifice, because love of God means letting the ego go.

Malukdas has said that the birds do not work, that the python does not hunt for a job, and yet God provides for them in abundance. But people have misunderstood these words. They say Malukdas is telling us not to do anything. This is not the correct interpretation at all. Birds work; they work from sunrise to sunset. They build nests; they search for grain. What Malukdas means is that the birds are not conscious of themselves, that when "I am" is not there the desire to acquire disappears.

The attitude of "These are mine" must vanish, and when this is gone the love of God develops. When this development has reached fulfillment and the feeling of "I am not" has been generated, then the revolution about which I have been speaking takes place.

There is a Sufi song that tells the tale of a lover who knocks at his beloved's door. "Who is there?" is asked from within. His answer is, "It is I, your lover." There is no reply. He knocks again, saying, "Please answer." After a long pause he hears, "Go away. There is not enough room in his house for two." He leaves.

Years pass. Summers and winters and rainy seasons come and go; countless moons rise and countless moons set. Finally he returns and knocks at the door once again. The same question comes from within. This time he answers, "You alone." The song says the door swings open then.

Had I composed the song I would have thought the time had not yet come for the door to open. The awareness of "you" still indicates the existence of "I". I would have told the young man to go away once again, and the song would go on a little longer.

When the lover says "You alone" silence would prevail once more. He would wait a while and then say, "Let the door be opened now. It is not me any longer, only you alone are." From inside the voice would say, "He who is conscious of one is still conscious of two. He who remembers 'you' still remembers 'I'. In this room there is only room for one." The lover would go away.

Days would dissolve into years, but still he would not return, because he would now have no idea that he was to go anywhere at all. He would have no idea he was supposed to return to his beloved. Finally the young lady herself would go to him and say, "My love, come! The door is open."

Just as "I" vanishes, "you" also vanishes—and what remains is the present, what remains is what you have always been seeking. After the elimination of "I" and "you" what remains is God.

Where "I" and "you" disappear is the starting point of the beginningless and endless existence. It is a limitless ocean of consciousness: it is the being of God himself. You can know it; you can live in it. You are in it. You stand in it already, you live in it already—but you do not realize it. You do not feel it within you; you do not recognize it outside you. You are too full of "I". Relieve yourself of this burden. The man who is empty of "I" is the only man who is really full. Get rid of your I-ness. Eliminate it completely.

It is to this end that I have spoken of the three keys, of the three rungs on the ladder to God. When you merge into love you dive into the fullness of the void, into the fullness of emptiness. Move ahead step by step. Get lost in love drop by drop. And at the last, lose yourself in love as a raindrop loses itself in the ocean. Are you not aware that when it loses itself the tiny raindrop becomes the vast and boundless ocean?

Accept life. It is the gracious gift of God. Never fight with life; never flee from it. Love life. There is no greater conquest possible than the victory of love.

Life is a single entity. The realization of this oneness in its entirety is love.

BOOKS PUBLISHED BY RAJNEESH FOUNDATION INTERNATIONAL

BOOKS PUBLISHED BY RAJNEESH FOUNDATION INTERNATIONAL

For a complete catalog of all the books published by Rajneesh Foundation International, contact:

Rajneesh Foundation International
P.O. Box 9
Rajneeshpuram, Oregon 97741 USA
(503) 489-3462

THE BAULS

The Beloved (2 volumes)

BUDDHA

The Book of the Books (volume 1 & 2)
the Dhammapada

The Diamond Sutra
the Vajrachchedika Prajnaparamita Sutra

The Discipline of Transcendence (4 volumes)
the Sutra of 42 Chapters

The Heart Sutra
the Prajnaparamita Hridayam Sutra

BUDDHIST MASTERS

The Book of Wisdom (volume 1)
Atisha's Seven Points of Mind Training

The White Lotus
the sayings of Bodhidharma

EARLY DISCOURSES

And Now, and Here (volume 1)

Beware of Socialism

The Long and the Short and the All

The Perfect Way

HASSIDISM

The Art of Dying

The True Sage

JESUS

Come Follow Me (4 volumes)
the sayings of Jesus

I Say Unto You (2 volumes)
the sayings of Jesus

KABIR

The Divine Melody

Ecstasy: The Forgotten Language

The Fish in the Sea is Not Thirsty

The Guest

The Path of Love

The Revolution

RESPONSES TO QUESTIONS

Be Still and Know

From Sex to Superconsciousness

The Goose is Out

My Way: The Way of the White Clouds

Walking in Zen, Sitting in Zen

Walk Without Feet, Fly Without Wings and Think Without Mind

Zen: Zest, Zip, Zap and Zing

SUFISM

Just Like That

The Perfect Master (2 volumes)

The Secret

Sufis: The People of the Path (2 volumes)

Unio Mystica (2 volumes)
the Hadiqa of Hakim Sanai

Until You Die

The Wisdom of the Sands (2 volumes)

TANTRA

The Book of the Secrets (volumes 4 & 5)
Vigyana Bhairava Tantra

Tantra, Spirituality & Sex
Excerpts from The Book of the Secrets

Tantra: The Supreme Understanding
(Tilopa's Song of Mahamudra)

The Tantra Vision (2 volumes)
the Royal Song of Saraha

TAO

The Empty Boat
the stories of Chuang Tzu

The Secret of Secrets (2 volumes)
the Secret of the Golden Flower

Tao: The Golden Gate (volume 1)

Tao: The Pathless Path (2 volumes)
the stories of Lieh Tzu

Tao: The Three Treasures (4 volumes)
the Tao Te Ching of Lao Tzu

When The Shoe Fits
the stories of Chuang Tzu

THE UPANISHADS

I Am That
(Isa Upanishad)

The Ultimate Alchemy (2 volumes)
Atma Pooja Upanishad

Vedanta: Seven Steps to Samadhi
Akshya Upanishad

Philosophia Ultima
Mandukya Upanishad

WESTERN MYSTICS

The Hidden Harmony
the fragments of Heraclitus

The New Alchemy: To Turn You On
Mabel Collins' Light on the Path

Philosophia Perennis (2 volumes)
the Golden Verses of Pythagoras

Guida Spirituale
the Desiderata

Theologia Mystica
the treatise of St. Dionysius

YOGA

Yoga: The Alpha and the Omega
(10 volumes)
the Yoga Sutras of Patanjali

Yoga: The Science of the Soul (volumes 1-3)
(Originally titled Yoga: The Alpha and the Omega)

ZEN

Ah, This!

Ancient Music in the Pines

And the Flowers Showered

Dang Dang Doko Dang

The First Principle

The Grass Grows By Itself

Nirvana: the Last Nightmare

No Water, No Moon

Returning to the Source

A Sudden Clash of Thunder

The Sun Rises in the Evening

Zen: The Path of Paradox (3 volumes)

ZEN MASTERS

Hsin Hsin Ming: The Book of Nothing
Discourses on the faith-mind of Sosan

The Search
the Ten Bulls of Zen

Take It Easy (2 volumes)
poems of Ikkyu

This Very Body the Buddha
Hakuin's Song of Meditation

INITIATION TALKS
between Master disciple

Hammer On The Rock
(December 10, 1975 - January 15, 1976)

Above All Don't Wobble
(January 16 - February 12, 1976)

Nothing To Lose But Your Head
(February 13 - March 12, 1976)

Be Realistic: Plan For a Miracle
(March 13 - April 6, 1976)

Get Out of Your Own Way
(April 7 - May 2, 1976)

Beloved of My Heart
(May 3 - 28, 1976)

The Cypress in the Courtyard
(May 29 - June 27, 1976)

A Rose is a Rose is a Rose
(June 28 - July 27, 1976)

Dance Your Way to God
(July 28 - August 20, 1976)

The Passion for the Impossible
(August 21 - September 18, 1976)

The Great Nothing
(September 19 - October 11, 1976)

God is Not for Sale
(October 12 - November 7, 1976)

The Shadow of the Whip
(November 8 - December 3, 1976)

Blessed are the Ignorant
(December 4 - 31, 1976)

The Buddha Disease
(January 1977)

What Is, Is, What Ain't, Ain't
(February 1977)

The Zero Experience
(March 1977)

For Madmen Only (Price of Admission: Your Mind)
(April 1977)

This Is It
(May 1977)

The Further Shore
(June 1977)

Far Beyond the Stars
(July 1977)

The No Book (No Buddha, No Teaching, No Discipline)
(August 1977)

Don't Just Do Something, Sit There
(September 1977)

Only Losers Can Win in this Game
(October 1977)

The Open Secret
(November 1977)

The Open Door
(December 1977)

The Sun Behind the Sun Behind the Sun
(January 1978)

Believing the Impossible Before Breakfast
(February 1978)

Don't Bite My Finger, Look Where I am Pointing
(March 1978)

Let Go!
(April 1978)

The Ninety-Nine Names of Nothingness
(May 1978)

The Madman's Guide to Enlightenment
(June 1978)

Don't Look Before You Leap
(July 1978)

Hallelujah!
(August 1978)

God's Got a Thing About You
(September 1978)

The Tongue-Tip Taste of Tao
(October 1978)

The Sacred Yes
(November 1978)

Turn On, Tune In, and Drop the Lot
(December 1978)

Zorba the Buddha
(January 1979)

Won't You Join the Dance?
(February 1979)

You Ain't Seen Nothin' Yet
(March 1979)

The Shadow of the Bamboo
(April 1979)

The Sound of One Hand Clapping
(March 1981)

OTHER TITLES

The Book
an introduction to the teachings of Bhagwan Shree Rajneesh
Series I from A to H
Series II from I to Q
Series III from R to Z

A Cup of Tea
letters to disciples

The Orange Book
the meditation techniques of Bhagwan Shree Rajneesh

Rajneeshism
an introduction to Bhagwan Shree Rajneesh and His religion

The Sound of Running Water
a photobiography of Bhagwan Shree Rajneesh and His work, 1974-1978

This Very Place The Lotus Paradise
a photobiography of
Bhagwan Shree Rajneesh and His work, 1978-1984

BOOKS FROM OTHER PUBLISHERS

ENGLISH EDITIONS

UNITED KINGDOM

The Art of Dying
(Sheldon Press)

The Book of the Secrets (volume 1)
(Thames & Hudson)

Dimensions Beyond the Known
(Sheldon Press)

The Hidden Harmony
(Sheldon Press)

Meditation: The Art of Ecstasy
(Sheldon Press)

The Mustard Seed
(Sheldon Press)

Neither This Nor That
(Sheldon Press)

No Water, No Moon
(Sheldon Press)

Roots and Wings
(Routledge & Kegan Paul)

Straight to Freedom (Original title:
Until You Die)
(Sheldon Press)

The Supreme Doctrine
(Routledge & Kegan Paul)

The Supreme Understanding (Original title:
Tantra: The Supreme Understanding)
(Sheldon Press)

Tao: The Three Treasures (volume 1)
(Wildwood House)

UNITED STATES OF AMERICA

The Book of the Secrets (volumes 1-3)
(Harper & Row)

The Great Challenge
(Grove Press)

Hammer on the Rock
(Grove Press)

I Am The Gate
(Harper & Row)

Journey Toward the Heart (Original title: Until You Die)
(Harper & Row)

Meditation: The Art of Ecstasy
(Harper & Row)

The Mustard Seed
(Harper & Row)

My Way: The Way of the White Clouds
(Grove Press)

Only One Sky (Original title: Tantra: The Supreme Understanding)
(Dutton)

The Psychology of the Esoteric
(Harper & Row)

Roots and Wings
(Routledge & Kegan Paul)

The Supreme Doctrine
(Routledge & Kegan Paul)

Words Like Fire (Original title: Come Follow Me, volume 1)
(Harper & Row)

BOOKS ON BHAGWAN

The Awakened One: The Life and Work of Bhagwan Shree Rajneesh
by Swami Satya Vedant
(Harper & Row)

Death Comes Dancing: Celebrating Life with Bhagwan Shree Rajneesh
by Ma Satya Bharti
(Routledge & Kegan Paul)

Drunk On The Divine
by Ma Satya Bharti
(Grove Press)

The Ultimate Risk
by Ma Satya Bharti
(Routledge & Kegan Paul)

Dying For Enlightenment
by Bernard Gunther (Swami Deva Amitprem)
(Harper & Row)

Neo-Tantra
by Bernard Gunther (Swami Deva Amitprem)
(Harper & Row)

FOREIGN LANGUAGE EDITIONS

DANISH

TRANSLATIONS

Hemmelighedernes Bog (volume 1)
(Borgens Forlag)

Hu-Meditation Og Kosmisk Orgasme
(Borgens Forlag)

BOOKS ON BHAGWAN

Sjælens Oprør
by Swami Deva Satyarthi
(Borgens Forlag)

DUTCH

TRANSLATIONS

Drink Mij
(Ankh-Hermes)

Het Boek Der Geheimen (volumes 1-5)
(Mirananda)

Geen Water, Geen Maan
(Mirananda)

Gezaaid In Goede Aarde
(Ankh-Hermes)

Ik Ben De Poort
(Ankh-Hermes)

Ik Ben De Zee Die Je Zoekt
(Ankh-Hermes)

Meditatie: De Kunst van Innerlijke Extase
(Mirananda)

Mijn Weg, De Weg van de Witte Wolk
(Arcanum)

Het Mosterdzaad (volumes 1 & 2)
(Mirananda)

Het Oranje Meditatieboek
(Ankh-Hermes)

Psychologie en Evolutie
(Ankh-Hermes)

Tantra: Het Allerhoogste Inzicht
(Ankh-Hermes)

Tantra, Spiritualiteit en Seks
(Ankh-Hermes)

De Tantra Visie (volume 1)
(Arcanum)

Tau
(Ankh-Hermes)

Totdat Je Sterft
(Ankh-Hermes)

De Verborgen Harmonie
(Mirananda)

Volg Mij
(Ankh-Hermes)

Zoeken naar de Stier
(Ankh-Hermes)

BOOKS ON BHAGWAN

Bhagwan: Notities van Een Discipel
by Swami Deva Amrito (Jan Foudraine)
(Ankh-Hermes)

Bhagwan Shree Rajneesh: De Laatste Gok
by Ma Satya Bharti
(Mirananda)

Oorspronkelijk Gezicht,
Een Gang Naar Huis
by Swami Deva Amrito (Jan Foudraine)
(Ambo)

FRENCH

TRANSLATIONS

L'éveil à la Conscience Cosmique
(Dangles)

Je Suis La Porte
(EPI)

Le Livre Des Secrets (volume 1)
(Soleil Orange)

La Meditation Dynamique
(Dangles)

GERMAN

TRANSLATIONS

Auf der Suche
(Sambuddha Verlag)

Das Buch der Geheimnisse
(Heyne Taschenbuch)

Das Orangene Buch
(Sambuddha Verlag)

Der Freund
(Sannyas Verlag)

Sprung ins Unbekannte
(Sannyas Verlag)

Ekstase: Die vergessene Sprache
(Herzschlag Verlag, formerly Ki-Buch)

Esoterische Psychologie
(Sannyas Verlag)

Rebellion der Seele
(Sannyas Verlag)

Ich bin der Weg
(Rajneesh Verlag)

Intelligenz des Herzens
(Herzschlag Verlag, formerly Ki-Buch)

Jesus aber schwieg
(Sannyas Verlag)

Jesus -der Menschensohn
(Sannyas Verlag)

Kein Wasser, Kein Mond
(Herzschlag Verlag, formerly Ki-Buch)

Komm und folge mir
(Sannyas Verlag)

Meditation: Die Kunst zu sich selbst zu finden
(Heyne Verlag)

Mein Weg: Der Weg der weissen Wolke
(Herzschlag Verlag, formerly Ki-Buch)

Mit Wurzeln und mit Flügeln
(Edition Lotus)

Nicht bevor du stirbst
(Edition Gyandip, Switzerland)

Die Schuhe auf dem Kopf
(Edition Lotus)

Das Klatschen der einen Hand
(Edition Gyandip, Switzerland)

Spirituelle Entwicklung
(Fischer)

Vom Sex zum Kosmischen Bewusstsein
(New Age)

Yoga: Alpha und Omega
(Edition Gyandip, Switzerland)

Sprengt den Fels der Unbewusstheit
(Fischer)

Tantra: Die höchste Einsicht
(Sambuddha Verlag)

Tantrische Liebeskunst
(Sannyas Verlag)

Die Alchemie der Verwandlung
(Edition Lotus)

Die verborgene Harmonie
(Sannyas Verlag)

Was ist Meditation?
(Sannyas Verlag)

Die Gans ist raus!
(Sannyas Verlag)

BOOKS ON BHAGWAN

Rajneeshismus - Bhagwan Shree Rajneesh und seine Religion
Eine Eiufuhrung
Rajneesh Foundation International

Begegnung mit Niemand
by Mascha Rabben (Ma Hari Chetana)
(Herzschlag Verlag)

Ganz entspannt im Hier und Jetzt
by Swami Satyananda
(Rowohlt)

Im Grunde ist alles ganz einfach
by Swami Satyananda
(Ullstein)

Wagnis Orange
by Ma Satya Bharti
(Fachbuchhandlung fur Psychologie)

Wenn das Herz frei wird
by Ma Prem Gayan (Silvie Winter)
(Herbig)

Der Erwachte
by Vasant Joshi
(Synthesis Verlag)

Rajneeshpuram - Fest des Foiedeus und der Liebe
(Sannyas Verlag)

GREEK

TRANSLATION

I Krifi Armonia (The Hidden Harmony)
(Emmanual Rassoulis)

HEBREW

TRANSLATION

Tantra: The Supreme Understanding
(Massada)

ITALIAN

TRANSLATIONS

L'Armonia Nascosta (volumes 1 & 2)
(Re Nudo)

Dieci Storie Zen di Bhagwan Shree Rajneesh
(Né Acqua, Né Luna)
(Il Fiore d'Oro)

La Dottrina Suprema
(Rizzoli)

Dimensioni Oltre il Conosciuto
(Mediterranee)

Estasi: Il Linguaggio Dimenticato
(Riza Libri)

Io Sono La Soglia
(Mediterranee)

Il Libro Arancione
(Mediterranee)

Il Libro dei Segreti
(Bompiani)

Meditazione Dinamica:
L'Arte dell'Estasi Interiore
(Mediterranee)

Nirvana: L'Ultimo Incubo
(Basaia)

La Nuova Alchimia
(Psiche)

Philosophia Perennis
(Alkaest)

La Rivoluzione Interiore
(Mediterranee)

La Ricerca
(La Salamandra)

Il Seme della Ribellione (volumes 1-3)
(Re Nudo)

Tantra: La Comprensione Suprema
(Bompiani)

Tao: I Tre Tesori (volumes 1-3)
(Re Nudo)

Tecniche di Liberazione
(La Salamandra)

Semi di Saggezza
(SugarCo)

BOOKS ON BHAGWAN

Rajneeshismo
una introduzione a
Bhagwan Shree Rajneesh a sua religione

Alla Ricerca del Dio Perduto
by Swami Deva Majid
(SugarCo)

Il Grande Esperimento:
Meditazioni E Terapie Nell'ashram
Di Bhagwan Shree Rajneesh
by Ma Satya Bharti
(Armenia)

L'Incanto D'Arancio
by Swami Swatantra Sarjano
(Savelli)

JAPANESE

TRANSLATIONS

Dance Your Way to God
(Rajneesh Publications)

The Empty Boat (volumes 1 & 2)
(Rajneesh Publications)

From Sex to Superconsciousness
(Rajneesh Publications)

The Grass Grows by Itself
(Fumikura)

The Heart Sutra
(Merkmal)

Meditation: The Art of Ecstasy
(Merkmal)

The Mustard Seed
(Merkmal)

My Way: The Way of the White Clouds
(Rajneesh Publications)

The Orange Book
(Wholistic Therapy Institute)

The Search
(Merkmal)

The Beloved
(Merkmal)

Tantra: The Supreme Understanding
(Merkmal)

Tao: The Three Treasures (volumes 1-4)
(Merkmal)

Until You Due
(Fumikura)

Rajneeshism
an introduction to
Bhagwan Shree Rajneesh and His religion

PORTUGUESE (BRAZIL)

TRANSLATIONS

O Cipreste No Jardim
(Soma)

Dimensões Além do Conhecido
(Soma)

O Livro Dos Segredos (volume 1)
(Maha Lakshmi Editora)

Eu Sou A Porta
(Pensamento)

A Harmonia Oculta
(Pensamento)

Meditacão: A Arte Do Extase
(Cultrix)

Meu Caminho:
O Comainho Das Nuvens Brancas
(Tao Livraria & Editora)

Nem Agua, Nem Lua
(Pensamento)

O Livro Orange
(Soma)

Palavras De Fogo
(Global/Ground)

A Psicologia Do Esotérico
(Tao Livraria & Editora)

A Semente De Mostarda (volumes 1 & 2)
(Tao Livraria & Editora)

Tantra: Sexo E Espiritualidade
(Agora)

Tantra: A Supreme Comprensao
(Cultrix)

Antes Que Voce Morra
(Maha Lakshmi Editora)

Extase: A Linguagem Esquecida
(Global)

Arte de Morrer
(Global)

SPANISH

TRANSLATIONS

Introducción al Mundo del Tantra
(Colección Tantra)

Meditación: El Arte del Extasis
(Colección Tantra)

Psicológia de lo Esotérico:
La Nueva Evolución del Hombre
(Cuatro Vientos Editorial)

¿Qué Es Meditación?
(Koan/Roselló Impresions)

Yo Soy La Puerta
(Editorial Diana)

Sòlo Un Cielo (volumes 1 & 2)
(Colección Tantra)

El Sutra del Corazon
(Sarvogeet)

Ven, Sigueme (volume 1)
(Sagaro)

BOOKS ON BHAGWAN

El Riesgo Supremo
by Ma Satya Bharti
(Martinez Roca)

SWEDISH

TRANSLATION

Den Väldiga Utmaningen
(Livskraft)

RAJNEESH MEDITATION CENTERS, ASHRAMS AND COMMUNES

RAJNEESH MEDITATION CENTERS, ASHRAMS AND COMMUNES

There are hundreds of Rajneesh meditation centers throughout the world. These are some of the main ones, which can be contacted for the name and address and telephone number of the center nearest you. They can also tell you about the availability of the books of Bhagwan Shree Rajneesh – in English or in foreign language editions. General information is available from Rajneesh Foundation International.

A wide range of meditation and inner growth programs is available throughout the year at Rajneesh International Meditation University.

For further information and a complete listing of programs, write or call:

Rajneesh International Meditation University
P.O. Box 5, Rajneeshpuram, OR 97741 USA
Phone: (503) 489-3328

USA

RAJNEESH FOUNDATION INTERNATIONAL
P.O. Box 9, Rajneeshpuram, Oregon 97741.
Tel: (503) 489-3301

UTSAVA RAJNEESH MEDITATION CENTER
20062 Laguna Canyon Rd., Laguna Beach, CA 92651.
Tel: (714) 497-4877

DEVADEEP RAJNEESH SANNYAS ASHRAM
1430 Longfellow St., N.W., Washington, D.C. 20011.
Tel: (202) 723-2188

CANADA

ARVIND RAJNEESH SANNYAS ASHRAM
2807 W. 16th Ave., Vancouver, B.C. V6K 3C5.
Tel: (604) 734-4681

SHANTI SADAN RAJNEESH MEDITATION CENTER
P.O. Box 374, Station R, Montreal, Quebec H2S 3M2.
Tel: (514) 272-4566

AUSTRALIA

PREMDWEEP RAJNEESH MEDITATION CENTER
64 Fullarton Rd., Norwood, S.A. 5067. Tel: 08-423388

SATPRAKASH RAJNEESH MEDITATION CENTER
4A Ormond St., Paddington, N.S.W. 2021
Tel: (02) 336570

SAHAJAM RAJNEESH SANNYAS ASHRAM
6 Collie Street, Fremantle 6160, W.A.
Tel: (09) 336-2422

SVARUP RAJNEESH MEDITATION CENTER
303 Drummond St., Carlton 3053, Victoria. Tel: 347-3388

BELGIUM

VADAN RAJNEESH MEDITATION CENTER
Platte-Lo-Straat 65, 3200 Leuven (Kessel-Lo).
Tel: 016/25-1487

BRAZIL

PRASTHAN RAJNEESH MEDITATION CENTER
Caixa Postal No. 11072, Ag. Cidade Nova,
Rio de Janeiro, R.J. 20251.
Tel: 222-9476

PURNAM RAJNEESH MEDITATION CENTER
Caixa Postal 1946, Porto Alegre, RS 90000.

CHILE

SAGARO RAJNEESH MEDITATION CENTER
Golfo de Darien 10217, Las Condes, Santiago.
Tel: 472476

DENMARK

ANAND NIKETAN RAJNEESH MEDITATION CENTER
Stroget, Frederiksberggade 15, 1459 Copenhagen K.
Tel: (01) 139940, 117909

EAST AFRICA

AMBHOJ RAJNEESH MEDITATION CENTER
P.O. Box 59159, Nairobi, Kenya

GREAT BRITAIN

MEDINA RAJNEESH BODY CENTER
81 Belsize Park Gardens, London NW3.
Tel: (01) 722-8220, 722-6404

MEDINA RAJNEESH NEO-SANNYAS COMMUNE
Herringswell, Bury St. Edmunds, Suffolk 1P28 6SW.
Tel: (0638) 750234

HOLLAND

DE STAD RAJNEESH NEO-SANNYAS COMMUNE
719 Prinsengracht, 1017 JW Amsterdam
Tel: 020-221296

INDIA

RAJNEESHDHAM NEO-SANNYAS COMMUNE
17 Koregaon Park, Poona 411 001, MS. Tel: 28127

ITALY

VIVEK RAJNEESH MEDITATION CENTER
Via San Marco 40/4, 20121 Milan. Tel: 659-0335

JAPAN

SHANTIYUGA RAJNEESH MEDITATION CENTER
Sky Mansion 2F, 1-34-1 Ookayama, Meguro-ku, Tokyo 152.
Tel: (03) 724-9631

UTSAVA RAJNEESH MEDITATION CENTER
2-9-8 Hattori-Motomachi, Toyonaki-shi, Osaka 561.
Tel: 06-863-4246

NEW ZEALAND

SHANTI NIKETAN RAJNEESH MEDITATION CENTER
119 Symonds Street, Auckland. Tel: 770-326

PUERTO RICO

BHAGWATAM RAJNEESH MEDITATION CENTER
Box 2886, Old San Juan, PR 00905.
Tel: 765-4150

SWEDEN

DEEVA RAJNEESH MEDITATION CENTER
Surbrunnsgatan 60, S11327 Stockholm. Tel: (08) 327788

SWITZERLAND

KOTA RAJNEESH NEO-SANNYAS COMMUNE
Baumackerstr. 42, 8050 Zurich. Tel: (01) 312 1600

WEST GERMANY

BAILE RAJNEESH NEO-SANNYAS COMMUNE
Karolinenstr. 7-9, 2000 Hamburg 6. Tel: (040) 432140

DORFCHEN RAJNEESH NEO-SANNYAS COMMUNE
Dahlmannstr. 9, 1000 Berlin 12. Tel: (030) 32-007-0

SATDHARMA RAJNEESH MEDITATION CENTER
Klenzestr. 41, 8000 Munich 5. Tel: (089) 269-077

WIOSKA RAJNEESH NEO-SANNYAS COMMUNE
Lutticherstr. 33/35, 5000 Cologne 1. Tel: 0221-517199

Rajneesh Foundation International

presents

Rajneeshism

An Introduction to Bhagwan Shree Rajneesh and his Religion

Edited by Academy of Rajneeshism

Revised Second Edition

"Man is now living in his most critical moment and it is a crisis of immense dimensions. Either he will die or a new man will be born. Rajneeshism accepts the challenge and is making the only world-wide effort to transform human consciousness . . ."

$3.00 paperback 78 pages

ISBN 0-88050-700-4

Please make payment to:

Rajneesh Foundation International

P.O. Box 9, Rajneeshpuram, OR 97741 U.S.A.